E. Nesbit: A Biography

Other Books by Doris Langley Moore

E. Nesbit

A BIOGRAPHY

Revised with new material by

Doris Langley Moore

Chilton Books

A DIVISION OF CHILTON COMPANY

Publishers

Philadelphia and New York

To GLANVILL BENN

this souvenir of March 19th 1931
when he delighted a young author
by commissioning a biography

Acknowledgments

In the preparation of this work the author laid to her account a triple debt. First and foremost she was, and remains, under obligation to a band of helpers whose personal knowledge of E. Nesbit formed the basis and the main structure of the story it has been her privilege to tell. Second, she must renew her thanks to those who so generously permitted her to make use of copyright material in their control; and third, to those whose aid simplified her researches in the British Museum and elsewhere.

Of all the many whose services were freely asked and given in all three capacities, the biographer's heaviest responsibility is to the members of the Bland family itself, now represented only by E. Nesbit's great-grandchildren; but at the time when the book was written those were unborn, and there were Mr. Paul and Dr. John Bland, Mrs. Clifford Sharp, and Mr. T. T. Tucker, E. Nesbit's second husband. Without their invaluable help, such a biography must have remained incomplete in every aspect.

To all those who sanctioned the printing of letters and other documents acknowledgments have been made in footnotes or in the text. For information on the life, times, and personality of E. Nesbit and subjects bearing upon these the author is gratefully indebted to a numerous company, the ranks of which have, alas, greatly thinned since the material was first gathered, but the list is here left in its original form:

Professor E. N. da C. Andrade, F.R.S., Miss Enid Bagnold (Lady Jones), Mr. Oswald Barron, Mr. C. W. Beckett, Mrs. Paul Bland, Mr. Peter Blundell, the Rt. Hon. Miss Margaret Bondfield, Miss May Bowley, Miss Ada Breakell, Sir Ernest A. Wallis Budge, D.Litt., Miss Mavis Carter, Mr. Stephen Chant, Mr. G. K. Chesterton, Mrs. Joseph Conrad, Mr. Albert Coumber, Mrs. Elsa Courlander, Mr. Noel Coward, Miss Clemence Dane, the Lord and Lady Dunsany, Mr. Havelock Ellis, Mrs. Welby Everard, the Fabian Society, Mr. F. Ambrose Flower, Mrs. Alma Murray Forman, Mr. E. M. Forster, Mr. Gerald Gould, Mr. Russell Green, Mr. and Mrs. Noel Griffith, Mr. Hubert Griffith, Mr. Ernest W. Haslehust, Mrs. Hildegarde Hawthorne Oskison, Mrs. P. T. Heady, Mr. Graily Hewitt, Miss A. Olive Hill, Miss Alice Hoatson, Mr. Laurence Housman, Mr. F. E. Jackson, Mr. Edgar Jepson, Mr. R. Brimley Johnson, Mr. J. Langley Levy, Mr. Richard le Gallienne, Mr. Angus MacPhail, Mr. Bower Marsh, Mr. H. R. Millar, Mrs. Naomi Mitchison, Mrs. A. T. Moore, Mr. H. W. Nevinson, the Rt. Hon. the Lord Olivier, Mr. Edward R. Pease, Mrs. Thomas Platt, Mr. Vernon Rendall, Mrs. F. E. Ringland, Miss Berta Ruck, Mr. Henry Savage, Miss Athene Seyler, Miss Evelyn Sharp, Mr. Clifford Sharp, Mr. George Bernard Shaw, Mr. F. H. Sikes, Miss Florence R. Simpson, Sir John Squire, Miss G. B. Stern, Mr. A. A. Sykes, Mrs. Vincent Taylor, Mrs. A. M. Thorndike, Dame Sybil Thorndike, Mr. Gustave Tuck, Miss Anne Verrall, Commander Arthur Watts, and Mr. H. G. Wells.

what I could of it in an article in *Good Housekeeping,* and had the text copied in full and sent to E. Nesbit's daughter, to whom these reminiscences of her mother's were quite unknown. Mrs. Philips handed them some time later to Miss Noel Streatfeild, who put them to good use in her book, *Magic and the Magician.* I have drawn further upon them in the early chapters here, two of which are entirely new.

Though E. Nesbit's own direct account adds much to our knowledge, it has called for very little in the way of correction to my first version; and that reflects great credit on the veracity of her circle—so different from the circles surrounding those other famous personalities with whom I have been concerned, Byron and Marie Bashkirtseff. I was fretful long ago, as I checked one set of notes against another, at what I have since recognized as minor slips in the focus of memory for which every biographer must be alert. I had not yet sifted the evidences of a Trelawny, a Blessington, or a Stendhal, nor compared Marie Bashkirtseff's published journal with her manuscript. Now I can appreciate the high quality of almost all the testimony I collected about E. Nesbit—a being who had the singular good fortune to inspire neither malice nor roseate idealization.

But if I was lucky enough to find trustworthy witnesses to every stage of her life from girlhood onwards, I had to face some unforeseeable difficulties. Who could have supposed the author of those charming and luminous children's tales had lived through so many dramas and melodramas? Not I when I wrote my careful, formally worded letters asking for assistance from those who had been named to me as her intimates. I was young enough to think authors must resemble their characters, and I began by picturing her like the serene and inconspicuous mothers in her stories. The complexities of her circumstances were unfolded gradually in the course of months, and set me, again and again, the problem of trying to tell the truth and yet avoid offending a number of indispensable helpers of diverging views and different generations.

The oldest whose approval had to be won was Mr. Tucker,

A Retrospective Introduction

The months I have spent revising a book first published in January 1933 have brought vividly back to me the ardent adventure of writing it, the obstacles, the privileges, and the constant element of surprise that pervaded the experience from beginning to end. Re-reading the letters, the verbatim notes of interviews I somehow managed to keep intact through all the vicissitudes of the last thirty-five years, I seemed to come face to face again with the providers of that mass of documentation, some of them so delightful and almost all of them so gifted. Few of the distinguished company remain, and I, still in my twenties when I began the task, am ending it some little way beyond the threshold of old age; but to be able to end it at all is what I hardly looked for.

Now that not one is left who can be hurt by any allusion in these pages, I owe it to my readers to fill in some facts and names which were necessarily suppressed while the subject of my biography had children and a husband living, and while uninhibited frankness might have embarrassed her friends. I have also added information about her childhood which was not in my possession until—ironically—just after a pocket edition of my book went to press in 1951. (See p. 6.)

Since it was too late then to mention my discovery, I made

Contents

her second husband, in his mid-seventies, lovable and kindly; the youngest Dr. John Bland, not much over thirty when I met him, a scientist, detached and unemotional. Between these two was Mr. Paul Bland, fifty-odd and much less outspoken, his sister Iris (Mrs. Philips) in her late forties—at first rather cautious with me—and, a few years younger, Rosamund, married to the progressive and outspoken Clifford Sharp, who had emphatic views of how I should paint my portrait.

The Sharps and John were ready for all facts to be given with the candour which, by the 1930's, had become a required feature of serious biography; Iris was tolerant, if less forthcoming; and old Mr. Tucker's breadth of mind was remarkable, though his love and loyalty made him particularly sensitive. Mr. Paul Bland, while never interfering, was noticeably reticent. His communications were strictly accurate but they were limited. It came as a painful shock to him (I was told by one of his sisters) to learn from the copy of his parents' marriage certificate which I innocently produced that he had been conceived substantially before the wedding. Without a word being spoken, I refrained in the book from mentioning the date of his birth. There were other matters I could not leave out, and he was the sole member of the family who did not write warmly to me when the work appeared in print.

He was a stockbroker—not, I think, on a very large or flourishing scale. He had been thrust into business early in life by his father, Hubert Bland, perhaps through some ambition at variance with the latter's professed Socialist beliefs, perhaps through indifference. Less lucky than John who, unknown to himself, was Bernard Shaw's protégé, Paul never had the happiness of following his bent at Oxford or Cambridge. He passed from school to his wage-earning job, from his job to active service in the First World War, and back again to uncongenial employment.

He struck me as spiritually misplaced, having reacted strongly against the Bohemianism of his upbringing, yet never really at home in the world of city business men in which his lot had so capriciously been cast. I felt more sympathy for him than he could ever have guessed, for I had been told his father had disliked him—actually "hated him" according to Clifford Sharp —and, though he would never have expressed such a sentiment to an outsider, he assuredly had good reason for hating his father. He must have realized while still a youth that the household was a permanent *ménage à trois* in which his mother usually got the worst of any situation which called for sacrifice; and he could not have been unaware that, besides the lady living on the premises, his father had other mistresses.

I have altered little that I originally wrote about Hubert Bland, because I think my opinion of him can be read between the lines now as it could then. I brought forward his good points and stressed the admiration in which he was widely held because to do otherwise would have been to yield to prejudice —nor can I deny that I was under the necessity of not antagonizing his favourite children, his son-in-law, and his friends.

Rosamund may be said to have adored him, and Clifford Sharp had, as a young man, been one of his disciples and still retained his early hero worship intact. Both were insistent that I should represent him as altogether the superior of his wife, who clung to him, they said, and could do nothing without him. I have letters of theirs to this effect, and had to tread very warily whenever there was any question that praise for her might be at his expense. John Bland was much more dispassionate, but his anxiety lest I should fail to do justice to his father was plain enough. The family was conscious, in short, that his character was vulnerable, and prepared—at least the younger members— to spring to his defence.

A year or two after my book came out, H. G. Wells, in the second volume of his autobiography, disregarded their feelings and attacked Bland ruthlessly, telling much more bluntly than I of his "essential preoccupation," his "inner compulsion to be a Seducer—on the best eighteenth century lines." Wells's account is not without signs that he was paying off an old score, but it is the same in substance as what I had heard from others who were more objective.

In company, in public, Bland talked and wrote of social and political problems and debated with a barrister-like effectiveness, but when I was alone with him, the fundamental interest insisted upon coming to the surface. . . . He would talk about it. He would give hints of his exceptional prowess. He would boast. He would discuss the social laxities of Woolwich and Blackheath, breaking into anecdotes, "simply for the purpose of illustration." Or he would produce a pocket-worn letter and read choice bits of it—"purely because of its psychological interest." He did his utmost to give this perpetual pursuit of furtive gratification the dignity of a purpose. . . . "I am a student, an experimentalist," he announced, "in illicit love."

"Illicit love"! It had to be "illicit" and that was the very gist of it for him. It had to be the centre of a system of jealousies, concealments, hidings, exposures, confrontations, sacrifices, incredible generosities—in a word, drama. What he seemed to value most was the glory of a passionate triumph over openness, reason and loyalty. . . .[1]

It is only fair, since I quote this passage reflecting unfavourably on Hubert Bland, to mention that Wells himself was not guiltless of the foibles he so sharply depicts, and that the quarrel which severed him from the Blands, after an eager friendship, was the outcome of his overtures to Rosamund when she was in—or only just out of—her teens and he a married man many years her senior. Bland did not tolerate seduction or attempted seduction practised by anyone but himself, and especially when his daughter was the object. (Of other people's daughters he was less considerate, and another great quarrel was, for that reason, with the father of one of Rosamund's schoolfriends.)

The excuse generally made for him by his contemporaries and near-contemporaries, including Bernard Shaw and Noel Griffith, was that he was sexually so constituted that one woman alone could not fill his demands: but Wells was proba-

---

[1] Quoted by permission of the executors of H. G. Wells, and Messrs. Victor Gollancz Ltd.

bly more astute when he guessed that Bland's conquests were a way of getting even with the "wit and freaks and fantasies of his wife," whose talents were more abundant than his own, and who, as Wells pointed out, "earned the greater part of the joint income," a situation still fraught with pitfalls and much more so then.

A man who is persistently unfaithful to a woman whom he will not let go is surely seeking to stifle troublesome self-doubts. E. Nesbit's own infidelities took place under huge provocation, and must have been to some extent a way of living down the humiliation Bland inflicted on her. How much he knew of them it is impossible to assess. When she was infatuated with Bernard Shaw, Bland (so Shaw himself told me) took no notice; but then, he must have guessed that the physical side of the affair would be on a somewhat rarefied plane. She had other lovers less abstemious, and that fact too was a delicate one for me to handle.

As I never thought the time would come when I could be explicit about it, I made no very probing investigations into that aspect of her life, but neither did I altogether neglect it. I have been too unsure about the precise circumstances to write without reserve even in the present edition. It may be said here, however, that she did make some half-hearted attempts to break up a marriage which cost her so many tears, but Bland was determined not to lose her. I heard on good authority that she was once on the verge of eloping with the attractive young Richard le Gallienne, who was about eight years her junior but romantically in love with her. That would have been about 1890, and was probably the first attachment of any importance after Shaw in the 1880's. It is a topic on which I cannot be positive because there was also Noel Griffith, who was her lover in no merely platonic sense for a period after 1887 when he met her, and before 1895 when he married Nina Freeling, a lady who became one of her close friends, and who made a very valuable contribution to this book.

E. Nesbit had the rather rare knack of remaining on the best of terms with ex-lovers; but this was possibly because, her deepest affections being bound up with her husband, she was able to take partings lightly. Yet if her love affairs were gestures, they were vigorous and meaningful gestures while they lasted, and since she was the absolute reverse of promiscuous, they were not mere passing fancies.

She dreamed often of escaping, with the help of some strong and protective man, from Bland's mesmeric influence. As late as about 1905 she implored Dr. Wallis Budge, the Egyptologist, to take her away, but although he thought her, middle-aged as she then was, most handsome and captivating, his position at the British Museum rendered any such measure too extravagant to contemplate. She wept at his refusal, but saw him a number of times afterwards, and their relations—more than friendship, less than love—only ended through his having to go to an excavation in the Near East. He was one of the people I came to know well in the course of my work, and could count on as a reliable informant; but of course there was no question of publishing what he told me until many years had elapsed.

There was one slightly earlier episode which remains, through my own fault, in tantalizing mystery. On p. 170 will be found my sole reference to Douglas Kennedy, the young man for whom, in 1902, she composed the very happy poetry I have quoted. Soon after my book came out, he wrote to me disclosing how fondly he remembered her. My answer led to his sending me a few curious lines of hers which I could only interpret as a love letter. He said he had hundreds of her letters, of which he was willing to let me have a discreet selection by post, or he would produce *all* for me to examine if I could arrange a meeting. I should have taken the trouble to do so without delay, but at the end of my lengthy and arduous task, my condition was one of utter lassitude. I never met Mr. Kennedy and never even asked to see the proffered selection. It was only in 1966 that I came upon his interesting correspondence, misfiled. Let me hope this unique cache of Nesbit letters still exists and will become available.

How so intensely attractive and much-courted a woman could have been content scarcely ever to possess more than half a husband—sometimes substantially less—may be explained as much by the epoch in which she lived as by his fascination (though I am bound to say that Rosamund described him as "irresistible"). Today such conduct as his could not fail to lead to the divorce court, but in England then adultery was insufficient grounds for a divorce unless the petitioner was a man. When a woman sought release, adultery had to be accompanied by cruelty, and that word was interpreted in a gross physical sense. Besides, E. Nesbit in her generosity had from the first practised a course which would have been called condoning. Indeed there was every legal obstacle and every social one too, and so, no rescuer coming forward, she stuck it out.

Opinions differed very much as to whether she was wise or foolish. Bernard Shaw said: "No two people were ever married who were better calculated to make the worst of each other." Clifford Sharp, on the other hand, wrote to me that, even as a "triangle," the marriage "worked extraordinarily well in practice for 99/100ths of the time, allowing E.N. to run about as she liked in her restless manner." But we must bear in mind that he never met any of the three till they were in middle life and had mellowed and worked out a *modus vivendi*. Wells may have been displaying his usual percipience when he summed up the effect of Bland's intricate web of entanglements thus:

> All this E. Nesbit not only detested and mitigated and tolerated, but presided over and I think found exceedingly interesting.'

It had taken her many years to reach that comparative detachment.

In my first edition I never mentioned Alice Hoatson by name in any context that was capable of giving her pain. She was old and ill, and she had no idea that her own children had told me of her place in the triangle, nor that I knew the secret of their parentage, which E. Nesbit had gone to such elaborate and self-abnegating lengths to conceal. In her communications to me (which were made, I fancy, under pressure from her son John

Bland) she was simply the affectionate and helpful friend; and it is only fair to acknowledge that E. Nesbit's literary career must have been greatly furthered by her ministrations. To be able to lay aside at any time the burden of domestic and nursery supervision is a boon that every professional woman will envy. If E. Nesbit sometimes complained to her very intimate friends that "the Mouse," as they called her, was inclined to presume, to take more upon herself than she was entitled to, it was no more than might have been said, in moods of irritation, about any other lady-housekeeper. Two women could hardly live at such close quarters without occasional friction. Miss Hoatson may now and then have felt slighted and shown too clearly that, if not mistress of the house, she was not without power over its master; but for the most part she fitted into the rôle she had allotted herself. "The humble satellite of a comet," so she spoke of herself in one of her letters to me.

It was thus that people invariably saw her. Clifford Sharp described her as "a cheerful, useful nonentity," whom no one either liked or disliked. His wife, Rosamund, actually Miss Hoatson's daughter, said, "She was a little unsophisticated mouse of a person, up from Yorkshire, and she came into this brilliant company, was dazzled by it, and succumbed, first to E. Nesbit's charms and then to Hubert's." Not having been born at the time, she was writing from hearsay or supposition. My story in Chapter VI of E. Nesbit's first meeting with one who was destined to be her lifelong friend and adversary, supporter and tormentor, is based precisely on Miss Hoatson's own account, which is certainly a true one as far as it goes. She was not a naïve provincial girl, but had been in London several years as a journalist when, about 1885, she joined the meagrely financed little household of the young Blands and thenceforward shared their fortunes.

I heard from other sources that they had advertised for a companion-help to look after their two children, John and Iris. (A companion-help living as one of the family cost less than a nurse or governess and required less waiting on.) Miss Hoatson unexpectedly applied for the post, timorous in manner and dressed in a shade of grey which caused them to say they would nickname her "the Mouse." "In that case," she retaliated, "I'll call you the Cats." And so it was that Hubert and Edith, when all was well between them, came to address each other as "Cat" and their factotum as "Mouse." Her retort does not sound very mouse-like, and I doubt if it was ever genuinely her nature to subjugate herself except out of policy. Even when their means were narrow, the Blands' home was always a hive of interesting activity and visited constantly by the most amusing and talented of the left-wing set. To become one of that vital band must have seemed well worthwhile, though it meant accepting with apparent willingness the status of "satellite."

It was naturally out of the question to make such observations as these while Miss Hoatson and her children were alive. Not that she seemed to have awakened much affection in them. John Bland, in fact, told me that the reason why it was at last decided to enlighten him as to their real relationship was because, as an adolescent, he was so persistently rude to her. Rosamund's attitude was more pitying than loving. It must have been a blow to each in turn to learn that their clever, famous, adventurous, and lively—albeit difficult—mother was a benevolent impostor, and to have to substitute for her the insipid person who had always been an unconsidered part of their background.

Rosamund had barely forgiven the deception by the time I met her. She was always vehemently on her father's side, and seemed to think it a justification of his conduct that it was E. Nesbit "who first persuaded her [Alice] to go about with him, in order to get him to give up another lady. . . ." John was less bitter, but he admitted having many quarrels with his mother-by-adoption while growing up. I am afraid the rewards of quixotic actions are much as Cervantes painted them.

Subdued as my revelations were, some reviewers expressed their disapproval at my having treated these private matters at all, and a few suggested that I had done so without the consent of the family, which was very far from the case. Proofs or typescripts were submitted in advance to all still accessible who figured prominently by name in the book, the members of the family first and foremost. It may be imagined with what trepidation I dispatched those copies and waited for their return.

Among the verdicts I most dreaded was that of Bernard Shaw, for it had not been easy to enlist his aid. On my first approaching him, I had received a reply with the well-known signature of his secretary, Miss Patch, but unmistakably a Shavian composition:

> "Mr. Bernard Shaw desires me to say that as Edith was an audaciously unconventional lady and Hubert an exceedingly unfaithful husband he does not see how a presentable biography is possible as yet; and he has nothing to contribute to a mere whitewashing operation." [2]

That was on May 8, 1931. I could not afford to let such a key witness evade me, one of the few remaining whose friendship with the Blands dated back to their youthful struggles in the 1880's, when he too was obscure and impecunious. I wrote the most earnest appeal of which I was capable. I humbled myself as I would have done for no one else. "Please, Mr. Shaw, do not be so unkind as to make me face publishers and public with your refusal." By November he was still adamant and I increasingly troubled, for almost everyone I saw gave—and rightly—some reason why I ought to consult him.

In the end I practised a little ruse. I had to ask his permission to reproduce one of three letters of his which had been preserved. Of course I could have sent him copies of them, but I kept them back, and, having briefly outlined them, went on to say that I was also desirous of quoting a letter by E. Nesbit herself, in which she described him "in terms of admiration not unmingled with criticism. . . . She was delighted with you but singled out one or two personal characteristics for rather critical comment." I would, I said, let him see the remarks before they were published if he so wished: meanwhile they were being typed.

[2] Quoted by permission of the Public Trustee and the Society of Authors, and Miss Blanche Patch.

Mr. Shaw did not immediately succumb to this not very subtle wile, but his answer, via Miss Patch, conveyed a glimmer of hope. He said he would like all quotations and even all references to be submitted to him and that the topic had its difficulties and he might be able "to help a little"; and he showed his change from negative to positive by adding two or three lines of useful advice. I wrote at once offering to bring my documents in person. This elicited one of Shaw's famous postcards in his own neat hand saying the matter was one he could not write about at reasonable length and that he would be at home the following day, November 11th, from 5:30 to 6:00 P.M.

He was at the highest pinnacle of his renown and it was natural for him to try and protect himself against encroachments on his time, but once he had decided that my cause was good, no one could have been more practical and obliging. I remember how solicitously he asked if I was sure I had a proper arrangement for the publication of my book before undertaking it, anxious as he always was that young authors should make sound business transactions. His manner was so gracious and so affable that I could not bear to let him see the whole of E. Nesbit's early strictures, which are now printed in full for the first time: I read them aloud to him, slightly bowdlerizing them. He raised no objection to my publishing her comments on his untrustworthiness and want of veracity, these weaknesses having been outgrown, I should say, too long ago for him to feel any defensiveness about them. The mass of information he gave me was the most exact that I received from anybody. His memory at seventy-five seemed quite unfaltering, and has remained unfaulted when checked by other data.

I took his conversation down in Pitman's shorthand, as I did almost all the other conversations in my notebooks. Even people who are inclined to speak loosely will become careful and responsible when they see their utterances being committed to paper word for word. Shaw was so accustomed to being reported verbatim that it had the effect—such was my impression—of stimulating him, and he grew endearingly expansive. Time went by the board. I have notes, passing far out of Nesbit territory, which would be misplaced here; but I take, as the least irrelevant specimen, his words, just as he spoke them, about Harold Cox, a member of the young Socialist group who had by now become the most orthodox Conservative. They may be appended to my long footnote on pp. 84–85, concerning a communal farming experiment that failed:

People used to go down and pay him visits [Cox at his unproductive farm], and the agricultural labourer and his daughter slept on the floor. This went on for some time, and at last an aunt of Cox's turned up. She took him to task about the labourer's daughter, who was a very pretty girl. The aunt said: "Harold, you are a very attractive young man, especially to a girl like that who has never been associated with a gentleman before. You must be careful, for her sake as much as for your own."

Cox was flattered and impressed. When he returned to the house, the young lady, who was always called "The Garden Industry," was standing at a window. Cox cried: "Oh, do stay where you are! Don't move, please!"

The girl really was infatuated with him. When he gave up the farm, the girl went to America and made enough money at dressmaking to come back and have a look at Cox—and she was very disappointed.

Cox went out to India and became a great exponent of Socialism. He had a burst of spelling reform too before the War. Later he dropped Socialism entirely and became a *Morning Post* Conservative.

It was in this easy, unpretentious style that a man of so great a stature as Shaw gave me a picture of characters and events on the Socialist scene of almost half a century before, about which I had everything to learn at setting out.

I have kept the proof copy in which he wrote his few but pertinent corrections. The phrase about returning E. Nesbit's love with "a heartlessness which he knew how to make amusing" is his own and it replaced a stilted one of mine. He put into more forceful terms my comment early in Chapter IX about her habit of interrupting discussions at Fabian Society meetings, and he reworded entirely my fumbling description of Hubert

Bland's strength-testing feat with an army rifle: but he censored nothing.

To avoid embarrassment to the family, I had refrained from touching on the financial assistance he had given after Hubert Bland's death. Not till the present edition did I say anything of this, and perhaps even now there is something I ought to add. Under the influence of her Bacon-is-Shakespeare frenzy (it was carried to such lengths that it can be called nothing less) E. Nesbit became for a time uncreative and applied to him so often for money that he eventually warned her she must count on him no more, but should adjust her scale of living to her diminished means. She was, he told me, "very angry" with him about that, but I am glad to say she made her peace when she stabilized herself by her second marriage. It would have been absurd if so happy an association had ended with an irrational grievance.

Shaw thought E. Nesbit a wonderfully attractive woman, and several times repeated it. When I asked him how he had reacted to her being in love with him, he answered, smiling, "Well, I didn't say 'How dare you!'" But to my question, whether he had been in love with her, his reply, still smiling, was: "No, I've never been in love with anybody—much."

If Mr. Shaw, having been difficult of approach, was encouraging and communicative when I came face to face with him, Mr. Wells was altogether the reverse. To see him was delusively easy. I wrote my customary letter, very stiff in tone, very clearly meant to persuade the recipient of my correctness. (It should be known to the reader that the only work of mine likely to have been heard of was called *The Technique of the Love Affair,* and I had to live it down.) In a matter of hours I had a telephone call from his secretary inviting me to go to tea at Mr. Wells's Baker Street flat. I had been a devoted admirer of his from the age of twelve, when I read *The First Men in the Moon,* and I was elated at the prospect of receiving his assistance. My disappointment on being admitted to his drawing-room was profound. Not only was he entertaining others beside myself; he actually expected me to interview him in front of them!

There was a visitor from New Zealand—a lady novelist whose name he could not recollect when he introduced us, an American who had come with a letter of presentation from someone he (Wells) scarcely seemed to recall, and a shy, amiable Swedish gentleman who was hoping to interest him in a simplified language system. All were as new to our host as I was, none could have felt pleased to find the others there. I had the impression that the New Zealand lady in particular was glowering with irritation at my arrival and determined to outstay me—which she did. I have never had the slightest doubt that my own invitation to the tea party was a deliberate device to stave off such questions as I might have put to him in private, and it succeeded completely.

Mr. Wells's generous compliments to my book in his autobiography were, I fancy, his way of making amends for an almost churlish reception. My notes made at the time remind me that he appeared bent on destroying my pretensions to become E. Nesbit's biographer as well as coolly patronizing about E. Nesbit herself. He began by demanding sceptically who did I think would buy the book? He went on to enquire whether I had known her personally, and when I replied "No," he asked if that was a good basis on which to start a biography. This with his other guests listening. I was astonished at his inquisitiveness as to how I came to be engaged in this writing, who would publish it, and why. Looking back, I see that he must have been worried as to whether I intended to indulge in scandalous revelations concerning his quarrel with the Blands—of which, as it happened, I had as yet barely heard, so that the peculiar tone he took with me was unaccountable.

The only agreeable thing about the occasion—for even the tea was black and lukewarm—was his evident pride in being able to have E. Nesbit's letters extracted without a moment's delay from files kept by his secretary. He read each one carefully before handing it to me, and kept back certain ones; but he allowed me to publish what I asked for, only requesting that "old squabbles" should be ignored.

The following comment at the end of my few jottings that day may shed as much light on Wells as on myself at twenty-eight: "I wore my brilliantly coloured dress of Rodier fabric, and a new yellow hat. I rather felt we might have hit it off pretty well tête-à-tête." I met him, in fact, years later on an occasion not connected with any aspect of his past and he was very genial, so I conclude the rift at Well Hall must have left an emotion that had been rankling still at our first encounter.

This Introduction would be of inordinate length if I were to surrender to all the temptations of reminiscence. I should deviate into telling how Mr. Noel Coward regretted that E. Nesbit had never seen *Bitter Sweet* and *Post Mortem,* as he thought she would have liked them both, and even—I slightly doubted this—*Private Lives;* how awestruck I was at John Bland's masterly command of Russian, only to learn that his songs were in a convincing gibberish that he made up as he went along; how Sir Ernest Budge (as he had by then become) gave me an amulet like the one in E. Nesbit's tale, and how I stood one morning outside the drawing-room of the Forum Club and said to myself, to savour it to the full, "The man I shall meet in there is positively E. M. Forster"—those and a horde of other happy recollections.

Everything went much faster in those days. Books were quite commonly published two or three months after being finished. Writers who took it for granted that clerical and household tasks would be done by others could keep up a pace unattainable in such hampering times as these. And it was of more advantage to my work than I was then aware to live in Yorkshire at an inconvenient distance from the capital, because it forced me to concentrations of effort that could probably not have been achieved if I had been able to arrange my interviews at leisure, and if the quarries I was after had felt free to be casual as to when I might catch them. That all my research was done, all my chapters written, all permissions gathered in, and the volume in the bookshops, well within two years after I had first approached the publishers with my idea now seems incredible.

A party was given by Mr. Noel Griffith, a barrister-at-law, to celebrate publication. It took place in the Temple, at his beautiful old chambers in Pump Court: and it was marked by a sad and secret little crisis. I tell of it now not for the sake of the anecdote, but because the older I grow, the more does every incident that can contribute to our acceptance of human nature as it is seem to me worthy of preservation.

Clifford Sharp, charming, clever, valorous, was a victim of the malady of alcoholism, which, after long struggles on both sides, had recently caused his wife to leave him and his important post as founder-editor of the *New Statesman* to be withdrawn from him. He had periods of perfect sobriety—as when I first met him—but the probability of a lapse caused us some anxiety in inviting him to the party. When all the company was assembled, Mr. Griffith drew me aside in consternation. Clifford Sharp had just arrived, and was already so undisguisably and pitiably drunk that it would be reckless to let him stay. He (our host) had pretended there was no party in progress, that Sharp must have mistaken the date. He begged me to go and support his story, and keep a conversation going while he fetched his son and got a taxi.

I hurried to the kitchen, whither Mr. Griffith had been obliged to lead him to prevent his being seen in so unhappy a state, and—among the plain evidences of our festivity with a babel of voices only too audible—I guiltily commiserated with him on having come on the wrong evening. It seemed a long time before Hubert Griffith (E. Nesbit's godson) appeared in his overcoat, heroically ready to steer the poor guest, reluctant, bewildered and near collapse, back to his house in the north of London. Few of those present had the least inkling of the contretemps. I never saw Clifford Sharp again; he died not long after. What especially touches me is that he had written such an article about my book for the *News Chronicle* as must have been meant to set me up and reward me for all my labour, and perhaps his chief object in coming to the party was to give me the pleasure of anticipation.

It was the Sharps who prevailed on me to allude to my subject in her adult years as "E. Nesbit"—though I have altered a good many of these references in the present edition as they never came really easily to me. Those who have not written biographies might be surprised to know what a problem may lie in simply the naming of one's principal characters. My heroine passed her childhood under the pet name Daisy, gradually became Edith, and then was Miss Nesbit. After that she was known as Mrs. Bland in private life and E. Nesbit professionally. In her last years she was legally Mrs. Tucker, but signed herself, formally, E. Nesbit Bland-Tucker.

One cannot in every second chapter use a different designation. I would have preferred a straightforward "Edith" for most of the book, but I could hardly, when a very young woman, take liberties with the Christian name of one whose children were much older than I. There were few at any time who did so. Her closest friends addressed her by deferential nicknames: to the less intimate she was always Mrs. Bland or Mrs. Tucker. So the compromise of the pen-name was adopted—after I had firmly refused to write of her as "E.N."

Once the family had satisfied themselves that I would not do injustice to Hubert Bland, we settled down comfortably to such comparatively minor arguments. Apart from Paul Bland's natural reserve—though even he was much more helpful than hindering—I met with none of the opposition biographers so often have to endure from the relations and friends of those whose lives they seek to commemorate. There were hazards, but I am struck at this distance of time by the fewness of the rebuffs I received. Almost no one, except Mr. Wells, even enquired how or why it came about that I had set myself this task.

In case anyone should ask it now, the answer is simple yet rather strange. As a child I read E. Nesbit's books as children do, enjoying tremendously, remembering, being influenced, but not troubling to notice the name of the author! There was thus no continuity in my reading; but when I married, my mother-in-law often spoke to me of the favourite books she had read aloud to her children, and how they had loved the "Nesbits," and suddenly I realized they were the books I too had loved in childhood and I started to read them again. I came across volumes I had never seen before. I collected "Nesbits" with avidity, and was disappointed to learn how hard it was to trace the smallest fact about her in print. When she had been dead only three or four years and I had published nothing but a translation of Anacreontic odes—that was before the prose work I have mentioned—I formed the resolution to become her biographer.

One day I happened to express my enthusiasm to Mrs. Vincent Taylor, the wife of the dear old tutor with whom I still used to read Greek (exquisite euphemism for my slow toil with a lexicon at my elbow). To my delight, she replied that she had known Mrs. Bland when they had both been young, and gave me a prepossessing verbal portrait of her. That was my first "contact," but fairly soon after I recognized, in a moment of belated perception, that the Hubert Griffith I had met —who was an author and dramatic critic—must be the selfsame Hubert Griffith to whom *The Phoenix and the Carpet* was dedicated. From then on, by the sort of luck or providence which I have now come to count on, I trust not presumptuously, wherever I turned I found trails that led directly to my more and more alluring subject.

At last I took courage and wrote a long, importunate, and fervent letter to E. Nesbit's publishers, Messrs. Ernest Benn. I told them I was sure she was "destined for posterity," that I had several friends who had known her, that I was "terribly afraid" someone else would undertake the book before me, and that the commission to write it could come from no one so properly as from themselves, and that I believed I might deserve the adjectives "lucid," "dispassionate," and "accurate-minded." I stated that Monday, March 9th (1931), was my only convenient day for seeing them.

The answer was signed by Mr. Glanvill Benn, who yielded gracefully—and I think willingly—to the kind of pressure that youth alone has the energy and the self-confidence to exert. I hope the reader will decide that he was right.

D. L. M.
London, 1966.

E. Nesbit: A Biography

1   *Parentage and Family Associations*

Edith Nesbit was born on August 15, 1858, at 38 Lower
Kennington Lane, a street with large houses and spacious gardens, soon destined to be replaced by Victorian terraced dwell-
ings and petty shops—which are now overshadowed by blocks
of council flats. She was the youngest of six children, the first of
whom, however, was a half-sister. It is a long time since
Kennington could boast any rural surroundings; nevertheless,
in the forties and fifties of the last century Edith's father, John
Collis Nesbit, was able to maintain a large and quite celebrated
agricultural college there—the first, I believe, that existed in
England.

Edith was decidedly fortunate in her early circumstances, for
her father was a prosperous and respected man—her mother a
kind, affectionate, and intelligent woman. Her ancestry, though
not illustrious, could very well bear examination—good yeoman
stock, as the saying goes; and both her grandfather and her
father were men of considerable distinction.

Anthony Nesbit, born in Northumberland in 1778, the son of
a farmer, had earned his living in his youth both as a schoolmaster and a land-surveyor, being employed in the Yorkshire
towns of Whitby, Malton, Scarborough, Bridlington, and Hull
successively. After following his diverse occupations for a time

at Farnley, near Leeds, he set up a school of his own in Brad-ford, and appears to have done pretty well there; though his re-moval to Manchester seven years later—in about 1821—would seem to indicate that the then immature Yorkshire woollen cen-tre did not afford him the scope he desired in either of his pro-fessions.

In Manchester he remained for twenty years, the head of a school in the Oxford Road, which soon became well known for his able though severe tuition. Then he removed to London where, with his adult sons, John and Edward, to act as his assistants, he opened that "Classical, Commercial, and Scientific Academy" in Lower Kennington Lane where his grand-daughter was born seventeen years later. At intervals through-out his career as headmaster, he published educational works with marked success. One of them, a mathematical primer, was reprinted many times and used in schools until the present century, while his once celebrated treatise on land-surveying went through at least a dozen editions. In 1841 he brought out an *Essay on Education,* in which both his sons had collaborated. Although it would be unfair to deny that some very sound and strikingly modern views on school training are set forth in this book, it is remarkable chiefly for its quaintnesses. There is a passage, for example—one of many equally uncompromising—which explains how the prehistoric animals, just then begin-ning to interest enquiring laymen, had become extinct: Noah, it would seem, had simply omitted to take specimens of them into the Ark. In this brisk manner every problem over which the theologists and geologists were then in conflict was disposed of.

Like most of his contemporaries in the scholastic world, Anthony Nesbit was a stern disciplinarian, heavy-minded and, according to some reports, heavy-handed. He regarded corporal punishment as a necessity, and his views on the lighter forms of juvenile recreation are censorious. "Beware," he writes in his *In-troduction to English Parsing* (1817), "of reading tales and novels, for they generally exhibit pictures that never had any ex-istence, except in the airy imaginations of the brain."

Fortunately for him, and perhaps for us, he did not live to

learn that his own son's child was to divert generations of children with some of the most airily imaginative "tales and novels" ever written. Among the books he recommended to the perusal of girls are Burton's *Lectures on Female Education,* Mrs. Hannah More's *Strictures on the Modern System of Female Education,* Mrs. Taylor's *Maternal Solicitude for a Daughter's Best Interests,* and *Practical Hints to Young Females on the Duties of a Wife, a Mother, and the Mistress of a Family.* Nothing could better serve to remind us of our debt to E. Nesbit than the study of this list. While warning his readers of light literature, however, he is favourably disposed towards music, as being particularly calculated to relieve the mind after intense study, and drawing he describes as "an elegant accomplishment which may be considered an amusement if it be not too closely followed."

One of his peculiarities, vouched for by the late Thomas Nesbit, an ex-pupil and a family connection, was that he rose punctually at three each morning and retired at seven in the evening—a habit which was possibly not much appreciated by the servant who had to prepare his early breakfast.

John Collis Nesbit became yet more widely known than his father. Very early in life he began to exhibit scientific abilities, and at the age of fifteen (that is, in 1832) he constructed a galvanic battery which was purchased by the Mechanics' Institute for thirty guineas—a handsome sum in those days for an untrained lad to earn. By this success he vanquished strong parental opposition, and was enabled to attend Sturgeon's famous lectures on electricity and galvanism, and to study chemistry under the great John Dalton,[1] discoverer of the fateful atomic theory.

Besides taking over a large part of the work of his father's school when it was established in London in 1841, he began lecturing on scientific subjects while still in his twenties, and had considerable talent as a speaker. In the *Dictionary of National*

---

[1] Dalton, whose scholarly papers include a treatise on colour-blindness, must have found young Nesbit an interesting subject, for he happened to be completely colour-blind.

Biography he is described as having been one of the first to introduce the teaching of natural science into the ordinary school course, and each pupil received practical instruction in chemistry in his laboratory. He was especially interested in chemistry as applied to agriculture—a branch of science little known before his day; and he undertook analyses of soils and fertilizing agents for farmers, and commercial analyses for manufacturers.

Eventually his father's "Academy" was converted into a "Chemical and Agricultural College" under his sole direction. A census of 1851 shows that, in that year, the school had seventeen boarders, three teachers besides the Nesbits, father and son, one commercial clerk and three resident maids. In 1845, when only twenty-seven years old, John Nesbit had become a Fellow of the Chemical and Geological Societies, and from that time onward he published books on agricultural chemistry, some of which were extremely successful, and contributed papers to the learned periodicals. He was an expert on the subject of soil fertilization, about which he gave much instruction by writings and lectures. In the course of his studies he seems to have travelled widely, and in 1855 he discovered valuable beds of coprolites in the Ardennes.

His services to agriculture were evidently rated high, for in 1857 he was presented with a microscope and a set of plate, purchased by subscriptions from the farmers of England. He died in 1862 after a lingering illness, and at the early age of forty-four, when his daughter, Edith, was less than four years old. His father had predeceased him by about three years.

The eulogistic obituary notice in the *Illustrated London News* contains this passage:—

> In all departments of scientific and practical agriculture he earned great popularity as a lecturer. He had the happy faculty of terse illustration, and threw an energy and manliness of tone into his subject and delivery which lent a charm and interest to what, under duller treatment, would have been a mere string of dry details. . . . He delighted to gather students round him and stir up their enthusiasm for a science which he loved so well, and the

high positions which many of them have since attained prove that as teacher, as well as lecturer and author, he has not laboured in vain.

It is clear that John Nesbit was a versatile and very brilliant man, and in the absence of any evidence of exceptional talent among Edith's maternal ancestors, the Aldertons of Hastings, it may be assumed that she inherited the finest of her gifts from her father, who in his turn was indebted to a stern but scholarly parent. A capacity for scholarship seems often to be metamorphosed, in the child who inherits it, into the imaginative quality which is an indispensable part of genius. In creative power John Nesbit far surpassed his father, Anthony, and his daughter, Edith, surpassed them both.

The family was altogether a clever one. Edward Planta Nesbit, Anthony's second son, also essayed authorship, assisting his father in one or two scholastic works, and publishing separately a critical examination of the New Testament called *Christ, Christians, and Christianity,* which seems to have been well received. Alfred Nesbit, Edith's brother, followed his father into the field of analytical chemistry, and for some years had a laboratory in London: he patented two or three inventions, including an improved ink for cancelling postage stamps and a method of preventing the fraudulent alteration of bank cheques. But none of his experiments appears to have been practically followed up except, perhaps, the colouring of natural flowers by means of aniline dyes. Other and remoter members of the family showed themselves possessed of various abilities which, if not separately very outstanding, provide cumulatively an excellent example of the effects of heredity.

Edith, as I have said, was the youngest of six, one of whom, John Nesbit, a boy of precocious brilliance, died when he was only six years old, earlier than Edith could remember. The others were Saretta Green, the only child of Mrs. Nesbit's first marriage ("Saretta" was a euphemism, I believe, for the then common name of Sarah), Mary, Alfred, and Henry. Mary was destined to fall a sacrifice to consumption before she was twenty—a sacrifice such as almost every Victorian family was compelled to make.

At the time when I launched out on my first researches not long after E. Nesbit's death, I could find out little about her childhood, and in the original chapters relating to it, the material was perforce thinly spread. Her descendants were unanimous in informing me that it was rather from memories of her own emotions and adventures in early years than from adult observations that she had built up the verisimilitude which distinguishes her best work, and that her principal child-characters were based on recollections of her brothers and her sister (the half-sister was grown up long before Edith had left the nursery): but plain facts, such as a biographer requires, were hard to come by. It was not till twenty years later that, browsing through a very battered volume of *The Girl's Own Paper,* I discovered—tormentingly enough just after a new edition of my book had gone to press—that she had written no fewer than twelve articles of childhood reminiscences, running as a serial from October 1896 to September 1897. They were entitled *My Schooldays,* but as she did not go to school till she was seven, I must begin by telling what I learned about her early infancy from family sources and letters.

After being widowed for the second time, Mrs. Nesbit took over the control, financially at least, of the Agricultural College, and kept it going for several years. She was assuredly a very capable woman and not the helpless female of Victorian mythology. In religion both she and her husband must have been somewhat unconventional, because Edith's baptism did not take place until she was old enough to stand at the font and to express herself in a sort of comprehensible language. In 1858 and thereabouts the sacrament was generally administered within the first weeks of the child's life, and as illness, supposing there had been any, would only make the necessity appear more urgent, it is to be assumed that Edith's parents could not have been orthodox.

It was at the belated christening ceremony that she first exhibited a kind of whimsicality very much her own. While waiting with the sponsors for the clergyman she managed secretly to take off her little kid shoes, and when she was lifted up to receive the sprinkling of water she dropped them both into the font, remarking audibly that they were meant "for boats."

This is the earliest authentic anecdote about her that has come my way. The next belongs to a slightly later time, when she was three or four years old, and offers a good example of the manner in which her mind perpetually wandered back to her own childhood when she planned those books upon which her reputation rests. There is a passage in *The Treasure Seekers* which describes how that unfortunate child, Albert-next-door, was stuck fast in the ground—through a "mistake" of the kind the Bastable family was prone to make—and had to be dug out. The origin of this incident seems to have been a trick played upon her by her brothers.

There was to be a tea-party at their home, and they had been all dressed up in their best clothes, and put out in the garden with instructions "to be good and keep clean" until the visitors arrived. Daisy—to call her by the name then most familiar— was clad in flimsy white stuff, and the wide flounced skirts, supported by half a dozen starched petticoats, which formed the party costume of a little girl in those days, inspired one of her brothers with the idea that they ought to "plant" her and pretend she was a flower. So, protesting vigorously, she was dug into the earth beside a gooseberry bush, and the brothers, several years older and consequently much stronger than she, did their work so thoroughly that her rescue by infuriated adults was not accomplished without some difficulty and the temporary destruction of the party frock.

A high-spirited girl with two elder brothers is likely to get up to a good deal of mischief, and Daisy found temptation from either Alfred or Henry almost irresistible. She was the sort of sister—like Alice, perhaps the most lovable of the renowned Bastables—to whom brothers give their confidences.

It was probably shortly before she went to her first school that Alfred and Henry decided to run away from home—a step which I suppose every child worthy the name has sometimes contemplated. They told their secret to Daisy, and considering that Alfred was four years her senior, and Henry three, it speaks much of her daring resolution that, when she offered to accompany them, they did not refuse. Provisions were collected from the larder; jars of jam and of preserved food, loaves, and all else that they considered necessary to subsistence, together with their favourite possessions, were tied in a tablecloth and they prepared very seriously for their departure. But when they tried to set out the huge bundle was too heavy to carry, and as they could not bring themselves to leave behind anything it contained they were obliged to abandon their scheme.

E. Nesbit carefully preserved throughout her life the first letter she ever received from her mother and, since these little relics are in a very special and tender sense illuminating, I venture to quote it in full. As her father was still living when it was written, she could not have been more than three years old:

My Pretty Little Daisy,
How kind of you my darling to help to send me a nice Handf. I shall be so glad to have you down in my bed and hug and kiss you for it.

I shall soon be home now and I shall bring you a Baby doll which I have bought for you. It has blue Eyes and flaxen hair and is dressed like a little baby in long clothes with a white Costume Hood and Cloak. You will be so pleased with it. Mama longs to bring it home to her darling little Daisy.

Mama hopes her little pet's cold is gone. Nurse must take great care of you and Alf this cold weather. Good night my dear little girl. Papa and Mama send you lots of love and kisses.

2   *Early Miseries*

The series of articles, *My Schooldays,* to which I have alluded began with a preamble which affirmed that everything in them was "written from my most clear and vivid recollection."

> When I was a little child I used to pray fervently, tearfully, that when I should be grown up I might never forget what I thought, felt, and suffered then. Let these pages speak for me, and bear witness that I have not forgotten.

The reminiscences that follow are largely of distresses, disappointments, loneliness, and stark terror. Knowing that works of art are often produced, like pearls, as a means of enduring an irritant in the system, we ought not to be surprised to learn that E. Nesbit's books for children owe their particular lustre and humour to the despairs of her own childhood. But we are more than that; we are taken aback. Surely those sunlit adventures cannot be anything but the reflections of youthful happiness?

On the contrary, they are a brilliantly successful dispersal of long-menacing shadows. Her schooldays were so bitterly miserable that schools, schoolwork, the behaviour of children in classroom or playground, were almost totally excluded from the pages meant for enjoyment.

It must have been in 1865 that Mary first showed symptoms of decline, and Mrs. Nesbit, to give her the benefit of sea air, took a house in Brighton. With her hands full, she decided to send the youngest child, Daisy as she was still called, to a local boarding school run by a Mrs. Arthur. It was, apparently, a badly managed place, where the pupils had considerable opportunities for maltreating one another. Daisy was unmercifully bullied by an odious little girl who, on the very first day, ruined a doll's tea-set of pewter which she (Daisy) had proudly brought with her. She did this by biting each piece of the thin metal into "a formless lump," and then threatening:

". . . If you say a word about it, I'll say you did it and pinched me as well. And Mrs. Arthur'll believe me, because I'm not a new girl and you are."

I turned away without a word, and I never did tell—till now. . . . She tortured me unremittingly.

No children so frightening ever darken E. Nesbit's fictitious tales. It could not have been more than a summer term that she spent at Mrs. Arthur's, but at seven a few months are longer than the same number of years in maturity.

I remember the hot, white streets, and the flies, and Brill's Baths, and the Western Road,[1] and the bitter pang of passing, at the end of a long procession, our own house, where always someone might be at the window and never anyone was.

I used to go home on Saturdays, and then all the bitterness was so swallowed up in the bliss of my home-returning, that I actually forgot the miseries of my school life, but I was very unhappy there.

She admits fairly that Mrs. Arthur and the big girls were kind to her, but she was overjoyed when, after catching measles, she was taken home wrapped in a blanket.

When she was better, the family went to a cottage in Buckinghamshire for the summer holidays, and the contrast was

[1] Brighton's principal shopping street.

rapturous. Her brother Alfred gave her a white rabbit in a hutch he had made himself, and Harry promised she could "go shares" in two dormice that he kept in a tea caddy. It was enchantment to breakfast on new-laid eggs and honey in the comb and fresh raspberries, with her mother "in a cool cotton gown" pouring out tea: yet she suffered acutely from the mysterious inability to reveal her aversions and her griefs. She wanted, for example, to reject a dress of the same tartan as her hated enemy of the school-yard had worn, but could not bring herself to say why, and so was obliged dismally to submit to it.

> I have often wondered what it is that keeps children from telling their mothers these things—and even now I don't know. I only know I might have been saved many of these little-big troubles if I had only been able to explain.

It is curious that, with so vivid a memory, she never suspected, when bringing up her own children, that they too had difficulties in communication.

The next school, where she spent a year, was spoiled for her by an unpleasant teacher. It was "a select boarding establishment for young ladies and gentlemen at Stamford, and I venture to think that I should have preferred a penal settlement." Miss Fairchild, the owner and headmistress, was kind and beautiful and had a notably charming mother, but Miss ———— (she remains nameless) was hateful. With humiliating insistence she deplored Daisy's intractable and untidy hair and the dirtiness of her hands.

> I can see now the little willow-patterned basin of hard cold water, and smell the unpleasant little square of mottled soap with which I was expected to wash them. I don't know how the others managed, but for me the result was always the same—failure."

To make her sense of shame more poignant, she spoiled Miss ————'s best dress by hiding a doll's bath full of water in her wardrobe—for which, with a fellow culprit, a small boy, she was punished by going without dinner and learning a long psalm. A hundred years ago a school-teacher's clothes were not likely to have been very numerous, and the drastic offence may have called for a drastic deterrent: but even for dirty hands Daisy frequently—or so it seemed in her recollection—had to have breakfast in isolation, while day after day one meal or another was forfeited because she could not understand long division.

> I should literally have starved, I do believe, but for dear Mrs. Fairchild. She kept my little body going with illicit cakes and plums and the like, and fed my starving little heart with surreptitious kisses and kind words.

An excessive use of the loaded word "little" suggests that natural self-pity was being over-indulged. Her "little head" was sore from futile brushing, her "grubby little hands" were vainly concealed beneath her pinafore. This too tremulous note is wonderfully avoided in E. Nesbit's later work. The writing of the series must have proved a valuable catalyst. The vapour of her indignation was finally distilled into a peculiar savour, sharp but never acrid, which counteracts the sweetness that might have become cloying.

The second term at Miss Fairchild's was happier than the first. Daisy had learned in the holidays how to make dolls' bedsteads, and, to provide draperies for them, she recklessly cut up her adult half-sister's Christmas present, a sash of green Japanese brocade.

> I acquired many marbles and much gingerbread, and totally eclipsed Cissy Thomas who had enjoyed the fleeting sunshine of popular favour on the insecure basis of paper dolls.

Her mother scolded her gently for the spoiled sash and gave her new ones, as well as rich pieces of material to pursue her hobby, but in the term that followed—

> No one wanted dolls' beds any more; and Cissy Thomas had brought back a herbarium. . . .

Long division set in again. Again, day after day, I sat lonely in the schoolroom—now like a furnace—and ate my dry bread and milk and water in the depths of disgrace. . . . Night after night I cried myself to sleep in my bed—whose coarse home-spun sheets were hotter than blankets—because I could not get the answers right.

Is she perhaps overcharging this picture of what she calls "the heart-broken misery of a child, to whom the present grief is eternal"? The worst school curriculum must consist of something beside arithmetic lessons, and even E. Nesbit, bad as she was at figures all her life, could not have got every sum wrong. If she took some dramatic license with gloom, it was to heighten the brightness of the scene when she received an unlooked-for visit from her mother—who, it must be borne in mind, was living and able to read these articles. The occasion was meant to be valedictory, for Mrs. Nesbit was about to take her elder daughters abroad, but—

. . . I clung about her neck, and with such insistence implored her not to leave me—not to go without me, that I think I must have expressed my trouble without uttering it, for when, after three delicious days of drives and walks, in which I had always a loving hand to hold, my mother left Stamford, she took me, trembling with joy like a prisoner reprieved, with her. And I have never seen—or wished to see Stamford again.

No dates are given, but according to correspondence of the time, the migration took place in 1867, so Daisy must have been nine or nearly so. Mary, for whose sake the journey was undertaken, tells the story herself in a letter of January, 1868, to her father's brother (the author of the book on Christianity), who had long been settled in Australia.

"The doctors," she says, "agreed that it would be scarcely safe to spend the cold months in England, and out of the question to do so in such a cold, bleak place as Brighton; so as soon as I was able to bear the passage, we left home and have been moving from place to place down the West Coast of France, without, until now, having found a place uniting the advantage of suitable climate, pretty scenery, and moderately cheap expenditure."

She goes on to tell their itinerary—first Rouen, where they "revelled in the magnificence of old Gothic churches" and where Mary, whose favourite heroine was Joan of Arc, "was especially charmed with the antiquities relating to her era"; then Paris where they stayed a fortnight, spending three days at the Great Universal Exhibition, which disappointed them, and eleven days visiting the Louvre, the Luxembourg, and the other noted sights. Paris became cold, and they hastened to Tours, where there were "excellent shops and very pleasing society." Mrs. Nesbit wanted to spend the winter there, but the others, eager to see the Pyrenees, urged the brave woman onward to Bordeaux, sending their heavy luggage in advance and stopping at whatever places they thought attractive on their route— Poitiers, Angoulême, St. Emilion, and elsewhere.

At sixteen Mary wrote gaily and eloquently, absolutely unaware that one member of the party was at that very time afflicted with an obsession of fear just short of breakdown. Daisy had been in a very low state of nerves on leaving England.

My mind was, I suppose, a little upset by my soul's sorrows at Stamford and my body's unspeakable discomforts on board the channel boat [the night crossing from Newhaven to Dieppe when she had been exhaustingly seasick], and I was seized with a horror of the words *Débit de Tabac* which I had noticed on our way from the station; I associated them with the gravestone of my father, I don't know why. I can only conjecture that the last syllable of *Débit* being the same as that of our name may have had something to do with it.

In a nightmare that followed, her father's ghost exhorted her to erase from his tomb the awful inscription ("Tobacconist's shop" if only she had known it!). That was, she says, her first encounter with fear of the dead or the supernatural, and she thought she owed it to "the chatter of some nurse-maid, long forgotten."

Though she was disturbed, the daytime still yielded its pleasures. She could to some extent share Mary's appreciation of Gothic churches, and she was glad to be given a silver brooch in the form of a daisy at the Paris Exhibition—which, on the whole, she found "large, empty, and very tiring." The enjoyments of children are as unpredictable as their woes. She was more gratified to see gloves being made at Poitiers, and to be measured for a pair of her own in kid of that lively blue so typical of the 1860's; and she treasured for years a little framed painting of a church bought for her by her mother at Rouen from a woman in a white coif who sold crucifixes, medals, and rosaries at a stall. This gift from a Catholic source is evidence of Mrs. Nesbit's freedom from the bigotry of the middle-class British matron of her epoch. She also allowed her children to visit a convent, where Daisy expected to find nuns walled up, and was relieved to be welcomed in "a trim well-kept garden and a pleasant house, where kindly-faced women in black gowns and white guimpes walked about, breviary in hand."

Like every highly sensitive child, she was always subject to the terrors of the imagination, and at Bordeaux they were given a dreadful stimulant. Before she could bring herself, at the age of thirty-eight, to relate how this draught of poison was administered, she made a compulsive pause, and devoted the whole of one long chapter to other occasions of fear, going back to the very first she could remember. It was a catharsis, and—though nothing is more unlikely than any acquaintance on her part with the work of Dr. Freud in Vienna—she knew it to be such. What is very odd is that so painful a record should have found its way into a magazine for girls, the prevailing tone of which was both gentle and cheerful.

She recaptured the shock of seeing her father, who died before she was four, playing at "wild beasts" with her brothers.

> He wore his great fur travelling coat inside out, and his roars were completely convincing. I was borne away screaming. . . .
> Then came nursery charades. I was the high-born orphan whom gipsies were to steal, and my part was to lie in a cradle, and at the proper moment to be carried away shrieking. I under-

stood my part perfectly—I was about three, I suppose—and had rehearsed it more than once. Being carried off in the arms of the gipsy (my favourite sister) was nothing to scream at. . . .

Unfortunately, however, there had been no dress rehearsal, and when on the night of the performance the high-born orphan found itself close to a big black bonnet and a hideous mask, it did scream to some purpose, and presently screamed itself into some sort of fit or swoon, was put to bed, and stayed there for many days which passed dreamlike. But that old woman haunted my dreams and haunts them still indeed. . . .

One used to lie awake in the silence, listening, listening to the pad-pad of one's heart, straining one's ears to make sure that it was not the pad-pad of something else, something unspeakable creeping towards one in the horrible dense dark. One used to lie quite, quite still, I remember, listening, listening. . . .

Her pillow was wet, she said, with the dews of her agony of apprehension.

My nurse—ah, how good she was to me!—never went downstairs to supper after she found out my terrors, which she very quickly did. She used to sit in the day nursery with the door open "a tiny crack" and that light was company, because I knew I had only to call out, and someone who loved me would come and banish fear.

Daisy's brothers, in the thoughtlessness of their own infancy, sometimes scared her badly, chasing her round the garden with a "terrible object"—the double head of a malformed calf which, mounted as a curiosity, their father kept in a sort of farm shed where he worked.

But one of my father's pupils to whom I owe that and many other kindnesses, one day seized me under his arm and the two-headed horror in the other, and thus equipped, pursued my brothers. They fled shrieking. . . . I never feared it again.

Adults, young and old, were almost invariably more sympathetic than mid-Victorian children were accustomed to find them, and that is doubtless why the attractive ones so easily out-number the unattractive in her tales for juveniles. Mr. Kearns, a teacher at the Agricultural College, dealt with one of her anxieties in the wisest possible manner. It was caused by the skin of an emu hanging on the wall, with black feathers that moved in the draught. When he saw that she covered her eyes in passing it—

He took me on his shoulder, where I felt quite safe, reluctant but not resisting, to within a couple of yards of the emu.

"Now," he said, "will you do what I tell you?"

"Not any nearer," I said evasively.

"Now, you know it won't hurt you. . . . Will you stroke it, if I do first?"

I didn't want to.

"To please me."

That argument was conclusive, for I loved him. Then we approached the black feathers, I clinging desperately to his neck, and sobbing convulsively.

"No—no—no—not any nearer!" But he was kind and wise, and insisted. His big hand smoothed down the feathers.

"Now, Daisy. You know you promised. Give me your hand." I shut my eyes tight, and let him draw my hand down the dusty feathers. Then I opened my eyes a little bit.

"Now you stroke it. Stroke the poor emu!" I did so. "Are you afraid now?" Curiously enough, I wasn't. Poor Mr. Kearns paid dearly for his kindness. For several weeks I gave him no peace, but insisted on being taken, at all hours of the day and night, to "stroke the poor emu."

Her association with this lovable man, who afterwards became Public Analyst of Sheffield, was in the period between her father's death and the removal to Brighton. After they left Kennington, she noted that her terrors became "more ordinary." She would dream of falling houses, crumbling precipices, and would wake with grateful relief, but the worst nightmares, the atrocities that could not be banished from the mind on awakening, ceased for a time to trouble her, and the woes of school life took their place.

The travels in France, which she had prepared for with "delicious thrills of anticipation and excitement," provided the experience that brought her nervousness back in its most acute form. It was one that would have proved traumatic even to a child of stolid constitution. By the time they reached Bordeaux, she was "tired of churches and picture-galleries, of fairs and markets," and when she heard that her sisters were going to see some mummies, she begged to be taken.

> My fancy did not paint mummies for me apart from plate-glass cases, camphor, boarded galleries, and kindly curators. . . .

That she should have wished to see any mummies at all, even "cousins" of those in the British Museum, seems peculiar in one who, at much the same age, found the Egyptian rooms horribly sinister and frightening; but few children are without a strain of morbid curiosity as long as daylight lasts.

> I was consumed by a fever of impatience for the three days which had to go by before the coming of the day on which the treasure might be visited. My sisters, who were to lead me to these delights, believed too that the mummies would be chiefly interesting on account of their association with Bloomsbury.
>
> Well, we went—I in my best blue silk frock, which I insisted on wearing to honour the occasion, holding the hand of my sister and positively skipping with delicious anticipation. There was some delay about keys, during which my excitement was scarcely to be restrained.

Such an ecstasy at the prospect of inspecting mummies hardly seems plausible. She is overdoing the gaiety this time as, in previous passages, she has overdone the gloom: but the very fact that she set the stage so carefully to insure the full impact of the impending disaster, shows how harrowingly she still felt it.

> . . . We went through an arched doorway and along a flagged passage, the old man who guided us explaining volubly in French as we went.

"What does he say?"

"He says they are natural mummies."

"What does that mean?"

"They are not embalmed by man, like the Egyptian ones, but simply by the peculiar earth of the churchyard where they were buried."

. . . The passage began to slope downward. A chill air breathed on our faces, bringing with it a damp earthy smell. Then we came to some narrow stone steps. Our guide spoke again.

"What does he say?"

"We are to be careful, the steps are slippery and mouldy."

I think even then my expectation still was of a long clean gallery, filled with the white light of a London noon, shed through high skylights on Egyptian treasures. But the stairs were dark, and I held my sister's hand tightly. Down we went, down, down!

"What does he say?"

"We are under the church now; these are the vaults."

We went along another passage, the damp mouldy smell increasing, and my clasp of my sister's hand grew closer and closer. We stopped in front of a heavy door barred with iron, and our guide turned a big reluctant key in a lock that grated. "Les voilà," he said, throwing open the door and drawing back dramatically.

We were in the room before my sisters had time to see cause for regretting that they had brought me. The vision of dry boards and white light and glass cases vanished, and in its stead I saw this:

A small vault, as my memory serves me, about fifteen feet square, with an arched roof, from the centre of which hung a lamp that burned with a faint blue light, and made the guide's candle look red and lurid. The floor was flagged like the passages, and was as damp and chill. Round three sides of the room ran a railing, and behind it—standing against the wall with a ghastly look of life in death—were about two hundred skeletons, hung on wires, like the one you see at the doctor's, but skeletons with their flesh hardened on their bones, with their long dry hair hanging on each side of their brown faces, where the skin in drying had drawn itself back from their gleaming teeth and empty eye-sockets. Skeletons draped in mouldering shreds of shrouds and grave-clothes, their lean figures still clothed with dry skin, seemed to reach out towards me. There they stood, men, women, and children, knee-deep in loose bones collected from the other vaults of the church, and heaped around them. On the wall near the door I saw the dried body of a little child hung up by its hair.

I don't think I screamed or cried, or even said a word. I think I was paralysed with horror, but I remember presently going back up those stairs, holding tightly to that kindly hand, and not daring to turn my head lest one of those charnel-house faces should peep out at me from some niche in the damp wall.

Her memory had played one or two tricks on her. The Church of Saint Michel, where she and many other hapless children were treated to so grisly a spectacle, had had its exterior burial ground cleared towards the end of the eighteenth century and the bodies removed into a crypt where they were preserved by the singular dryness of the atmosphere. The damp and mould it was irresistible to imagine were not present, but the place was none the less ghastly for that. In nearly thirty years that had passed since that dismal day, she had never enquired the name of the building, nor learned the facts the guide book could have told her. Deliberate ignorance was perhaps a natural protection. The simple remedy of "stroking the poor emu" is not likely to be effective when the object of fear is so incorrigibly repugnant as the contents of a charnel house.[2]

Daisy's "stupor of fright" passed unnoticed. (It does not seem to have occurred to her then or later that the sixteen-year-old Mary, if not the fully grown-up Saretta, might also have been in a state of repressed shock.) The family dressed for the hotel evening dinner, and she was left to have her light supper in the bedroom.

It was a high room, and very imperfectly lighted by the two wax candles in silver candlesticks. There were two windows and a curtained alcove, where the beds were. Suddenly my blood ran cold. What was behind that curtain? Beds. "Yes," whispered

[2] In girlhood Lady Bessborough, the mother of Lady Caroline Lamb, had a similar experience. She was made to touch one of the corpses, and the effect on her nerves was deplorable.

something that was I, and yet not I; "but suppose there are no beds there now. Only mummies, mummies, mummies!"

A sudden noise; I screamed with terror. It was only the door opening to let the waiter in. He was a young waiter, hardly more than a boy, and had always smiled kindly at me when we met, though hitherto our intercourse had not gone farther. Now I rushed to him and flung my arms round him, to his amazement and the near ruin of my bread and milk. He spoke no English and I no French, but somehow he managed to understand that I was afraid, and afraid of that alcove.

Once again the world of adults proved completely dependable.

He set down the bread and milk, and he took me in his arms and together we fetched more candles, and then he drew back the awful curtain, and showed me the beds lying white and quiet. . . . I hope he did not get into any trouble that night for neglected duties, for he did not attempt to leave me till my mother came back. He sat down with me on his knee and petted me and sang to me under his breath and fed me with the bread and milk, when by-and-by I grew calm enough to take it.

All good things be to him wherever he is! I like best to think of him in a little hotel of his own, a quiet little country inn standing back from a straight road bordered with apple trees and poplars. . . . I like to believe that now he has little children of his own, who hold out their arms when he opens the door, and who climb upon his knees clamouring for those same songs which he sang, out of the kindness of his boyish heart, to the little frightened English child, such a long, long time ago.

Even if only eighteen or nineteen in 1867, the rescuer must have been approaching fifty in 1897, the year this contribution was written, and his children were no longer likely to be at the knee-climbing stage; but it must have been hard for her to picture him as anything but a young man. Whatever may have happened to him, he remains the *preux chevalier* among waiters, and an influence on her life that must have been more important than she knew, helping her to at least a comparative freedom from the sense of class distinction which, in so many late-Victorian and Edwardian children's books, supplies an uncongenial element.

> The mummies of Bordeaux were the crowning horror of my childish life. [she sums up] It is to them, I think, more than to any other thing that I owe nights and nights of anguish and horror, long years of bitterest fear and dread. All the other fears could have been effaced, but the shock of that sight branded it on my brain, and I never forgot it.

She had already given grim instances of the forms her horrors took—corpses lying under white sheets, a luminous skull, a skeleton arm, contrived from a bedroom gas globe and a metal bracket seen in dim light. She dwelt almost lovingly on the "frozen terrors of the long, dark nights when I was little and lonely. . . ." It all seems to make rather harsh reading for young schoolgirls, but the spontaneity—amounting sometimes to sheer carelessness—of the writing shows that she was more concerned to purge her own imagination than to gratify the subscribers to the magazine. Until after she had children of her own, she said, she remained mortally terrified of the dark, and, as a grown woman, was "tortured" by memory.

> My children, I resolved, should never know such fear. And to guard them from it I must banish it from my own soul. It was not easy, but it was done. It is banished now, and my babies, thank God, never have known it.

As to this, she was unduly optimistic. Her children, like all children, were subject to deep and nerve-racking anxieties which they were just as unable to share with her as she had been to share hers with her mother. One effect, however, her determination to shield them did have. They always regarded her as utterly intrepid. Her daughter Iris was quite incredulous when I told her of discovering these articles which laid so much stress on fear. She assured me I must have mistaken them: her mother had been a most daring and dauntless child.

Daring, unquestionably. Her high courage is shown even in her consenting to stroke the sinister emu skin because she had promised to: and in all adventures where she could play an active part, she was as mettlesome as any of the children she portrayed. But, when of necessity passive, she had no defence against the most cruel sensibility.

Her sufferings ultimately resulted in an extraordinary dichotomy in her creative work. On the one hand, she wrote for adults a number of gruesome stories—more genuinely "horrid" than any tale by Mrs. Radcliffe or Mary Shelley, yet singularly ineffectual and now deservedly forgotten; on the other, she produced a kind of literature for children that was serenely protective and free from the least hint of her own insecurity, not outgrown till she was in her thirties. When the fears engendered in her childhood were at last dispelled, it was, she wrote, as if she had come into the splendour of noontide after having lived long years in an evil enchanter's castle. She could not speak "soon nor lightly" of what had befallen her there.

3 *Childhood in France*

After ten days in Bordeaux, Mrs. Nesbit and her daughters went on to Arcachon, and thence to Pau, where they took rooms in a pension. Daisy by now was dismally bored with travel.

> . . . I believe all children are—so large a part of a child's life is made up of little familiar playthings and objects; it has little of that historic and artistic sense which lends colour and delight to travel. I was tired of wandering about, and glad to think we were to stay in Pau for the winter.

Both the boredom and the more secret trouble of her mind were lightened by going to a charity bazaar and acquiring a dazzlingly dressed doll which could be turned from a brunette to a blonde by changing its wig.

> Here let me make a confession, I had never really loved any doll. My affections up to that time had been lavished on a black and white spotted penny rabbit, bought at a Kentish fair; but when I saw Renée, it seemed to me that if I could love a doll, this would be the one. . . .
>
> The bazaar pleased me. It was got up by English residents, and their fancy-work was the fancy-work of the church bazaars in

England, and I felt at home among it, and when my eyes rested on Renée I saw the most delightful object I had seen for many weeks. I looked and longed, and longed and looked, and then suddenly in a moment one of the great good fortunes of my life happened to me. The beautiful doll was put up to be raffled, and my sister won her. I trembled with joy as she and her wardrobe were put into my hands.

I took her home. I dressed and undressed her twenty times a day. I made her play the part of heroine in all my favourite stories. I told her fairy tales and took her to bed with me at night for company, but I never loved her. I have never been able to love a doll in my life.

Arrangements were now made for Daisy to live with a little girl of her own age in a French family. She was reconciled to the prospect of parting from her mother by an assurance that she would become capable of writing her letters in French, and she pictured herself "crushing" the odious teacher at Stamford with that accomplishment.

Marguerite Lourdes, her new companion, a pretty flaxen-haired child, turned out most congenial, and Madame Lourdes, who could not speak a word of English, "knew the universal language of love and sympathy."

I learned French in three months. All day I was with Mme. Lourdes or Marguerite. . . . It was French or silence, and any healthy child would have chosen French as I did. They were three happy months. I adored Marguerite, who was, I think, the typical good child of French story books. . . .

I do not think we ever got into wilful mischief. For instance, our starving the cat was quite unintentional. We were playing bandits . . . and it occurred to us that Mimi would make an excellent captive princess, so we caught her and put her in a hamper at the end of the cellar, and when my mother called to take us home to tea with her, we rushed off and left the poor princess still a prisoner.

Madame Lourdes, failing to find the cat that night, concluded that it had run away or met with an accident, and, to spare their feelings, avoided mentioning it, so that it was not until two nights later still that Daisy recalled their interrupted game.

> . . . I started up in bed about midnight and pulled Marguerite's yellow pigtail wildly. "Oh, Marguerite," I cried, "poor Mimi!" I had to pull at the pigtail as though it was a bell-rope. . . . Then she sat up in bed rigid with a great purpose.
>
> "We must go down and fetch her," she said.
>
> It was winter; the snow was on the ground. Marguerite thoughtfully put on her shoes and her dressing-gown, but I, with some vague recollection of bare-footed pilgrims, and some wild desire to make expiation for my crime, went down bare-footed in my nightgown. The crime of forgetting a cat for three days was well paid for by that expedition.

For Daisy, who had only recently had the shock of finding herself in the charnel house at the Bordeaux church, the guilty journey to a distant and pitch-dark cellar that opened from a courtyard in front of the house, was a feat of immense courage. It was rewarded by their finding the unfortunate animal alive.

> I remember so well the feeling of her soft warm fur against my cold little legs. I caught the cat in my arms, and as I turned to go back to the house, my half-frozen foot struck against something on the floor. It felt silky, I picked it up. It was Renée. . . . She also had been shut up here all this time, and I had never missed her!
>
> We took the cat and my doll back to bed with us and tried to get warm again. Marguerite was soon asleep, but I lay awake for a long time kissing and crying over the ill-used cat.
>
> I didn't get up again for a fortnight. My bare-footed pilgrimage cost me a frightful cold and the loss of several children's parties to which we had been invited. Marguerite, throughout my illness, behaved like an angel.

There is generally, in E. Nesbit's groups of children, one whose conduct leans towards virtue and whose sense of responsibility seldom wavers. The prototype is Dora Bastable, and perhaps *her* prototype was Daisy's friend, so lovingly remembered from the days at Pau. No one else in her early life quite fits the picture of a maternal child with an active but not repressive social conscience. Daisy herself became an incorrigibly daring and irresponsible tomboy; and as for her much admired sisters, they had always belonged in her eyes to the adult world, and though they must have been drawn upon for her literary creations, it is unlikely that they figure in her books as juvenile characters.

Daisy's one quarrel with Marguerite ended in a Bastable reconciliation.

We were going to a children's party and my best blue silk was put out for me to wear. "I wish you wouldn't wear that," said Marguerite hesitatingly, "it makes my grey cashmere look so old."

Now I had nothing else to wear but a brown frock which I hated. "Never mind," I said hypocritically, "it's better to be good than smart, everybody says so," and I put on my blue silk.

When I was dressed, I pranced off to the kitchen to show my finery to the cook, and under her admiring eyes executed my best curtsey. . . . It ended in a tub of clothes and water that was standing just behind me. . . . As I scrambled out, I saw Marguerite in the doorway, smiling triumphantly, and heard her thin little voice say, "The blue silk can't mock the poor grey cashmere now!"

An impulse of blind fury came upon me. I caught Marguerite by her little shoulders, and before the cook could interfere I had ducked her head-first into the tub of linen. Mme. Lourdes behaved beautifully; she appeared on the scene at this moment and, impartial as ever, she slapped us both, but when she heard from the cook the rights of the story, my sentence was "bed." "But Marguerite," said her mother, "has been punished enough for an unkind word."

And Marguerite was indeed sobbing bitterly, while I was dry-eyed and still furious. "She can't go," I cried, "she hasn't got a dress!"

"You have spoilt her dress," said Mme. Lourdes coolly, "the least you can do is to lend her your brown one." And that excellent woman actually had the courage to send her own daughter to a party in my dress, an exquisite punishment to us both.

Marguerite came to my bedside that night; she had taken off the brown dress and wore her little flannel dressing-gown.

"You're not cross now, are you?" she said. "I did beg mother to let you come, and I've not enjoyed myself a bit, and I've brought you this from the party."

It was a beautiful little model of a coffee-mill made in sugar. My resentment could not withstand this peace-offering. I never quarrelled with Marguerite again.

This must have been in the New Year of 1868. Up to near Christmas time, Mrs. Nesbit had been paying Daisy frequent visits, but Mary's health was showing signs of deterioration, and on medical advice they moved to Biarritz, leaving Daisy behind.

"I am much better now than I was," Mary wrote to her uncle on January 26th, "but by no means quite strong yet. It is a great drawback to me now not to be able to go on with my studies—just at the age when I should enjoy them most.

"While at Biarritz we made a little excursion into the Spanish frontier—S. Sebastian and Irun. We had glorious weather and enjoyed our trip immensely; going part of the way by train, and part by that much pleasanter mode of travelling, the top of a diligence.

"Mamma was so intensely disgusted with the Spanish inns and accommodation, that she declares she will never enter Spain again on any pretext whatever unless we are accompanied by some able protector, who will manage to arrange all things comfortably for us."

After this jaunt, evidently more agreeable to the girls than to their weary mother, they settled for a while at Bagnères-de-Bigorre, a resort full of streams and minor cataracts, and in February or March Daisy was sent for. Glad as she was to rejoin her family, she wept grievously at parting from the French household, none of whom she was ever destined to see again.

A servant looked after her on the journey, and dried her tears by reminding her of the present of knitted cuffs that she was carrying to her mother, her own zealous handiwork.

They were of a size suitable to the wrist of a man of about eight feet, and the irregularities at the edge where I had forgotten to slip the stitch were concealed by stiff little ruchings of blue satin ribbon. I thought of them with unspeakable pride.

We reached Bagnères after dark, and my passion of joy at seeing my mother again was heightened by the knowledge that I had so rich a gift to bestow upon her.

In her eagerness to display the offering, she turned the contents of her box upsidedown, and Mrs. Nesbit did not fail to open the carefully folded wrappings with every demonstration of surprise and pleasure, which her elder daughters echoed.

. . . I went happy to bed. When I was lying between the sheets, I heard one of my sisters laughing in the next room. She was talking, and I knew she was speaking of my precious cuffs. "They would just fit a coal-heaver," she said.

She never knew that I heard her, but it was years before I forgave that unconscious outrage to my feelings.

She does not say which sister made this unlucky blunder. Probably it was Saretta. Mary's pathetic death three years later would scarcely have permitted the grudge to linger: and, in fact, an adulatory poem which Daisy wrote some time before that shows that Mary inspired the most romantic attachment in her.

The tiny anecdote, taken with others which have been quoted, reveals the magic by which E. Nesbit transmuted what began as a long memory for injuries into the sensitive understanding of a child's emotions that was of such advantage to her in her writing. She outgrew all ideas of unforgivingness but used her recollection of her poignant feelings to re-create at will those daydreams of supernatural power by which the vulnerable compensate themselves for their helplessness.

Although Saretta's laughter had hurt her, their day-to-day relations were not seriously impaired. Sitting on the elder girl's knee she would beg for a fairy tale as if no wound rankled.

My sister had a genius for telling fairy stories. If she would only write them now as she told them then, all the children in England would insist on having her fairy stories and none others.

This half-sister fourteen years Daisy's senior must have been a significant influence, but although Saretta did some writing and it was expected that she would have a literary career, I have been unable to trace even so much as one of her letters.

Mrs. Nesbit's resolution never again to risk the hardships of Spanish travel weakened when they had all grown a little tired of their picturesque but unexciting watering-place, and Daisy was overjoyed to learn that they were to drive over the mountain roads in an open carriage bound for Spain. But while they were en route, they learned that one of the boys was ill with whooping-cough, and the horses heads were turned northwards.

In her January letter, Mary had mentioned that her brother Harry was in poor health and that her mother was thinking of sending for him. Whether it was he or Alfred who had contracted the infection, Mrs. Nesbit determined to go back to England.

On their drive towards Bagnères de Luchon, they stopped to look at a castle which had "a great square tower without door or window." Though the castle itself was ruined, the tower was still strong and apparently impregnable. They walked round it trying in vain to find a door, and their driver told them, in all earnestness or so Daisy thought, that there was treasure buried there, and that one day a wind would blow down the walls and the people of the village would share the hoard and become kings of France. The strange legend and the singular impenetrability of the structure made a very deep impression on her, and she often meditated on finding the entrance, taking possession of the treasure, and buying rich gifts for all her family, as well as driving about herself in a chariot drawn by four tame zebras with silver harness.

Thirty-six years later this French tower, and its treasure too, were introduced into *The Phoenix and the Carpet,* but by that time, 1904, it was a motor car that seemed the conveyance most worth having—at any rate to the boys in the story.

The principal adventure of their journey through an almost medieval part of France was an alarming one. They began the drive from Aurillac to Murat late in the afternoon because Saretta and Mary wanted to see the mountains of Auvergne by moonlight.

We had a large open carriage, with a sort of rumble behind and a wide box-seat in front. The driver, a blue-bloused ruffian with plausible manners, agreed to take us and our luggage to Murat for a certain price, which I have forgotten. All our luggage was packed on his carriage; we, too, were packed in it, and we started. About five miles from the town the driver halted, and came to the door of the carriage.

"Mesdames," he said, "a young relative of mine will join us here, he will sit on the box with me."

My mother objected that, as we were paying for the carriage, we had a right to refuse to allow his friends to enter it.

"As you will, madame," he said calmly, "but if you refuse, I shall place you and your boxes in the middle of the road, and leave you planted there."

Three English ladies and a little girl alone in a strange country, five miles from any town, what could we do? My mother consented. A mile or two further on two blue-bloused figures got up suddenly from their seat by the roadside.

"My father and brother-in-law," said our driver.

My mother saw that protest was vain, so these two were stowed in the rumble, and the carriage jolted on heavily. We now began to be seriously frightened. . . . In the next few miles two more passengers were added to our number, a cousin and an uncle. All wore blue blouses, and had villainous-looking faces. The uncle, who looked like a porpoise and smelt horribly of brandy, was put inside the carriage with us, because there was now no room left in any other part of the conveyance. The family party laughed and joked in a patois wholly unintelligible to us. I was convinced that they were arranging for the disposal of our property and our bodies after the murder. My mother and sisters were talking in low voices in English.

"If we only get to the half-way house safe," she said, "we can appeal to the landlord for protection," and after a seemingly interminable drive we got to the half-way house.

It was a low, roughly-built, dirty auberge, with an uneven,

earthen floor, the ceiling, benches and tables black with age, just the place where travellers are always murdered in Christmas stories. My teeth chattered with terror, but there was a certain pleasure in the excitement all the same.

We ordered supper; it was now near midnight, and while it was being prepared, my mother emptied her purse of all, save the money required to pay the driver, and a ten-franc piece to pay for our suppers. The rest of the money she put into a canvas bag which hung round her neck, where she always carried her banknotes.

The innkeeper was a woman, and when she brought them a clean cloth, new milk, new bread, and honey, they were disarmed into telling her their fears of continuing the journey: but it turned out that she was the driver's mother and hot in defence of his right to give his relations a lift whenever he pleased.

"You paid him to take you to Murat, and he will take you to Murat; but there was nothing said about not taking anyone else, and he says now that he won't take you on to Murat unless you pay him double the fare you agreed to. His horses are tired!"

"I should think they were," muttered my sister, "considering the number of extra passengers they have dragged."

My mother emptied her purse on the table. "You see," she said, "here is only the money I promised your son and enough to pay for our suppers; but when we get to Murat I shall find money waiting for me, and I will give you what you ask."

I believe this conduct of my mother saved us, at any rate from being robbed by violence. The inn stood quite by itself in one of the loneliest spots in the mountains of Auvergne. If they had believed that we were worth robbing, and had chosen to rob us, nothing could have saved us.

We started again. My mother now began to make light of the adventure, and my terror subsided sufficiently for me to be able to note the terrible grandeur of the scenery we passed through.

It seems improbable that a family of four was in danger of being robbed with violence at an inn which, however isolated, was the known half-way house between two towns—one of which, even in those days, was big enough to have a railway station. Mrs. Nesbit's so soon making light of the adventure suggests that she might have been angry at being cheated rather than actually afraid for their lives. But as they proceeded through dark tunnels and roads built between steep cliffs, Daisy was petrified with dread lest the driver and his accomplices should "spring out upon us and kill us there and then," and she was by no means sure when she wrote up the incident that the perils of that night were imaginary. Even without so intimidating a driver, the journey in a lamp-lit carriage, solitary among the "black chasms and mysterious gorges" of Auvergne, was an odd event in the life of an English child of nine.

The change that a hundred years have brought to the traveller is illustrated in her last anecdote about the tour. The inn at Murat was repulsively filthy.

> The sheets were grey with dirt and the pillows with the long succession of heads that had lain on them. . . . To go to bed was impossible. We sat round the fire waiting for daylight and the first morning train.
>
> My mother took me on her knee. I grew warm and comfortable, and forgot all my troubles. "Ah," I said with sleepy satisfaction, "this is very nice; it's just like home."
>
> The contrast between my words and the filthy, squalid inn must have been irresistibly comic, for my mother and sisters laughed till I thought they would never stop.

By the time she had reached her ninth chapter, E. Nesbit must have remembered for the first time since ending her second that she had entitled the series *My Schooldays*. The intervening six chapters had been entirely devoted to the much more congenial subject of her wanderings. Nor could she bring herself to allot more than a few lines to the boarding-school where she spent a few months on her return to England. She does not say where it was: only that there were no more than twenty girls there, and that "Mrs. MacBean was one of the best and kindest women in the world." There was also at least one Miss MacBean.

If I could have been happy at any school I should have been happy there. And I was not actively unhappy, for I lived on my mother's promise that in July I should go back to her again.

Where she was I did not know; but I knew she was looking for a pretty home for us all. I used to write letters to her addressed to St. Martin's le Grand, which I think I believed to be in Paris.

St. Martin's le Grand was, and is, the headquarters of the English Post Office, and it speaks volumes for Mrs. Nesbit's unsettled state that she gave no other address.

At last the news came that she had decided to live at Dinan in Brittany, and that in two short days I was to go by boat and join her. One day passed. The next day at dinner I was hugging myself on the thought of the morrow.

"Tomorrow," I said to the girl next to me, "I shall be going to my mother in France."

"Oh no, dear!" said the governess at the foot of the table. "Miss MacBean says you're not going till Wednesday."

With a crash my card-castle came tumbling about my ears. Wednesday might as well have been next year—it seemed so far off. I burst into passionate weeping just as the servant placed a large plate of steaming black-currant pudding before me. I saw through my tears how vexed Miss MacBean looked; she hadn't meant to break the news to me in this way.

"Come, Daisy," she said after a while, "don't cry, dear. Have some black-currant pudding—nice black-currant pudding."

"I don't want any black-currant pudding," I cried. "I hate it! I never want any pudding again!" And, with that, I rushed from the room; and from that day to this I have never been able to tolerate black-currant pudding.

Everyone was very kind to me; but there was not any one there who could at all understand the agony that delay cost me. I didn't care to eat, I didn't care to sleep or play or read.

When my mother met me at St. Malo on the following Thursday her first words were, "Why, how pale and ill the child looks!"

It will be judged that Daisy's feelings were not only unusually intense, whether for joy or woe, but also—even allowing that a deferment of days stretches further before a child than an adult—that she was rather immature emotionally. This habit of abandoning herself without restraint to her feelings, perhaps the outcome of her mother's and sisters' indulgence, remained with her for many years. Her angry retreats from the table in the midst of meals became a recurring event in her own household.

She was recompensed for the misery of the postponement by the bliss of the journey's end:

> . . . The consciousness that I was going home, not to a hotel, not to a boarding-house, but home.
>
> The small material objects that surround one's daily life have always influenced me deeply. Even as a child I found that in a familiar entourage one could be contented, if not happy; but hotels and boarding-houses and lodgings have always bored me to extinction. . . . I have a cat-like fondness for things I am accustomed to. . . .

The house at La Haye near Dinan was adjacent to a farm on one side and a large walled garden on the other.

> There never was such another garden, there never will be! Peaches, apricots, nectarines, and grapes of all kinds, lined the inside walls; the avenue that ran down the middle of it was of fig trees and standard peach-trees. There were raspberries, cherries and strawberries, and flowers mingling with the fruits and vegetables in a confusion the most charming in the world. Along the end of the garden was a great arcade of black, clipped yews, so thick and strong that a child could crawl on the outside of it without falling through. Above the dairy and coach-house was an immense hay-loft, a straw-loft over the stable and cowhouse. What play-rooms for wet days!
>
> Beyond the chicken-house was the orchard full of twisted grey apple trees beneath whose boughs in due season the barley grew. Beyond, a network of lanes, fringed with maiden-hair, led away into fairyland.
>
> My brothers eagerly led me round to show me all the treasures of the new home. There was a swing in the orchard, there were trees full of cherries, white and black.
>
> "And we may eat as many as we like," said Alfred.

Her description of the games and make-believe she and her brothers contrived was a valuable rehearsal for similar adventures brought into the tales she was soon to embark on, but the house she called "the dearest home of her childhood" makes no appearance in her fiction. Whether because she realized that a foreign *mise-en-scène* might not prove very evocative to English-speaking children, or whether the golden days in Brittany were too lush, too peaceful and prosperous, to stimulate the story-telling faculty, she nearly always chose to place her young characters in the scenes of her adult life, particularly the outer suburbs of London that she had lived in after marriage, Lewisham and Blackheath: and she often introduced financial stringencies which she had known as a married woman but never as a child.

The tenancy of the Dinan house must have lasted from July, 1868, till early in 1870, but such contentment seemed to spread its sunlight over a much larger tract of time.

The house was reputed to be haunted—like almost every other she was to inhabit—but, nervous as she was, she recalled the manifestations rather affectionately than otherwise. They took the form of a strange nocturnal clattering in the courtyard, as of spectral coaches going to and fro.

E. Nesbit thought a good deal about ghosts and believed in them all her life, having had an experience in Dinan which convinced her of their existence. One day, as she used to tell, she and her brothers went off on an excursion and lost themselves in a maze of small lanes that lay behind their house. After wandering about for some time they came to an ancient, half-ruined château standing back from the road. Creeping round the building to explore it, they discovered a door which was boarded up, and they were disappointed on peering through the cracks to see nothing but an empty room with a heap of straw on the floor. But while they looked, it became apparent to their terror that the straw was rapidly gathering itself together as though it were caught in a little whirlwind, and it began to spin itself into a kind of rope stretching towards the ceiling. They were so frightened that they ran screaming down the weedy drive, where near the great gates they came upon a cottage. As they reached it an old peasant woman came out and greeted them with the words, "Je vois, mes enfants, que vous avez vu *la dame qui file.*"

This story has the correct and traditional sequel. When at a later time curiosity got the better of fear and the children endeavoured to retrace their steps to the château, they were quite unable to find it, and after many fruitless expeditions were obliged to abandon their attempt.

The records of the Dinan home written for *The Girl's Own* do not contain anything but pleasurable experiences, so this one could not figure there. Nor was she able to tell another incident that her children heard of from her.

Mrs. Nesbit, probably in 1869, let the house for a season to the Kitchener family. At that date the future Lord Kitchener was a youth of eighteen or nineteen, and he and his brother took over the ponies belonging to Daisy and her brothers and used to race with them. Daisy's pony was beautifully white and was said to be the one Horatio Kitchener favoured. When Mrs. Nesbit and her children returned to their home, the white pony was found to have been lamed, and—rightly or wrongly—its aggrieved owner assumed the injury had been caused by hard riding. Lord Kitchener's illustrious deeds were seldom mentioned before her in later years without provoking some half-serious comment on "the boy who lamed my pony."

That pony was the crowning privilege of her life at La Haye, which, though somewhat idealized for magazine readers, really must have had more of the elements of freedom and happiness than often fell to the lot of a mid-Victorian child.

My mother, with a wisdom for which I shall thank her all my days, allowed us to run wild; we were expected to appear at meals with some approach to punctuality, and with hands and faces moderately clean. . . . But, as a rule, we were left to go our own way, and a very happy way it was. I don't mean that we were neglected; my eldest sister was always a refuge on wet days when a fairy story seemed to be the best thing to be had.

In the midst of all the parties, picnics and gaieties in which our elders were plunged, my other sister found time to read aloud to us, and to receive such confidence as we deemed it wise to make concerning our plans and our plays. . . .

A part of the infinite charm of those days lies in the fact that we were never bored, and children are bored much more often and much more deeply than their elders suppose.

A long chapter was consecrated to playing pirates and explorers with her brothers. Then once again her undertaking to recount her schooldays came back to her. Friends had persuaded her mother that she ought to be given more education, and it was arranged that she should go to a boarding-school in Dinan run by a Mademoiselle Fauchet.

. . . Owing to some misunderstanding I arrived five days before the other girls. Mademoiselle Fauchet kindly consented to overlook the mistake and keep me till the other girls arrived. I had a paint-box which pleased me for the first day, but the boredom of the other four days is branded on my memory in grey letters.

Before the school reassembled, she ran away in circumstances which rightly occasioned qualms of conscience; for she impulsively took advantage of being given a treat—an excursion with the teacher to La Fontaine. Her mother understood her feverish homesickness and did not send her back.

Try as she might, E. Nesbit could not work up any interest in schooldays, and, having reached her eleventh chapter, she left out her next school, a French convent, altogether. There are contemporary letters from her which illuminate that period better than retrospections, but I will follow her sequence of articles to the end before quoting them.

She speaks next of an episode of acute boredom some years further on, when she was sent to stay with friends of her mother's in north London. (This may have been in 1871, soon after Mary's last illness.) They lived in a dreary square with no activity beyond the windows but the passing of bakers' and butchers' carts. "The sordid ugliness of Islington" outraged her feelings when she went for a walk. The dining room with its mahogany and leather furniture, its Bible and family prayer book, depressed her when she stayed at home, and the drawing room, which was only used on Sundays, had nothing to engage her attention but a few illustrated gift books and albums and old bound volumes of *Good Words,* which she had read again and again. The piano was kept locked. Unlike any surroundings presided over by her mother, it was the Victorian household of legend.

The master of the house, a doctor, was, my mother tells me, a man of brains, but I only saw him at meals and then he seldom spoke. The lady of the house had a heart full of kindness, and a mind full of the court circular, she talked of nothing else. Her daughters were kind to me in their way, and the games I had with them were my only relaxation. The doctor talked very occasionally of his patients and this interested me.

Doctors in those days were in the habit of dispensing their own medicines or keeping an assistant to do so.

One night I went into the surgery and found the bottles of medicine, which his assistant had made up, standing in a row waiting for their white wrappers. I didn't in the least realize what I was doing when I thought to escape from my boredom by mixing the contents of these bottles in a large jug, and then in partially filling up the bottles again with the mixture. When I had filled and corked them all, I slipped away; it was done in pure mischief with no thought of consequences.

It seems incredible that a highly intelligent girl who must by now have been thirteen could have had "no thought of consequences" in playing such a dangerous trick, and, in fact, she extracted a good deal of drama from it, wondering in the night if some poor sick person would die as the result, urging herself to own up next morning, then deciding, after all, to wait and see what happened.

If anyone did die, and Dr _____ were accused of poisoning his patients, I would come forward in the court of justice, as people did in the books, and own that I, and I alone, had been to blame, making my confession among the sympathetic tears of usher and jury, the judge himself not remaining dry-eyed. This scene so much appealed to me that I almost forgot that before it could be enacted somebody would have to die of my mixture.

When I remembered this I wept in secret; when I thought of the scene in which I should nobly own my guilt, I secretly exulted. I was not bored now. Whatever else might be the effect of my mixtures, they had certainly cured my boredom.

Day after day passed by in spasms of alternate remorse and daydreaming; every day I expected Dr _____ to announce at dinner that some of his patients had breathed their last in inexplicable circumstances.

Either her concoction was harmless or the doctor refrained from discussing at table any untoward symptoms among his patients, or else—but this theory of her own seems far-fetched —someone had seen her foolish game in the surgery and made up a new batch of medicines.

. . . I shall never know, but in the reaction following my anxiety, boredom settled down on me more heavily than ever. I wrote a frantic letter to my mother begging her to take me away for I was so miserable, I wished I was dead.

Not having any stamps, Daisy entrusted the letter to her hostess for posting, and, with so honourable an upbringing as hers, it came as a shock to her to learn that this lady had opened and read her appeal.

I hope she was gratified by its contents. She added a note to my mother begging her to accede to my request, and to take me away at once. It was years before I forgave her for reading that letter, and to this day, I am afraid she has never forgiven me for writing it.

My mother was at Penshurst at the time; I was sent down to her in deep disgrace, and my mother received me with gentle reproaches that cut me to the heart.

My sister was exceedingly angry with me, perhaps with some cause, and pointed out to me how ungrateful it was to repay Mrs

——————by writing such a letter. I defended myself stoutly. . . . Though I was sorry for having hurt the feelings of one I knew had tried to be kind to me, I fear the verdict of my unregenerate heart was "serve her right."

Daisy's offence was for once taken seriously. The embarrassment between Mrs. Nesbit and the doctor's family must have been very distressing, and we may suppose Daisy's complaining letter had not been forwarded without the expression of some grievances on the other side.

After such rebukes as she had from Saretta, and some solitary reflections in Penshurst churchyard, where "the spirit of spring breathed softly" round her, it was not till next morning that Daisy was in the mood for apology. Then she presented herself "in charity with all men and all women except Mrs ——————"

"I am sorry if I have been naughty," I said to my sister; "I didn't mean to be, but—"

"That will do," she said, skilfully stopping my confidences, "now I do hope you are going to try and be a good girl, and not make dear mamma unhappy."

"I will be good," I said; "oh, I will indeed!" And as long as I stayed among the golden buttercups and silver may-bushes, I believe I was moderately good.

She was, by now, almost at the end of the considerable space the editor had allotted to her, and was obliged to apologize to her readers.

When I began to write of the recollections of my childhood, I thought that all those days which I remember could well be told in the twelve chapters. But the remembrances of that long ago time crowded thickly on me, and I wandered in the pleasant fields of memory, where time ceases to be. So the twelfth chapter is reached, and finds me still only ten years old, and finds me, moreover, with not one-tenth of the events of those ten years recorded.

She had forgotten that, in the last issue of the magazine, she had skipped "some years" to relate her bored sojourn at the doctor's. Obviously she had never at any stage given much thought to the form and content of the series; and now she lamented that it was too late to tell of her adventures in Germany and France during the war of 1870, of her English schools, and of much else that she had intended to set down. Still evading schooldays, she resolved at random to end with a description of her home in Kent. As this is chronologically very far out of order, I postpone drawing upon it till we reach the appropriate year.

I cannot recall that E. Nesbit ever again wrote with so little self-discipline; but, rambling and disorganized as those twelve articles were, they played a most vital part in her literary career. The vein of reminiscence she had tapped, the dialogues with her brothers she had reconstructed, must have shown her a new direction for her talents, and it was very soon after the publication of the final instalment that she began stories for children in an entirely new style, naturalistic, warmly personal in tone, and based, with whatever additives of humour and plot, on recaptured experience. The series ended in August 1897: it was in about October the same year that she began writing *The Treasure Seekers*.

4 *Education*

It must have been about spring, 1869, that Daisy and her brother Alfred were settled in schools near Dinan—Daisy's an Ursuline Convent, Alfred's a pensionnat for boys in the vicinity. Mrs. Nesbit had a kindly motive for choosing boarding instead of day schools. Saretta was at an age to find it a hardship to be tied to a group of very young children, and Mrs. Nesbit, entering into her feelings, gave her every chance to form her separate friendships. Opportunity for marriage too had to be borne in mind. Saretta was now twenty-four.

A little batch of early letters concerning Edith's sojourn at the Ursuline school unconsciously provides a portrait of an intelligent but irrepressible young creature who gave her guardians a good deal of trouble.

In the first, written when she was still ten, a certain easy eloquence is coupled with that air of patronage with which young children so often astonish and dismay their elders. It will be noticed, by the way, that one or two phrases have a distinctly Gallic ring, as if by now she thought rather in French than in English, while Mrs. Nesbit on the other hand appears to have known no French at all.

My dear Mamma [it runs], I got your letter from Alfred the other day but I would rather have had you and Minnie and Sister and Piggy pog and all the rest of the baggage. On the tenth Julie and I intend going to La Haye and there remaining till Monday, during which period I hope you will arrive to your poor little pet. The Mère Marie Madeline gives her full consent to this arrangement. She tells me to tell you that she thinks that I am a "Bon petit Diable." You must ask sister what that means. I think she will tell you that it means a "Good little Devil." This appellation does not really signify a Devil such as tempts the world but it is a pet name for the "brise fer" in "La Belle France." Sister [Saretta] would perhaps kindly explain the words you do not understand.

How many balls has Minnie [Mary] been to[?] You told me in your last letter to tell you about the fruit and flowers in the garden. I will tell you. There are not any strawberrys ripe yet except two which Julie found and ate at least she brought them to me and I ate one and she ate the other. The artichokes are nearly over and as for the roses why! each bush and the ground under it is like a great rose. The anemones are nearly over, the moss-roses lovly, the violets which we planted in a corner are grown all over the bed which is *mine*. There are lots of unripe plums, peaches, cherries, strawberries, gooseberries, currants and figs. Mamma do come home.

. . . I really must leave off so take much love from

> your young Diable
> Edie Nesbit
> Little Daisy.

Under the signature is a neat drawing of a daisy.
The next letter is in a slightly more sedate and mature style:

My dearest Mother,

Have you received any of my other letters yet. I hope so. Am I not to learn singing. I want to do so very much indeed. The nuns are all very kind to me though I have been very naughty, but I am very sorry and intend to be good now. . . . Every Thursday at present I spend my half franc in bonbons and eau de seldtz.

I have just received your letter and I really will be good I promise. How is that queen of dogs that splendid lady that estimable that lovely loveing loveable Trot. I hope Her Majesty is in bonne santé, that she has sufficientcy of velvet cushions to support her royal feet, an abundance of daintys to please her royal palate, and a sprightly family of hippopotami to be a comfort in her old age. How is the old mother owl I hope she is not ill. Alfred is in very good health and spirits. We are doing examinations now not for prizes but for medals and places. I am

6 for french
7 for Geographie
9 for reading
0 for hist de France

and that is pretty well for me.

Will you buy a locket for Minnie on her birthday and give it her from me put my hair and portrait in for her. I send *my* hair in case you have none—do put it in a locket, do. Why do you never write to me to tell me that I may be a Catholic. I know you will let me. Do write and say so. You say that you do not believe that Our Lord is body and soul in the Holy Communion? Well, at the last supper when our Lord took the bread and wine He did not say "This is the figure of my body this is the figure of my blood." He said this is my body this is my blood. This do in remembrance of me. What are you to do in remembrance of Him? What had He just done? He had changed bread and wine into his body and blood. The priests being the descendants of the apostles operate the change. I really have no more time so with love to you all

I remain
your little
Daisy.

There are signs in this of a more developed sense of humour than is usual in early childhood: but emphatic religious convictions—especially on such complex subjects as transubstantiation—are not, I imagine, uncommon. Anxious as I am never to give rein to my fancy, I cannot help picturing Mrs. Nesbit's face as she read this communication—the neatly coiffed head shaking in affectionate remonstrance over the confession, evidently not a new one, of naughtiness; the smile of appreciation for the passage about "that splendid lady," Trot, and for Alfred's health and spirits; another smile, not without a shade of fond irony, for the command to purchase a locket and present it, complete with hair and portrait, in Daisy's name; and at last, a perplexed frown for the little arrogant lecture on religious dogma.

But there is a postscript which must have restored good humour, for it can refer, I assume, to nothing but Daisy's imminent reform: "I think after my next letter you may safely send my parcel."

The last letter from the convent, dated November 3rd, 1869, is from the Mother Superior to one of Daisy's sisters (possibly for the reason that Mrs. Nesbit herself could not understand the French in which it was written). It concerns Daisy's departure to rejoin her family, living somewhere else in France, and there is very clear evidence in it that the nuns had found her a trying pupil, though they were obviously fond of her. There are references to the strange violence of her temper, and it is laid down as a condition, though gently, that there must be an improvement in this respect before she can be permitted to return; it is apparent that Mrs. Nesbit has been addressed before on this subject. Daisy had shocked the good sisters, too, by leaving behind her, besides two harmless pots of jam, a pair of empty wine bottles!

"I regret," the letter runs, "that Daisy should have taken wine; I believe this has been the cause of her tempers. It was her brother who brought it to her and the little girl wished to drink some of it."

Altogether, it would seem, Daisy had introduced an unwonted liveliness into the tranquil Ursuline Pensionnat, but whatever the nuns may have endured from her, she herself must have been happy there, for she wept bitterly when told she was to leave, and it was the only school she ever looked back upon without disfavour.

Exactly where Daisy was taken on leaving the convent is not recorded, but it is probable that she was put to school in Germany somewhere near her brothers. At any rate, we know that she did receive some slight part of her education there, and that she was in Prussia when the war with France broke out.

Her German school was ill-chosen; she was miserable there, and it is said that she made three attempts to run away. On one of them—fraught with a more desperate wretchedness than an adult mind can well understand—she sought to reach her brothers: but as a turnip stolen from a field was all she had to eat throughout a whole day she was obliged to go back of her own accord.

Two of her earliest attempts to versify belong to this epoch. They express her feelings with a pleasing terseness worthy of that admired poet, Noel Bastable. Here is the first poem complete:

> A German Household
> I like the cat I like the dog
> And the red plums with the boiled hog,
> I like the mountains and the Rhine
> And the apple sauce with the roasted swine.
> I like Jack Yorke and his father and mother,
> But not Mr. Morsbach nor Mrs. either.

Of the second I am unhappily only able to offer the last two lines:

> God! Let the Germans be suppressed
> So that Europe at last may have a rest!

Childish impressions being all but ineradicable, these days of unhappiness in Germany should be remembered when we discover that some of her progressive and humanitarian principles seemed to fail her when the Great War came. Her hostility was strengthened by more than one unpleasant experience in childhood. When the Franco-Prussian conflict had just become crucial, for instance, she went to some public place where her brothers were foolhardy enough to begin singing the "Marseillaise," and she has recorded that they were very severely treated by their audience.

It was, of course, imperative, when war had been declared, that she should be sent back to her family, then still living in France. The only means of getting her there was through neutral England, and she was shipped—apparently alone—to Southampton. What may have happened to Alfred and Henry at this time I am unable to trace, but there is no doubt that at

Southampton Daisy, a child just turned twelve, was placed on a boat bound for St. Malo where Mrs. Nesbit was to meet her. Unluckily, they were stranded in fog three and a half days, and Daisy was the only female passenger on board. In response to her appeal for reading matter she was supplied with all that the vessel, ill-equipped for long voyages, could yield—a set of nautical time-tables!

With nothing to see, nothing to do, nothing to read, and no one of her own sex or age to speak to, the solitary little girl wandered from deck to cabin and from cabin to deck throughout what she afterwards described as the three dullest days she ever spent.

Of the imaginative part of her life as a young child—her games, her mischiefs, her tastes, and favourite pleasures, so much appears in her own works about children that I shall not be blamed for leaving most of that ground untrodden. I give, however, a selection from the verses which she herself preserved as among the first she ever wrote.

This is the last stanza of a poem written, as she explains, "in characters about half an inch high" when she had only recently learned to write at all:

> And now good-by
> I wish I could fly
> if I had wings
> like the bird that sings
> i wood fly where you are
> Mama, Mama.

The verses about Germany, of which I have given samples, were written a few years after this. On returning to England in 1870 or 1871 she went through an extremely poetical phase, and produced, among a great number of other works, her first sonnet:

> To My Sister's Portrait
> It is so lovely! Yet that portrait shews
> But one half of her beauty, auburn hair

Falls o'er her shoulders and her throat, small fair
Soft hands, and a delicate Grecian nose!
Those eyes, those wells of truth and love and light
Speak volumes to a colder heart than mine.
They are as tranquil those blue eyes of thine
As summer sea beneath a moonlit night.
Thy cherry lips make happy slaves of those
Who hear thee speak through them their *Christian* name,
Some love thee sadly without hope of love,
Some give thee love while hoping for the same,
Some love thee with a love that cannot die
And, Maris Stella, such a one am I.

This she has called "an attempt to write poetry like other people. . . . Most of my verses at this age, however, are sincere
outpourings of the soul. One, a veritable *cri-de-cœur,* begins
vehemently:

'I know that I am ugly: did I make
The face that is the mock and jest of all?'

These lines from a narrative poem telling "how a shepherd
and a prince set out on a journey through a wood to find a mysterious bell" seem to me by far the most promising:

Said the poor shepherd lad,
  "Where go you?"
Said the King's son, "To find
  The bell. And you?"
"We can go together
  If you have a mind,
For the same thing you seek
  I go to find."

To close this chapter, which has brought me to E. Nesbit's
twelfth year, I give what must be still more interesting than
these early verses to those who feel that it was not as a poet that
she made her mark. It is a specimen of prose composition in the
form of a story—a story, alas! of which only a small part re-

mains. It is written on the paper of the Agricultural College, and belongs—if this fact and her handwriting be any fair guide—to infant years. Whether the action of the tale is original or a paraphrase of something she had read or heard I cannot say. Original or not, two points will strike the reader of this fragment—first the directness and economy of the style, a feature which she carried to a fine art in later years; and second that, at the age of six or seven, she had already a craving to express herself in literary form; for the story does not seem to be a piece of schoolwork, nor is it likely that so difficult a composition would be set for a child to whom a pen was still obviously a strange instrument:

A good many years ago there lived a very rich Roman. His name was Agrippa, and his wifes name was Claudia. They had one only daughter, but she was no comfort to them, she was so wild. She was very pretty, though. Her name was Mira.

She used to wrap herself in a dark thick cloak, and a white dress benieth it, pretty little blue sandals, and roses in her hair. She looked lovly then. One night, she went down the marble steps, opened the door and went out. She walked along till she came to the gates of Rome. The Porter who was there did not prevent her entering. She did so. As she walked along she saw many gay parties, coming out of the different houses. At last she saw one coming and thought she would go into a narrow passage that was near while they passed.

Mira looked around. Exactly opposite was a statue of a Goddess that looked lovely as life. She could not resist the temptation of running up to it and throwing her arms round its neck. But what was her astonishment when the figure slid on one side, and she saw a flight of steps she went down them for a long, long way, and Mira began to see a faint glimmer in the distance, at the end of the steps. I wonder what that dim light can be, said Mira to herself as she ran on. At last she came to it and she found that it was a round room with doors all round she opened one and there found herself at the entrance of a corridor lined with dead bodies. Mira walked on till she thought she heard a voice. Surely the dead cannot speak thought she. She walked on and she found that it was somebody praying she listened, they were not praying to Venus or Mars or Jupiter or any of her Gods. The thought came at last they were Christians, hated Christians. Oh, what should she do, perhaps if they found her . . . ?

Here the manuscript ends, and we are reluctantly obliged to leave Mira calmly wandering among the dead bodies.

5   *Girlhood and Marriage*

Within a few months or weeks of Daisy's roundabout voyage from Germany to France in 1870, the curiously unsettled family came to England. Mary Nesbit, aged eighteen now, was engaged at this time to Philip Bourke Marston, a young blind poet who was one of Swinburne's intimate friends. She moved, so E. Nesbit herself has written, in the set which contained Swinburne, the Rossettis, William Morris, Burne-Jones, Oliver Madox Brown, and many others whose names will occur to those familiar with mid-Victorian art and letters. Her portrait shows her as a beautiful girl with just such a gentle, yet firm, intelligent face as the pre-Raphaelite artists delighted in.

Daisy, at twelve or thirteen years of age, stayed with her sister for some little time in a house frequented by the members of this circle. She heard them talk about poetry, and her interest in giving poetical expression to her own thoughts was much heightened. It was here that she first ambitiously attempted the sonnet form, after a rough-and-ready explanation of it from one of the group. Her poetical tendencies did not, however, diminish her love of mischief, for many years later, recalling a visit to Tonbridge in 1871, she wrote to her mother: "You remember there was the thanksgiving for the recovery of the Prince of Wales—and I went out with the boys to see the illuminations, and we threw crackers into the gaping mouths of the trombone and cornopoeum—to the amazement and terror of the band!" She was on visiting terms with the Rossettis,[1] and at least on nodding terms with Swinburne, for he was in the habit of patting her benevolently on the head when he met her taking her daily rides on a friend's pony across Putney Heath. Of her encounters with Dante Gabriel Rossetti she would often make some mention in later years, referring to their having played games of hide-and-seek together in which, perhaps through some confusion of the issue, he had insisted on kissing the girls.

But Daisy was not long to remain in this stimulating society. Her sister, young, lovely, and attractive as she was, and apparently well fitted for a life of happiness, relapsed again into consumption. She was taken to Brittany and died at Ille-et-Vilaine towards the end of 1871. The young poet whom she was to have married was prostrated by the blow, which proved but the forerunner of a series of tragic bereavements. He survived her by many years, and yet only lived to be thirty-seven. In the *Oxford Book of Victorian Verse* he is represented by two poems of great charm.

After this bitter loss Mrs. Nesbit returned again to England and made her permanent home there, and it was while she was occupied with all the travail involved in giving up one establishment and searching for another that Daisy was sent for a short time to yet another boarding school in Brighton. She was not much happier there than she had been in Germany. An individualist with more initiative than is comfortable in a schoolgirl, she was as intolerant of all the little snobberies and conventions of a seminary as, later, she was intolerant of the snobberies and conventions of the social world. And she had that reluctance to submit to other people's discipline which we often find in those who themselves have the capacity to be good organizers. On a day which she always remembered as a joyful one she was fetched away to live at Halstead Hall in the Kentish village of Halstead, a few miles from Knockholt. Her mother had pre-

[1] Presumably Christina Rossetti and her mother. Dante Gabriel kept a separate household at Cheyne Walk.

pared a home there in which for some years the family was to
remain settled.

> "The Hall" it was called [she wrote in *My Schooldays*], but the
> house itself did not lend itself to the pretensions of its name. A
> long, low, red-brick house, that might have been commonplace
> but for the roses and the ivy that clung to the front of it, and the
> rich, heavy jasmine that covered the side. There was a smooth
> lawn with chestnut trees round it, and a big garden, where flow-
> ers and fruit and vegetables grew together, as they should, with-
> out jealousy or class-distinction. There never were such peonies as
> grew among our currant-bushes, nor such apricots as hung among
> the leaves on the sunny south wall. From a laburnum tree in a
> corner of the lawn we children slung an improvised hammock,
> and there I used to read and dream, and watch the swaying gold
> of leaf and blossom.

When I visited the house thirty years ago and more, it still
answered entirely to that description. The village was almost as
peaceful and pleasant as it must have been when the Nesbits
lived there nearly a hundred years ago. So many of the villages
of England have changed that I have not dared to go back.

In Daisy's time, long tranquil walks lay in every direction,
and for livelier amusement the children, now in early adolescence, resorted pretty frequently to a brand-new railway cutting
a couple of miles away. Her book, *The Railway Children*, must
owe something to her memories of games with her brothers
near—dangerously near—the Knockholt line. When Harry and
Alfred were at home every day was full of adventures and enterprises. When they were away at school, the pattern was a
quieter one.

> . . . There were nooks among the laburnums and lilacs that
> grew thickly round the pond, nooks where one could hide with
> one's favourite books, and be secure from the insistent and irritat-
> ing demands so often made on one's time by one's elders. For
> grown-up people never thought of spoiling their clothes by pene-
> trating the shrubbery. Here, on many a sunny day, have I lounged
> away the morning, stifling conscience with Mrs. Ewing's tales, and

refusing to remember the tangle of untidiness in which I had left my room involved. For I had a little room of my own, a little, little room, with a long, low window and a window-ledge, where bright plants in pots, encouraged by the western sun, withstood the intermittence of my attentions, and blossomed profusely.

My bookcase stood by this window, an old mahogany bookcase with a deep top drawer that let down to form a writing-table. Here I used to sit and write—verse, verse, always verse—and dream of the days when I should be a great poet like Shakespeare, or Christina Rossetti! Ah me, that day is long in coming. But I never doubted then that it would come.

Daisy hid her poems because she was afraid, she wrote in 1919,[2] of the mockery of her brothers. She showed them only her least sincere works, those that were not "heartwarm" but concerned only with experiences they had in common; for example, six hundred lines describing *A Walk up the Drachenfels*.

Besides the desk and the well-oiled key that formed so excellent a defence against "the boys"—for what young poet could ever set down a line with the possibility of even the best-loved brothers looking over her shoulder?—my little room had another feature, by turns a terror and a charm. A little trap-door in the ceiling led to that mysterious and delightful region between the roof and the beams, a dark passage leading all round the house, and leading too—oh, deep and abiding joy! to the door that opened on the roof itself. This, until the higher powers discovered it, was a safer haven even than the shrubbery.

Enclosed by four pointed roofs of tiles was a central space— safe, secluded—whence one could see the world around, oneself invisible, or at least, unseen. Another trap-door, from the linen-closet by the boys' bedroom, afforded them an equal access to this paradise. We kept a store of books and good things in the hollow of the roof, and many a pleasant picnic we enjoyed there.

Happy, vanished days, when to be on the roof and to eat tinned pineapple in secret constituted happiness!

[2] In *John o'London's Weekly,* 15 Nov.

Daisy's nerves must have been in much better shape than at any other time in her youth, for, by the coincidence upon which I have already remarked, the Halstead house, like that in Brittany, was reputed to be haunted, and in this case the reputation was so well established that a rector of the parish had actually paid an "official" visit to the place for the purpose of exorcizing evil spirits. A former occupant of the house, Edward Garnet Man, is said to have written for private circulation a monograph on the occult phenomena observed there. I have been unable to trace the book; but, in the 1930's, I talked with five or six old inhabitants of Halstead who were all emphatic in their confirmation of the ghostly legends I had heard.

In this house, despite its eerie associations, the Nesbits were destined to be very happy. They lived the life of country people of their class in that day in all its simplicity and respectability. As newcomers of only moderate affluence, they had no great position to support, but whatever was expected of them they did to the satisfaction of their neighbours and the village in general. They exchanged visits with the rector and his wife and with all the families of local importance; they were on formally correct terms with the "great houses" of the district, they went to church as often as was generally thought proper in that time and place, and there was certainly no hint of rebellion in their submission to a social code which we should now think pretty rigid and with which Daisy was to play havoc in a few years.

From Mrs. Sikes, the rector's wife, she borrowed books, devouring all the novels of Scott one after the other. She was always an avid and very catholic reader, but it will hardly surprise anyone acquainted with her work to know that stories of adventure and action were in childhood, and remained through most of her life, her favourites. But though uncommonly fond of reading, she never was what is called a bookworm. She had an enormous fund of physical energy, loved running, swimming, and games, and was more proficient in them than most young ladies of her day—even granting that the listlessness of Victorian womanhood had been greatly exaggerated.

It was in the seventies that the new game of lawn tennis was introduced into England under the name of Sphairistike. A tennis lawn had been improvised rather roughly at the Rectory, and Daisy and her brothers played on it.

Daisy had developed a taste for story-telling and was a favourite with the Rectory children because of the exciting tales with which she entertained them. But her adult half-sister, Saretta, had written some "little things" which, under the pen name Caris Brooke, were actually in print, and no one yet suspected that she would be eclipsed by a younger member of the family. Nevertheless, that younger member was already seriously thinking of a literary career, and was soon to embark upon it.

> . . . When I was fifteen I ventured to show some verses to my mother. She showed them to Mr. Japp, the editor of *Good Words* and the *Sunday Magazine,* and never shall I forget the rapture of delight and of gratitude with which I received the news that my verses had been accepted. By-and-by they were printed, and I got a cheque for a guinea, a whole guinea, think of it!

That is from *My Schooldays.* In the reminiscences written in 1919 for *John o'London's,* she is more explicit.

> The first poem I ever had published was a non-committal set of verses about dawn, with a moral tag. It was printed in the *Sunday Magazine.* When I got the proof I ran round the garden shouting "Hooray!" at the top of my voice, to the scandal of the village, and the vexation of my family.
>
> The next poem came out in *Good Words.* Then I sent a poem to another magazine. I asked my mother to tell me what to say in the covering letter to the editor. She dictated a suitable exercise in propriety, and I wrote it out very fair. But I thought it sounded cold and unconvincing. So I wrote at the end "P.S.—Do, *please,* take this!" He did, too.
>
> I was seventeen then.

She was telescoping two years of literary aspiration. The *Argosy* as well as *Good Words,* both famous periodicals in their day, issued her artless musings on uplifting themes, and while still in her teens she became a fairly prolific contributor of verses to magazines. This easy acceptance of work done with extreme facility, and often slipshod of its kind, must have been a serious setback to the development of her talent.

It was an uneventful, peaceful, pleasant time. The only really exciting thing was the presence, within a stone's throw of our house, of our landlady's son, who lived all alone in a little cottage standing in the fields. He was reported mad by the world, eccentric by his friends; but, as we found him, perfectly harmless.

His one delusion, as far as I know, was that he was the rightful owner, nay, more, the rightful tenant of our house, and about once in six months he used to terrify the whole household by appearing with a carpet bag at the front door and announcing that he had come to take possession. This used to alarm us all very much, because if a gentleman is eccentric enough to wish to "take possession" of another person's house, there is no knowing what he may be eccentric enough to do next. But he was always persuaded to go away peaceably, and I don't think we need have been so frightened.

Once while he was in the drawing-room being persuaded by my mother, I peeped into the carpet bag he had left in the hall. It contained three empty bottles that had held mixed pickles, a loaf of bread, and a barrister's wig and gown. Poor gentleman, I am afraid he was very eccentric indeed.

The few years that the Nesbits spent at Halstead were the happiest of Edith's life. Her irresponsible youth as "Daisy" was symbolically drawing to a close with a most drastic change in her circumstances. From a protected girl living a comfortable well-ordered life in a quiet village, she was to turn into the poorest of poor Bohemians in London, and the sole support of a sick husband and two babies. How it all happened it has proved scarcely possible to trace, and it will be necessary to have recourse to what it is generally desirable for a biographer to avoid—conjecture.

The first phase of the transformation seems to have been that somewhere in the late 1870's Mrs. Nesbit ceased to be a well-to-do woman. It has been said that she was ruined by her sons. In one venture and another they lost money, and always came to their mother to refund them. Alfred, the elder boy, was especially prodigal, and had the knack of making his mother give him whatever he pleased, and when she was left almost penniless it is certain enough that his sister, Edith, gave him from her own meagre purse substantial assistance.

The Halstead house could no longer be kept up, and the family migrated to London, where they lived at Barnsbury on a much reduced scale. Edith was at that time, or became soon afterwards, engaged to one Stuart Smith, for whom, however, it does not appear that she felt any very strong sentiment, for shortly after accepting his proposal she met Hubert Bland and immediately severed her other alliance.

Hubert Bland, a young man of some small independent means, came of ancient North Country stock. He had a strong, impressive personality, and was both good-looking and clever. Edith, like far too many other women, fell in love with him at first sight. There are two or three different versions of the manner of their first meeting. Edgar Jepson heard from Edith herself that they met at a picnic at which they shared the same plate of strawberries and cream, and fell in love in the process.

On the other hand, the late Miss Ada Breakell, whom Edith described in 1906, near thirty years after their first meeting, as "my dearest and oldest friend," recollected going with her to change a note at the bank where Stuart Smith was employed, and his introducing Hubert Bland to both of them as one of his colleagues, and she was sure he had never met Edith before that day. Perhaps, remembering only the glamour of the picnic and the shared plate of strawberries, Edith may not have thought the first semi-public encounter in the bank worth recording.

The year in which the fateful picnic took place was probably 1877, and the season, I suppose, must have been early summer. Of the courtship very little information has so far come to light. Indeed the whole of that period, three years in length, which followed Edith's departure from Halstead and ended in her wedding, presents to the biographer, in so far as dates and plain facts are concerned, a tantalizing lacuna.

The only correspondence belonging to this time which I was fortunate enough to secure consists of some letters written to Miss Breakell, a girl of about her own age, with whom she remained on intimate terms all her life. Miss Breakell lived in Manchester, where Saretta—who had become Mrs. John Deakin —was now settled with her husband; and Edith frequently went to stay with her there. On these occasions one of her favourite pleasures was to go rollerskating with Miss Breakell at the Manchester rink, and the two young girls became by degrees so fond of each other that Mrs. Nesbit invited her daughter's friend to spend a holiday with them in London—the first of several visits made and returned.

Edith was a most affectionate creature, and corresponded with Ada for years in terms of ingenuous sentimentality worthy of a Victorian heroine. Despite her precocity of experience—for she was soon, as will be seen, to endure extraordinary trials— Edith's mind did not mature early. (It is a striking fact that almost all her best literary work was done after she was forty.) The letters she wrote in her twenties read like those of a clever and observant child, endowed with eloquence enough to put its questionings into words, but naïve and simple in its reasoning. Her style was—and remained—unselfconscious to a fault, and she was prone at this time to derive a childlike enjoyment from phrases that sounded more profound than they were.

The letter from which I give some extracts here seems to have been written during her engagement, and possibly belongs to the year 1879, when she was twenty:

> How different I was this time last year!—Now I see the world through "larger, other eyes"—but the increased light brings with it infinitely increased sorrow. Do you not find it so?—See—I am in a moralizing mood—do you mind? I wonder if it is *hard* to be *great*. It seems to me that all our lives we are trying *not* to be great—I fancy the real obstacle to human greatness lies in the backwardness of the human mind to conceive it. Greatness is around us on all sides, but we are mistrustful of the fact, and

while its sun shines in upon us at every instant, we are for ever shading it off with our timid hands. Greatness is easy—not difficult—it is *giving up* ill—not acquiring good alone—but *oh!* to acquire is so unutterably more easy than to renounce. . . .

It's rather hard on you, is it not, to bore you with a letter like this. I *might* treat you worse though—as I treat Mr. Bland sometimes—with vicious and long expositions of one-sided views on every conceivable subject of non-interest to humanity. . . .

I am looking forward INTENSELY to your coming to us in the summer. Oh hasten, swallow, come back from the south and bring summer and Ada and all pleasant things. The joy of last year cries from its well ordered family vault—

"Who hath remembered me, who hath forgotten?
Thou has forgotten, oh summer swallow,
But the world shall end when *I* forget."

The next letter, written within a few weeks or months of the other, is much more natural and engaging, as well it might be since it describes "the most charming day I ever spent." It is interesting to observe that her attachment to Halstead, so reluctantly deserted, was already drawing her back there, and that she was eager to show her old home to her lover. She had passed beyond middle age before she ceased to make excursions to this village, which was hallowed by the dearest memories of her life.

Yesterday was awfully pleasant [she writes]. Mr. Bland and I went to Halstead and had *no end* of a "nice time"—we went into the woods—sat about—caught (and kissed) a chaffinch—had lunch in the kitchen of a funny old-fashioned Inn—came back to the station through the grounds of the Oakleys house, home by train and a sumptuous drive in a hansom cab to conclude the most charming day I have ever spent. The country was *fresh young* and *jolly. So were we.* When you come home we will run down to Halstead together, will we not? . . .

I wish I could give you some faint slight idea of the jolly larks we had yesterday—T'wer foine—we could not for a long time get *anything* to eat as a ghastly famine seemed prevalent for *miles* round Halstead—but at last we got into the queerest little 'Pub'—

and, having recd the usual answer "Not a thing in the house, sir"—we felt despair gnawing chill at our vitals and I think our faces of woe softened the heart of that Innkeeper, for he relented and said "If cold boiled ham—?" We pressed him to our bosoms (or felt like doing so) and fed—At the risk of seeming "young" I *must* reiterate. It was *fine!*

I hope your next letter will be as nice and long as the one wh. was forwarded to me last night. I *do* love you—Carita, and you *must* not think I am offended if I do not write sometimes for a little while. Remember I am *fiendishly* busy sometimes. Please write again as soon as you can. . . .

Goodbye—

Yours as much as her own

Daisy.

In another communication she is able to laugh at her own youthful philosophizing.

You'll bless me for sending you such a letter, but I can't help it [she says, after easing her mind with a quotation from Swinburne. "I'm sure to quote poetry sooner or later if I'm not restrained," she admits on another page.]. I'm worried with trying to *understand* things. What good is my life to me? What good can I do with it? *Can* I do *anything?*

Is life a dream, and death a reality?—Or is *death* the substance?

I think on—and on—and I *nearly* get an answer and then—just as I think I am attaining to what I so desire, it slips—and I lose my chance and then—I have only to "dry my eyes and laugh at my fall" and humbly begin my train of thought all over again—I shall never be answered—I think still and from my thoughts *gain* nothing—*attain* nothing, *see* nothing of all that my soul longs to grasp.

> "only I discern
> Infinite passion, and the pain
> Of finite hearts that yearn."

I'd better stop, I think. I shall only sink into a veritable miry slough, represented by my own ridiculous system of bad metaphysics—and, as I don't want to drag you down with me I won't go on—on paper—In my thoughts I sink or swim—alone——

Introspection is a luxury which demands a measure of idleness and freedom from material worries, and Edith did well to indulge in it while these yet remained to her. During the new life upon which she was about to embark we find little enough of introspection in her letters. Full ten years of unremitting preoccupation with material worries stretched before her. The most pessimistic prophet could hardly have foreseen what lay in wait for this pretty, talented, captivating girl, so happily engaged to a handsome, promising, and comfortably situated young man: nor could the most optimistic have imagined how gallantly she would overcome them.

And now we approach the termination of that engagement about which my stock of facts has been so visibly deficient. It is a relief, where such a dearth of information prevails, to be able to turn to the Record Office for a transaction which admits of no uncertainty. Edith Nesbit was married to Hubert Bland by a Registrar in the City of London on April 22, 1880. She was a few months less than twenty-two years of age, and her husband was twenty-five. His address is given on the certificate as 17 Devonshire Square, and hers as being at Oxford Terrace, Greenwich. By profession he is described as "Brush Manufacturer."

Neither Mrs. Nesbit nor any other member of Edith's family was at the wedding. The witnesses have names which never recur again in tracing out her life-story, and were as likely as not to have been collected casually, as witnesses often are. And there is one much more significant fact showing the absence of her kin. Edith's father being dead before she turned four, it is not surprising that she should have been unaware of his Christian name, which, for purposes of registration, she erroneously gave as "Henry." (He was actually, as the reader will recollect, "John Collis.") None of her seniors could have passed such a blunder unnoticed. In any case, her near relations would have been signatories to the register if present.

The civil wedding ceremony—an unconventional procedure in those days—was probably a hurried and private one. Edith was in the seventh month of pregnancy, a dreadful situation for a girl of good upbringing, and one not to be lived down without great discretion of conduct and, however belatedly, marriage lines. She must have suffered wearing anxiety, both in respect of Hubert Bland's tardiness in making amends, and because, for so frank and open a person as she, the deceptions she was obliged to practise could not have failed to go against the grain. She had, for example, to pretend even to friends as dear as her beloved Ada, that she had been married some time before.

Whether she took her mother into her confidence before the ceremony remains doubtful. Their usually excellent relations must have been disturbed for a time, because Hubert Bland was no favourite with his future mother-in-law. But Mrs. Nesbit was so gentle and affectionate a woman that, if there was an estrangement, it was soon healed. She was a frequent and cherished visitor to her daughter's house, and Edith somehow succeeded in maintaining a loyal devotion to both her husband and her mother.

6   *Misfortunes and Strivings*

I have said that Hubert Bland described himself on his marriage certificate as a brush manufacturer, but he was not destined to remain so. A very young and headstrong man, born into the leisured classes, with no commercial instincts whatever, he had been persuaded, shortly before his wedding, to leave the bank in which he then worked and invest all his capital in what was, as far as I can make out, a brush factory on a small scale. But the business had hardly been organized and the newly-married couple was but just settled down in a little house in Lewisham, when a double calamity overtook them of such magnitude as only a woman of Edith's character could hope to contend against. Bland succumbed to smallpox, and recovered from the danger of death only to learn that his partner had defrauded him in his absence, and that he was left penniless with a newly-born son added to the burden of his responsibilities.

The young wife and mother—she was twenty-two years old —braced herself for a desperate attempt to maintain her home. She had three resources for the support of her child and convalescent husband, and she must use them all. She could write, she could paint a little, she was good at the then popular art of recitation. By these three precarious means she was to pay the rent and feed and clothe herself and her family. At the same time, it being beyond her purse to keep more than one general servant, she must do part of the housework and look after her baby.

And yet the girl who shouldered these immense tasks so readily was not by breeding or temperament adapted to this life of drudgery. She was gently nurtured, gay, charming, a willowy, graceful creature, whose lovely face and figure were never seen but to be admired. No woman of such attractions ever sacrificed her youth with a more boundless prodigality. Child-bearing and every kind of toil that could earn or save a penny were to be her lot for many years to come.

In those days there were many professional elocutionists who gave performances at smoking concerts and various other public and private functions. Edith had a friend named Marshall Steele, who was much in demand for this type of work, and he was kind enough to get her engagements and to rehearse some duologues with her which they produced together. She appeared with him at numerous concerts, chiefly in working men's clubs, and wrote several of her own recitations—some of which, when published, became popular with other performers. She also did as much work as newspapers would pay her for, and in this Hubert Bland—who had a hitherto unsuspected talent for writing—was induced to collaborate with her. He became by degrees a journalist, an eminent one, and remained so till his death, but at the beginning it was she who was the mainspring of his literary activities.

Among the papers in which her earliest prose work appeared was *Sylvia's Home Journal,* and an interesting little history is attached to the acceptance of the first story she submitted to it. In 1881 a "ladies' paper" was very much more essentially a feminine affair, at least in the matter of its personnel and organization, than is often the case to-day. The editorial staff of *Sylvia's Home Journal* consisted of several gay and informal young women, approach to whom was not barred by commissionaires and office boys proffering slips of paper on which the caller is expected to state his business. One press-day in winter the ladies were hard at work in the editress's room preparing belated copy for the printer—all of them, that is to say, except the manuscript reader, Miss Alice Hoatson; and she was kneeling on the floor by the gas-stove making cocoa to be taken with a luncheon of sandwiches. These various occupations were interrupted by a knock on the door, and the young journalists were surprised by the entrance, not of the printer's boy whom they expected, but of a tall stranger in a black dress, pale as a ghost, shivering with cold, and altogether wearing a look of distress.

The visitor was, of course, E. Nesbit, who had come all the way from Lewisham on this particularly bleak and bitter day to offer a story, written by herself and Hubert, to the journal. Miss Hoatson hastily poured out the cocoa and handed a cup to the stranger, to whom she also tendered her box of sandwiches. She was obliged to take her own drink from the milk-jug, and to sit on the floor, since all the chairs in the room were now occupied. Edith was embarrassed when she realized what little sacrifices had been made for her comfort, but as Miss Hoatson protested that she liked the milk-jug, had more sandwiches than she could eat, and could remain nearer the fire by sitting on the floor, she did not reject the kindness offered. Meanwhile, the other ladies, having eaten their lunch and finished their morning's work, took their departure, the editress, Miss Graham, explaining that no decision could be made about the story until Miss Hoatson had reported on it, and assuring her that she need not hurry out into the cold if she preferred to remain before the fire. Edith looked relieved, so Miss Hoatson invited her to stay until she had finished some work of her own, promising that she would read and report on her story the same day. An hour's conversation revealed many points of congeniality between the two young women, and they parted with mutual assurances that they should soon meet again.

Miss Hoatson was as good as her word, and not only read the story that day but, finding it suited to the requirements of the paper, dispatched an encouraging personal note at once, saying that she was certain it would be accepted. The next morning, on going to the office, she was told that there was a lady waiting to see her, and on arriving in her room she discovered Edith walking up and down with an agitated air and looking, if anything, more ill and ghostly than the day before. "Oh!" she said urgently, "could you not give me back that story of mine that you accepted? There was another copy, and my husband took it to the *Weekly Dispatch* yesterday and we had a letter of acceptance this morning. It is to come out in next Saturday's edition, and we shall never get anything more accepted if they find it appearing in another place! I have brought a different story written by myself only—can you possibly let it be submitted instead?"

Such a proceeding was quite irregular, but as no entry had yet been made in the MS. book, Miss Hoatson was able to substitute the second story for the first, and to get it accepted without anyone being the wiser. This kindly act was the foundation of a life-long friendship; and a few years later Miss Hoatson was satisfied to leave her journalistic employment and throw in her lot with the Blands altogether. She was a member of their household for over thirty years.

Edith continued to send contributions to *Sylvia's Home Journal,* and was soon writing more or less regularly for the *Weekly Dispatch* as well. This was her principal source of income. The second was her painting. She called one day in winter at the office of a Jewish firm of colour printers in the City and asked if they would purchase hand-painted Christmas cards from her. Such cards were then very much in the fashion, and hers offered the special merit of original verses. The manager, impressed with her suggestion, handed her a packet of blank cards and told her to bring them back, duly painted, before a given date. Delighted, she took them home and worked at them in every available moment, but what with house and child and other duties as well she was two days late in completing the order.

She returned to the City office at closing time, and was greeted by a disappointed and angry manager: "You are too late," he said. "We don't take work that is behind time. I shall not require the cards now." She pleaded, but unavailingly: the office was about to be shut, and picking up the little bundle of paintings into which she had put her whole heart she went towards the door. But before she could reach it she burst into tears, and the manager suddenly perceiving the extent of her need yielded to humanity. He brought her back, paid her generously for the work, and ordered more; and so she went away, to use her own words, "as happy as a queen." It was an incident she never forgot. Many of her own innumerable acts of kindness might be traced to her excellent memory for such experiences as this.

Miss Breakell showed me several decorated cards from Edith's hand. Pretty, neatly done, quite free from the slightest aesthetic pretension, they are representative of the more ephemeral tastes of the decade—tastes which the artist herself was soon to outgrow. Yellow asters, marguerites, almond-blossoms or violets, in sprays and garlands, with miniature scenes inset amongst them—all the designs are redolent of the pre-Wilde eighties, and they are pleasantly matched by the verses.

It is significant alike of Edith's limitless energy and of her genius for friendship that, when the painting of greetings for Christmas and other seasons was one of her chief means of earning bread, she should have exerted herself to produce specially elaborate cards and poetry for her friends. The birthday verses I quote, written for Miss Breakell, appear on a semi-transparent card, bright with forget-me-nots and ferns, and are typical of many such compositions:

> Could love make worthy things of worthless
> My song were worth an ear,
> Its notes should make the days most mirthless
> The merriest of the year,
> And wake to birth all buds yet birthless
> To keep your birthday, dear!
>
> Could love make music worthy of you
> And match great singers' powers,
> Had even my love less heart to love you,
> A better song were ours,

With all the rhymes like stars above you
And all the words like flowers!

About a year and a half after the birth of their son, who had
been christened Paul, the young couple found themselves the
parents of another child, a girl: they named her Iris. No doubt
now that her husband was in good health again, Edith's financial position was something less precarious, but whatever
ameliorations there may have been were not to be long-lasting.
Another double calamity, scarcely less complete than the first,
was to fall upon this already over-burdened girl of twenty-four.

An untrustworthy servant, who had been asked to look after
the little boy Paul for a few hours, took him out, ostensibly for
a walk in the fresh air, but in reality to a house where there was
a case of smallpox in its most virulent phase. The child was not
only allowed into the sickroom, but even lifted on to the bed to
speak to the patient. Mysteriously enough he escaped the con-
tagion himself, but he carried the disease home, and—by an evil
miracle—his father was infected a second time. Such a recur-
rence must constitute, I suppose, a medical curiosity. Once more
Edith had to strive alone, not only against her husband's danger, but for money to supply the needs of her increased family.

And she had made, or was about to make, a discovery which
was at once preposterous and tragical. From a letter which fell
into her hands in this third year of her married life she learned
that Hubert Bland was still under promise of marriage to
someone whom he had known before his wedding, and who
was not even aware that he had a wife. This lady is said to have
kept a small business at Beckenham and, as by a final deft touch
to a situation which had all the elements of a music-hall joke,
her name was Maggie.[1]

Edith, grieved, amazed, but indomitable, decided to go and
see her, with the intention of explaining the "fiancé's" true position. She went—prepared, it may well be, to be disagreeable:

[1] I was told by another informant that "Maggie" was the paid companion of Hubert Bland's mother, but this seems hardly likely since,
in that case, she would have known of his marriage.

but when they stood face to face, and she realized that the unfortunate woman had been from first to last the victim of deception, and heard, too, that she actually had a child of which
Hubert was the father, all rancour vanished. Her only desire
was to befriend a fellow creature whose plight seemed even
more pitiable than her own. Befriend her she did by every
means in her power, and the two women, different as they were
in culture and in acquirements, were drawn together by a link
of sympathy which endured until Maggie's death eighteen years
later.

It is desirable in this place to say something of the character
of Hubert Bland. He was undeniably well-meaning, and—as
his intimates have unanimously agreed—a thoroughly likeable
man, but one who, to use a phrase not less expressive than vulgar, could not by any effort of nature leave women alone. And
like many men of this turn of mind, he had a charm for women
equally precarious to himself and to them.

It was part of his dangerousness that he shrank from inflict-
ing pain; and for this reason he had a radical incapacity for
breaking off with any woman who had become attached to
him. He could not bring himself to strike a final blow, and it is
thus that his friends explain the deceit practised upon the much-
wronged Maggie. His more-wronged wife, generous to a fault
in all her dealings, began from this time to have a very keen
perception of her husband's weaknesses and to suffer them not
uncomplaining, but yet with more indulgence than might have
been expected.

The condemnation of small minds, shocked because she
would not hate the women her husband had seduced, outraged
because she gave them friendship and help—this meant little to
the girl who had been strong enough to devote her youth and
beauty to a life of incessant and inglorious labour. To horrify
self-righteous respectability was to her rather a gratification
than otherwise. As time went on she drifted further and further
from the conventional world to which she had been bred, and
became more and more firmly fixed in that little sphere of
rebels which then proudly called itself Bohemia.

To say that she became a shining light of that sphere, which contained the liveliest and most brilliant people of the time, would be to exaggerate. Money-getting and the toil of keeping an understaffed house in order must have done much to prevent her from realizing all the possibilities of that commodity with which she was very richly endowed—personality. And this is a frustration for which, since we might otherwise have missed the art she learned in struggle and distress, we must be grateful. She loved admiration and, had she been untrammelled, she would probably have applied herself delightedly to the winning of social triumphs.

As it was, without attaining or seeking after celebrity, she entertained, and was warmly liked by many young members of the Bohemian set; and somehow found leisure in which to bestow on them hospitality of the most charming sort. Indeed, hospitality and a miraculous knack of making time's ends meet were to be Edith's particular specialities for the rest of her life. In these arts Hubert Bland, too, was adept, and he enjoyed as enthusiastically as herself the simple pleasures of the circle in which we find them established by 1884, the year when they helped to found the celebrated Fabian Society.

7 *The First Year of the Fabian Society*

Hubert Bland was deeply and sincerely interested in social questions, especially as they touched the welfare of the neglected labouring classes, and he never lost an opportunity of discussing such topics with acquaintances of a congenial turn of mind. He succeeded, with very little difficulty, in communicating this enthusiasm to his wife, and by a natural magnetism they attracted about them many people who shared their views. These views were then regarded as little less than seditious: one needed as much moral courage to confess to them as one might need to-day to confess to an out-and-out belief in the most extreme form of Communism. The outrageous young Blands were Socialists!

Moreover, they were active, indefatigable, and influential Socialists. Their names were among the first dozen or so to be registered on the membership roll of the Fabian Society, to which they belonged all their lives from the day of its foundation. Hubert Bland took the chair at the very first meeting the Society as such ever held, acted as treasurer and a member of the Executive for twenty-six years, was one of the famous Fabian Essayists, and in short played a very important part in the history of that organization.

Edward R. Pease recounted this history fully and lucidly in a book which is doubtless known to everyone who has studied the growth of English Socialism, and it is not my intention to attempt an invasion of that province. Some few facts, however, it will be expedient to give, and for these I was indebted both to Mr. Pease and to Mr. Bernard Shaw, who made a liberal and valuable contribution to my notes.

The Fabian Society grew out of a coterie called the Fellowship of the New Life, which had for its professed object "the cultivation of a perfect character in each and all." This was the sort of laudable but perhaps somewhat too far-reaching aspiration to which many extremely able young men were inclined in that epoch. (Among those who avowed this one were Havelock Ellis, the future exponent of sexual psychology, Edward Carpenter, the interpreter of humanist ethics, and J. Ramsay MacDonald, the first Socialist Prime Minister of Great Britain.)

The eighties were rich in cults and movements which, by natural reaction against the materialistic philosophy and theology of the older Victorians, aimed at various forms of mysticism, of spiritual development, or artistic regeneration.

These cults and movements, voicing undeniably high-flown sentiments and extravagant ambitions, may appear not a little naïve and foolish to us who know how vain most of such hopes have proved. But it is well to bear in mind that an interest in moral, religious, and aesthetic reform was then just as much a mark of mental distinction as—say—a reverence for theories of universal sexuality from the cradle to the grave has been in our time. The persons who joined literary societies, art-and-craft guilds, and Vita Nuova brotherhoods towards the end of the last century, were not earnest young suburban artisans, as they often are supposed to be to-day, but some of the best brains that the generation produced.

So much by way of apologia for the Fellowship of the New Life, whose object I have described, and whose principle was "the subordination of material things to spiritual." Now very early in the organization of the Fellowship there was a feeling among a section of its members—of which section Hubert Bland was one—that the reconstruction of society might be effected more adequately by a new and better distribution of material wealth than by a profound attention to the spiritual welfare of either the community or the individual. This dissension was friendly, but it was unmistakable; and so, at a memorable meeting on January 4, 1884, with Hubert Bland in the chair, a separate society named Fabian ("in allusion to the victorious policy of Fabius Cunctator") came into existence.

Edith was present on this occasion, and was noticed with admiration by someone whose attention, had she known it, would have flattered her. Havelock Ellis was kind enough to write me this impression: "I well remember . . . though it is so long ago . . . observing in the chair immediately in front of that I occupied a woman, young and beautiful it seemed to me, and certainly full of radiant vitality; she turned round and looked into one's face with a frank and direct gaze of warm sympathy which in a stranger I found singularly attractive, so that I asked afterwards who she was. I never spoke to her and never saw her again." Attractions remembered thus after a great lapse of time must have been of a very striking quality. There is no lack of evidence that they were so.

"She was, I suppose," Mr. Pease [1] has written, "the most attractive and vivacious woman of our circle." She attended meetings regularly for a considerable time, taking an intense interest in Fabian activities and personalities, as her letters show. The Society seems to have been for at least a year or two the very pivot of all that portion of her life which was spent outside her home.

And indeed it encroached not a little upon her home life, for members and potential members were frequently asked out to Lewisham to dine, and the hours spent in discussing politics were looked forward to delightedly both by Edith and her husband. In an undated letter to Miss Breakell, for instance, she mentions that Mr. Sidney Webb, of the Foreign Office (she

[1] The historian of the Society to whom I have made acknowledgments earlier in this chapter. He was one of the original Fabians and a member of the Executive.

must have meant the Colonial Office), was coming to dinner with the Reverend C. L. Marson, a clergyman actively interested in social reform, and that as "both are very clever" she expects to have "a nice evening." Olive Schreiner was one of her guests on the same occasion.

This letter also conveys news of purely feminine significance. "Now, Ada," she says, "I have something dreadful to break to you *gently*. A certain friend of ours says 'When a woman becomes "advanced" she cuts her hair.' I don't know whether I am 'advanced'—but I have *cut my hair off!!!!!!* I retain the fringe—but at the back it is short like a boy's. . . . It is *deliciously* comfortable . . . I have also taken to all-wool clothing which is also *deliciously* pleasant to wear." All-wool clothing was one of the vital proofs of belonging to the avant-garde.

It is a letter written probably in February, 1884—if only persons who are destined to be celebrated would have the kindness to date their correspondence!—that contains her first reference to the new Society:

> . . . On Friday evening we went to Mr. Pease's to tea, and afterwards a Fabian meeting was held. The meeting was over at 10—but some of us stayed till 11.30 talking. The talks after the Fabian meetings are very jolly. I do think the Fabians are quite the nicest set of people I ever knew. I wonder what you will think of them when you see them.
>
> . . . Yesterday Mr. Pease came at 3. His people are quakers and he has the cheerful serenity and self-containedness common to the sect. I like him very much. We went for a walk in the afternoon and got home about seven, supped, and had a long evening of talk, which was very nice.
>
> To-day Hubert and I and Paul went for a walk in the country. Hubert taught Paul to climb stiles, an accomplishment of which he (Paul) is very proud, as one always is of anything newly acquired. This afternoon we went to sleep, and this evening we have been diligently writing stories.

At about this time Miss Breakell went to Australia, and the extent to which the Fabian Society was engrossing Edith's attention may be judged from the fact that she treats of it more frequently and at greater length than any other topic in her letters. In spite of hard work and many domestic worries, she was making a valiant effort to master subjects connected directly or indirectly with Socialism and we find her, in March, 1884, writing after an agonizing visit to the dentist and an accident in which her little son had gashed his leg so badly as to require stitches in it:

> The Fabian Society takes up a good deal of my thoughts just now. I am also doing a good bit of serious reading—among other things Buchner's "Man," Mill's "Subjection of Women," Louis Blanc's "Historical Revelations"—and an intensely interesting book . . . called "Esoteric Buddhism" by Sinnett. You see my reading is rather mixed and miscellaneous—but it is the fate of most women only to be able to get a smattering, and I seem to want to read all sorts of things at once.

A few days after she wrote this the Fabians elected that Pamphlet Committee whose productions were to cause no little stir; and Edith, no doubt on account of her growing experience in the profession of letters, was made a member of it. The Society now looms larger than ever in her correspondence, and she becomes more and more explicit in describing it.

> I should like to try and tell you a little about the Fabian Society. [she says to her friend in Australia in the opening paragraph of her next (undated) dispatch.] Its aim is to improve the social system—or rather to spread its news as to the possible improvement of the said S.S. There are about thirty members—some of whom are working men. We meet once a fortnight—and then someone reads a paper and we all talk about it. We are now going to issue a *pamphlet*—and the last meeting was devoted to the discussion of that same. *I* am on the 'Pamphlet Committee'— Now *can* you fancy *me* on a committee? I really surprise myself sometimes. . . . The pamphlet[2] was written by Mr. Keddell—

[2] "The pamphlet" was the first tract of the Fabian Society—*Why are the Many Poor?*

the sec. of the society and a Mr. Phillips (working man) and revised by the com. and finally approved—after 3 hours of discussion—by the rest of the Socy. It will be printed next week. Personally, I don't think much of it—but you can't expect a working
man's style to be *much,* and his *facts* are all right. There are several working men in the Fabian—Mr. P[hillips] is a painter and
decorator. I like him so much.

She goes on to enumerate the various members by name, with
observations on their salient features which show that even in
her enthusiasm, she was by no means inclined to idealization.
Here are a few typical specimens from her commentary.

Mr. Watts—*might* have been Bones in an amateur Christie
Minstrel troup—but supposed to be very much in earnest. . . .
Mrs. and Miss Robins—exponents of the "gospel of love"—(not
religious)—Mr. Podmore—mouthpiece of Mrs. and Miss R.—may
be called the member for Robins . . . 3 Misses Haddon—old—
gospel of love—belong to a society called the Fellowship of the
New Life—and talk of "the highest moral possibilities" . . . Mr.
Bellingham Smith—writes plays—interested in social questions
and dried fruits—married—*very much.* Mrs. H.B.S. *very* youthful
and gushing (eldest son aged 19). . . .

There are two distinct elements in the F.S. [she continues],
the practical and the visionary—the first being much the
strongest—but a perpetual warfare goes on between the parties
which gives to the Fabian an excitement which it might other
wise lack. We belong—needless to say—to the practical party, and
so do most of our intimate friends.

. . . We spent a week end with the Keddells a little time ago. I
like him very much, but he has a passion for being thought *deep*
and *mystical,* which leads him to be rather aggravating at times.
His wife was beneath him in station and intellect—but I like her
very much.

This letter ends on the most astonishingly incongruous note it
would be possible to imagine:

I've just been reading "Jessica's First Prayer" to my maid (who
is a treasure), and I felt my eyes smart and my throat grow lumpy
towards the finish. Pathetic simplicity is a grand gift in writing.

At the end of March in the same year she makes one of her few references to literary work:

> Hubert and I have just done a story for Longman's which has been accepted and will appear in the Christmas Number. Hubert wrote the first part and we finished it together. £10. We have now finished the Social Cobweb.[3] I am sorry to say it for £3 0. 0. a week is not to be sneezed at. I suppose I shall go on writing poems for the W[eekly] D[ispatch]. Be sure and tell me which of them you like and which do not please you.

Feminine topics are not conspicuous, but neither are they entirely lacking in her letters. In this one she tells how she has made herself "a new dress of terra cottery crushed strawberry mixture nun's cloth with dark velvet bodice and *trappings*." "It does not suit me," she adds, "but is rather pretty and fits me perfectly." But she never lingers long over this sort of news. Her very next paragraph is about a debate she had just attended; and there is a scathing comment on the Lewisham Literary Society to which she belonged: "All its strength has run to title, and it has three secretaries who between them can never get a notice out in time." And she ends: "We are going out a good bit—to public meetings—to debates—to readings and to meetings of societies, 'human warious.' (The allusion is to Mr. Venus's collection of bones in *Our Mutual Friend*.)

Another reference to her means of earning money appears a week or two later:

> I am not doing any painting just now, I am sorry to say—so I try to write as many stories as I can—but it is uphill work— writing when you don't feel a bit inclined. I hope the Weekly D. will give me some more work later on in the year. We have just sent a joint story to "Belgravia"—of whose acceptance I feel some faint hopes. I still write poems for the W.D. . . .
> . . . Did I tell you I am writing nothing now by myself except poems? In all stories Hubert and I "go shares"—I am sure it is much better when we write together than when we write separately.

[3] A series of stories written by Hubert and Edith Bland together for the *Weekly Dispatch*.

Genius in women has nearly always blossomed early, but E. Nesbit, as I have said, did little work of value before she was forty: perhaps the lateness of her development may in part be accounted for by her having been obliged to write so much and so often when she didn't feel "a bit inclined." Turning out a weekly poem and collaborating in a large output of miscellaneous stories and articles are exertions not conducive to the maintenance of a high standard. She knew this herself, for in the same letter she says: "What seems to be the worst of my present life is that I have no time to do any *good* work." But it was of poetry that she was speaking; she still had no notion that it was in her power to create prose better than the very best of her verse.

All her prose work at this time—and, to be truthful, at almost any time—was done, as one of her oldest friends expressed it, "first and foremost to keep the house going." That she wrote quite insincerely, without any ideas, real or illusionary, about self-expression, is evidenced by the curious fact that she was always asking her friends to think of plots for her. "They are," she wrote, "our great difficulty. . . . They are so hard to hit upon—at least to *us*—though people who don't write always say that to think of a plot is the easiest thing in the world." In the eighties and nineties the short story which did nothing and attempted nothing beyond the unfolding of a simple plot was at the zenith of its popularity, and it is not surprising that a writer gallantly striving to get her living should have cast about in all directions for new subjects: but it is equally to be expected that stories written on quite extraneous themes will reveal little of their author's best capacities.

The letter I last quoted is, like some of the others, in the form of a diary, entries having been made on several separate days for two or three weeks before it was sent—a system adopted, no doubt, on account of the infrequency of the mails to Australia. The note for Easter Sunday is at once illuminating and touching, showing her as it does with her eyes turned wistfully on the country home where she had been so happy, and which she now constantly revisited. Remembering all she had experienced of material and emotional difficulty during her four years of wifehood, we shall not find the last words of the paragraph as extravagant as such remarks usually seem:

I have just got Iris to sleep, and laid her down and Paul is standing watching my scribbling pen—His quietness will not last long, so I will provide him with a box of bricks and then go on with this. It is so quiet—the *peculiar* stillness attaching only to Sunday *afternoons,* especially from 2 to 4. The maid has gone out for the day and I have just washed up the dinner things and am sitting in the kitchen. The kettle is singing on the fire and the kitten purring before it. I sit here in my "deck" chair, and my blue dress—and write to you. Charming domestic picture isn't it. Paul and his bricks make a feature in it. His continual "Look mother, look" only *emphasizes* the silence—like the hum of bees and the stirring of trees, leaves undisturbed the silence of a June day in the country. The country—ah! I was there yesterday. Hubert and I went to Halstead and had a long delicious time among the woods and primroses and dog-violets. But though Spring is well awake in these same woods they are not *green,* only *grey.* The dead grass is *grey*—the birch stems are *grey*—the hazel stems where the light catches them are grey. The pale green of the budding leaves blends in a curious way with the brown twigs, so that the trees look grey too—at a little distance, and the windflowers and wood sorrel are thick enough to make the ground look white as with frost or snow. We had a delightful day—and brought home no end of primroses. I got dreadfully sunburnt and am no end tired—but it was worth it. The woods were near Bath's. Harry [her brother] will remember them, where we used to picnic, in the old days. I seem to have lived three or four lives right *through* since those old times.

In the next entry she reverts to debates, public meetings, and the Fabians, and mentions several still interesting figures. H. M. Hyndman (1842–1921), who debated with Bradlaugh,[4] was

---

[4] Charles Bradlaugh (1833–1891), despite professed atheism and Socialism, succeeded in being elected to the House of Commons. He was an early propagandist for contraception. His liaison with Mrs. Besant did nothing to decrease the odium of society.

the founder of the Social Democratic Federation, one of the most active Socialists of his day, and very nearly a martyr to his cause, having been tried for sedition in 1886, on which charge, however, he was acquitted. J. Glode Stapleton was one of the few well-to-do members of the Fabian Society in its infancy, and the first of the Fabian debaters.

> On Thursday [she tells her friend], we went to a Debate on Socialism—Bradlaugh on one side and Hyndman on the other. Bradlaugh was weak and Hyndman was worse. Hynd. had a bad cold—but there was no excuse for Bradlaugh—He is innately *bestial*—Forgive my strong language. I do so *loathe* the man. (I have been smoking too much and I feel quite silly.) The Debate was at St. James Hall and I liked it because so many people I knew were there. All the Fabian lot. On Friday *was* the Fabian —not a very good meeting. The best part of it was the walk from Westminster to Charing Cross afterwards. Mr. Stapleton walked with me—and we had a real good talk on all sorts of things. I like Mr. Stapleton, though he is "newy," and doesn't answer Hubert's letters *under* a fortnight. He has given up Christianity on insufficient grounds, I think, and being unable to face the outer darkness and desolation of materialism has taken refuge in Spiritualism—and this is always cropping up in his talk in a most aggravating way . . .
>
> On Monday we went to a Woman's Right meeting where I was *infinitely* bored. I saw and heard (for the first time) Miss B[ecker] who is hideously like a *hippopotamus*—Yesterday, we went to a lecture on Socialism by Mr. Hyndman—who was *very good indeed*. Mrs. Annie Besant spoke—William Morris was there.

Edith, in 1884, was already a heavy smoker, and appeared at Fabian and other semi-public gatherings with her box of cigarette papers and tobacco under her arm. The habit was unconventional, but it does not seem to have been thought outrageous. At any rate, her friends, not all of whom were Bohemians, tolerated it without complaint. It is certain that she was not unique (Mrs. Besant actually smoked cigars at meetings); yet at the same time she must, I suppose, be regarded as one of the pioneers of public smoking for women.

There is in this long letter a description of a day's tasks, domestic and otherwise, which we may accept as typical:

> To-day I have washed my hair and have not been out. I have
> done 2 sheets "sides into middle," [5] written some paragraphs for a
> newspaper—cooked the dinner, nursed Iris for a whole hour in
> the vain hope of getting her to sleep. . . . I have also painted
> some cards. I am thankful to say I got some yesterday. I do hope
> the supply will now be kept up. We have just finished a story
> about a dream. I don't mind telling *you* that I feel an inward
> conviction that it will be refused.

That she could summon up the energy, after such days of
physical and mental labour as this, to spend her evenings at debates and committee meetings shows a most uncommon vitality.

The last letter of what may be called the Fabian series is also
likely to prove the most interesting to those who enjoy reading
private opinions of notable personalities. It was probably written early in 1885, by which date the Society had made very considerable strides towards importance. In March that year, Sidney Webb, afterwards Lord Passfield, and Sydney Olivier, the
future Lord Olivier, had been elected as members. A little later
Harold Cox, afterwards M.P., an editor, for many years, of the
Edinburgh Review, joined his friend, Olivier, who had been
born in the same year and educated at the same school, Tonbridge. In 1884 one of the meetings had been "made memorable
by the first appearance of Bernard Shaw"—so Mr. Shaw himself
truthfully recorded in the Minute Book.[6]

---

[5] It may be judged from her practising this wily expedient for repairing
badly worn bed-linen that Edith was well versed in housewifely arts.

[6] Mr. Shaw very kindly communicated this piece of information on the
manner in which he came to join the Fabian Society and to bring to it
his friend, Sidney Webb, who, in his turn, brought Olivier:

"At that time I had read Marx and become a strong Socialist, but I
was in doubt about throwing in my lot with the Social Democratic Federation—not because of snobbery, but because I wanted to work with
men of my own mental training. The Fabian Society's tract, *Why are*

The lady whom E. Nesbit was "trying hard not to dislike" and whom she was successful in eventually liking very much, was Mrs. Charlotte M. Wilson, a member of the Fabian Executive Council, who later became one of the foremost anarchists and the editor of their paper, *Freedom*. She contributed to an early Fabian tract, and was prominent in the Woman's Suffrage Movement. It would also appear that she was one of the originators of that other movement by which so many country cottages have been sophisticated into homes for town-bred people.

The said Society [Edith writes—her enthusiasm evidently in no wise abated after nearly a year and a half of regular attendance at meetings] is getting rather large now and includes some very nice people, of whom Mr. Stapleton is the nicest and a certain G. B. Shaw the most interesting. G.B.S. has a fund of dry Irish humour that is simply irresistible. He is a very clever writer and speaker —Is the grossest flatterer (of men, women and children impartially) I ever met, is horribly untrustworthy as he repeats everything he hears, and does not always stick to the truth, and is *very plain* like a long corpse with a dead white face—sandy sleek hair and a loathsome small straggly beard, and yet is one of the most fascinating men I ever met. Everyone rather affects to despise him "Oh it's only Shaw." That sort of thing you know, but everyone admires him all the same. Miss Hoatson pretends to hate him, but my own impression is that she is over head and ears in love with him. Then there is a very nice-looking young man with a romantic name, Sydney Olivier—who is just going to be married to a sister of another member, Harold Cox—who has a crooked face [she gives a little sketch of it in the margin] but is very nice. He has a co-operative farm near Aldershot, works on it himself and refuses to be addressed as Harold Cox *Esq*.[7] An interesting new member

the Many Poor? fell into my hands. The moment I saw the words 'Fabian Society' on it, I realized that here was a good title which immediately suggested an educated body, so I found out the Society's address from the tract, and turned up at Pease's rooms for the next meeting."

[7] Mr. Shaw gave me some lively reminiscences of Mr. Harold Cox's farming venture which seem well worth reproducing here for their own sake: "At Frensham Pond in Surrey Cox took a lot of land which was

is named Walter *Coffin* (!) He has a dark face, of the type wh. it is now the fashion to term "inscrutable"—whatever that may mean. I think he promises to be an acquisition. He has sent us tickets for a lecture on Garrick to be given tonight, but as it is raining I am afraid Hubert will, considering my cold, refuse to let me go—or rather to take me. Sidney Webb—another member—is no fool, and is in fact an absolute master of political economy but a face like a fat billy goat and a wild profusion of red spots do not contrive to give him an attractive appearance. Mr. Pease I think I have told you of before. He is the young stockbroker in the Prophet's Mantle. . . . Mrs. Wilson . . . was a Girton girl and is clever, and I am trying my very hardest not to dislike her. But it is difficult, as she is sometimes horribly rude, and will never speak to a woman if she can get a man to talk to. I don't mean that she is a *flirt*—she isn't, but I suppose women are not clever enough for her to talk to. She has a husband who is very nice, and a perfect gentleman. Did I tell you about their house? He is a stockbroker, and they used to live in a very charming and rather expensive house at Hampstead, but she at last declined to live any longer on his earnings (wh. she tersely terms the "wages of iniquity") and now they have taken a quite little cottage where she means to keep herself by keeping fowls! It is a charming and quite idyllic little farm. They have 2 rooms—study and kitchen. The kitchen is an *idealised* farm kitchen, where of course no cooking is done —but with a cushioned settee—open hearth, polished dresser and benches, and all the household glass and crockery displayed mixed

mere sand. He induced an agricultural labourer and his daughter to throw in their lot with him, Cox putting up the money for the experiment. They were to run the farm on a communal system. Cox's friends all told him he couldn't grow anything in the sand. He replied, 'I have selected this sterile and barren soil because I am going to show that it will yield as much as the richest and most fertile ground under the influence of Communism. All it wants is scientific agriculture.' Then he got the Army and Navy Stores catalogue and ordered barrels of guano, and scattered it over the sand. The result was not nil, but consisted of an enormous crop of radishes. The labourer came and said: 'What are we going to do with these radishes? We can't dispose of them.' This was perfectly true, so Cox decided to make jam of them, and ordered quantities of sugar from the stores. He was the inventor of radish jam."

up with aesthetic pots pans curtains chairs and tables—a delightfully incongruous but altogether agreeable effect.

It was at this cottage, as Mr. Pease has recorded, that the
Fabians for many years held "the most delightful of their social
gatherings." Its "aesthetic pots and pans" were then new and
striking. The aesthetic vogue was at the height of its short
but successful career, and Edith, as an "advanced woman," had
already adopted it, not only for herself but for her little daughter, now three or four years of age. Towards the end of the
same letter she says:

> I dress Iris in a kind of loose gown now—it comes a little below
> her knees and she looks so aesthetic and pretty in it. It is old gold
> colour. She has pinafores made after the same pattern.

For some years "aesthetic" was to be one of her favourite adjectives of commendation, and her little daughters, attired à la
Kate Greenaway and Walter Crane, were to experience much
embarrassment and discomfort among their school friends.

8   *Circa 1886*

The Blands, and especially Hubert, continued to take an active part in all the affairs of the Fabian Society, and were acquainted or intimately friendly with many of its members, and the members of other Socialistic organizations. They came into contact with Mrs. Annie Besant, later to be president of the Theosophical Society, then considered an outrageous young woman, Charles Bradlaugh, William Morris, Walter Crane, Prince Kropotkin, the famous anarchist, Sergius Stepniak, a somewhat mysterious Russian celebrated in his day for books on Nihilism, Mrs. Emmeline Pankhurst, Edward Carpenter, Graham Wallas, and a large number of others who held views on questions of art, religion, or politics, which were then regarded by the public as very odd indeed.

Early in 1886, Hubert Bland took over the editorship of a paper called *To-day,* which boasted many distinguished contributors, chief of whom was Mr. Bernard Shaw. Mr. Shaw's novels, *An Unsocial Socialist* and *Cashel Byron's Profession,* appeared in it as serials,[1] and besides these and several of the same writer's essays, there was a translation of Ibsen's *Ghosts,*

[1] Mr. Shaw gave me the following account of the manner in which his novels came to be thus published: "The paper was under the editorship of Belfort Bax and J. L. Joynes at the time, and was not doing too

the first that appeared in England, and numerous articles from other pens which then or later were famous—including those of William Morris, William Archer, Havelock Ellis, Edward Carpenter, and Walt Whitman (I am, of course, deliberately selecting only those names likely to be more or less familiar to the generality of readers: there were many others which carried as much weight in their time). For some years, in despite of small circulation, a very high standard was maintained.

By this time Bland was already a well-known figure, not to the public at large, but still among a fairly considerable section of it. He was an efficient chairman at numerous meetings, a useful lecturer, debater, and pamphleteer, and an excellent talker in private life. He was also endowed with a notable talent for hospitality, and married to a woman as adept in this art as himself. They were very poor—though their growing reputation in journalism had by now rendered their position a good deal easier—but most of their associates were in the same plight, and besides, they had the knack of making such matters as grilled herrings, or bread and cheese and beer, seem richly satisfactory.

At week-ends large gatherings of young reformers began to congregate at 8 Dorville Road in the Blackheath district; and there all the most advanced views of the day were discussed for hours at a stretch. Anyone who happened to be present at a mealtime was asked to take a seat at table; and this was truly Bohemian in those years when old-fashioned hospitality had long given place to the formal call and the carefully prearranged dinner-party. Edith, though relieved of some of the cares of the household by the services of Miss Hoatson, still had many domestic tasks to do, and she must have expended a good

well. I said to Joynes one day, 'It's impossible to keep this going as it is. I'll tell you what you ought to do—run a serial in it. It doesn't matter a rap what it is; nobody will read it. Now, I have a pile of old novels that no one will publish, and that are nearly in the wastepaper basket. Take one of those, and use it as a serial.' Joynes took the suggestion up, and I chose *The Unsocial Socialist,* because it was naturally the most suitable for that paper. It was through this that I came into contact with William Morris, who actually read the instalments and liked them. It was the first idea I had that they were not unreadable."

deal of energy on these entertainments, since even the least elaborate party involves some preparation and a certain amount of
after-work, and she had *three* children now to occupy her
attention.

For early in 1885, in the midst of all her other activities—her
painting, writing, reciting, housekeeping, and attendance at
meetings—she had mysteriously found time to give birth to a
son, on whom, with an eager enthusiasm, she had bestowed a
name intended to be of good omen—Fabian. Childbirth is, very
naturally, an event of such moment in the lives of most women
that perhaps it may seem as if I introduce the subject somewhat
casually. My intention in doing so is to attribute to it in this
work, as nearly as possible, that degree of importance which it
would appear to have held in her life. This must not be taken to
mean that she was other than a devoted and conscientious
mother. In many respects she was the sort of mother that every
child would desire to have—lively and amusing, generous without being over-solicitous, and affectionate without being importunate—but she was not, in the sentimental sense of the
term, strongly maternal.

She was fond—even passionately fond—of her children, but
they were by no means the primary interest of her life. A
woman of many resources, endowed with immense physical as
well as mental energy, she did not let childbirth divert her more
than was inevitable from her normal mode of living; nor did
she submerge herself in motherhood with reckless self-
abnegation. Those who have pictured this incomparable exponent of the child's psychology as the personification of
maternal zeal may be astonished and even disappointed; but such
a woman could hardly have produced works of art for which a
certain detachment of mind and a great deal of undisturbed
time were indispensable.

Yet if she was less moved by the advent of a child than mothers commonly are, she was not less appalled by the loss of one.
About a year after Fabian's birth she had a stillborn baby, and
grieved as much over it as if it had been her first-born. It was
buried in the garden of her home, a form of interment no

longer permitted. Hubert Bland prepared the grave, and Miss
Hoatson laid the dead child in a long basket which she decked
with flowers. Edith begged that she might be left alone with the
basket for a quarter of an hour, and her friend, who was acting
as nurse, doubtfully acquiesced. When she returned she found
Edith clinging to the baby desperately, in a frenzied determination not to part with it. The struggle to take it from her was
long and agonizing, and she only yielded it up at last when her
husband, terribly distressed, came to Miss Hoatson's aid.

Shortly after this loss, Edith had an illness which was the
occasion of an act of the most womanly kindness by Mrs.
Besant, who, brooking no denial, came to Lee and carried away
little Paul and Iris to her own home, so as to relieve the Bland
household of everything that might detract from the care
needed by its mistress.

Another valuable friend, and one who long remained so, was
Bernard Shaw, who at about this time was responsible for
Hubert Bland's getting his first regular journalistic work. Mr.
Shaw himself had been asked to undertake a weekly article for
a now extinct periodical; and it was a practice of his never to
reject an offer of this sort without trying to get one of his
friends accepted as substitute. At his suggestion, therefore,
Hubert Bland was given the job, and, making a success of it,
achieved by degrees a very wide repute.

Shaw's attractions, upon which Edith made comment in a letter recently quoted, did not leave her unmoved. His wit and
charm, his handsome figure, his rich voice, and—it may well
be—his extraordinarily pleasant Irish brogue, made a strong impression on her; and, emotional as she was and far from
happy in her home life (she had not yet learned how to resign
herself to her husband's growing tendency to infidelity), she
yielded herself to the luxury of being in love. Her sentiment,
which she made no attempt to disguise, elicited from its object
nothing but a heartlessness which he knew how to make amusing, and was soon happily transmuted into a gay and untrou-
bled friendship.

She addressed several fervent poems to him, which the necessity of earning money obliged her to sell to the newspapers and magazines she wrote for. It was desirable to suppress any evidence by which her friends might guess at the source of her inspiration, and she was not so serious as to be incapable of getting a good deal of fun out of this. On one occasion, as Mr. Shaw recalled, she had written him some verses in which she referred to his "maddening white face." Together they altered this phrase to his "maddening dark face," and thought his identity sufficiently well concealed.

It was probably shortly before Fabian's birth that Edith had the pleasure of preparing some of her work for book form. The first book of all, published in 1885, was a novel written in collaboration with Hubert Bland; it was called *The Prophet's Mantle,* and was published by them jointly under the pseudonym "Fabian Bland." It made no stir, and was altogether a rather abortive venture never repeated. I prefer to count her real literary debut as having been made with the first publication— apart from magazines and newspapers—of work which was exclusively her own. She began with poetry, and not, to be sure, on a very grand scale. The traditional "slim volume" of the young poet was, in her case, so exceedingly slim as to be hardly a volume at all, and she was not even the only contributor to it; but still there was print and there was binding, and these must always have their charm for a writer.

In those days there was a fashion for presentation booklets— the most diminutive imaginable—containing seasonable verses and decorated lavishly on almost every page with vignettes and floral ornaments. It was in this manner that E. Nesbit first saw her poetry between covers, and for some years, even when she could find a ready market for more ambitious work, she continued to supply material for such booklets from time to time. The earliest catalogued in the British Museum are four sets of *Songs and Sketches* appropriate to Spring, Summer, Autumn, and Winter respectively, and all printed at Nuremberg (where fancy typography was a special industry) in 1886. They were done in collaboration with Robert Ellice Mack, and include, besides many of E. Nesbit's own poems, a number by other hands.

But in the latter half of the same year her authorship took on a more impressive aspect. Longman's brought out a quite substantial volume of her poetry under the title *Lays and Legends,* and it enjoyed a very fair success. It would appear that the firm consulted Andrew Lang as to the advisability of accepting the book, and that he replied with the following cautious recommendation, which was doubtless a sound one:

> 1 Marloes Road,
> Kensington, W.
> July 18. (? 1886)

Dear Longman

I think the verses will make rather a big book, and they might be judiciously weeded. The socialistic ideas, especially, are repeated pretty often, and two or three pieces of that kind would be enough. There are several examples of sudden drops into prose, and of roughness in metre which might be improved. With a good deal of care given to the proofs, and with some energy in "cutting" the volume might please a fairly large public.

> Yours very truly,
> A Lang.[2]

How much "weeding" was done it is impossible to guess—perhaps not as much as the critic would have wished, for many poems were included in the selection which might have been dispensed with. Nevertheless, it was well received; reviewers hailed the writer as one from whom great things might be expected; and she received a number of those personal tributes which are capable of giving even more pleasure, and began to be talked about as a promising young poet.

There was already a fairly wide circle of readers who followed the work she was then doing pretty regularly for *Long-*

[2] Andrew Lang (1844–1912), celebrated folklorist and man of letters; wrote poetry, essays, novels, and children's books; he was a founder of the Psychical Research Society. This letter, like the others by the same writer which will appear in this book, was originally printed by kind permission of the late Mrs. Lang.

man's Magazine. One of these was H. Rider Haggard, himself an exceedingly popular writer at that time; and it must have been gratifying to her to receive this quite unexpected homage from him, just before the publication of *Lays and Legends:*

> 9 Gunterstone Road,
> West Kensington.
> 5 September 1886.

My dear Madam,

I hope that you will forgive me for doing a thing (which honestly I never have done before) namely writing to you to express my admiration of your poetry and the great pleasure which it has given me to read it. The immediate occasion which prompts me to write this is the reading of your poem in this month's Longmans but I have been a humble admirer of your poetic power ever since I read "Absolution" now some years ago.

Of course opinions differ about poetry, and I am the last to pretend that any value is to be attached to mine. But as one who writes himself I do know what is calculated to stir our human sympathy, and I must say that for sweetness and strength and beauty of imagery I know no verses from the pen of a modern writer of poems which appeal to me so much as your own. This then must be my excuse for writing to you as one very grateful for shade in the desert land of contemporary verse. Hoping to see some more from your pen before long, and also that I may some day have the pleasure of making your personal acquaintance, believe me dear Madam

> Very truly yours
> H. Rider Haggard.[3]

No doubt she sent him a copy of her book—it was a lifelong habit of hers even more than of most authors to make such presentations to her admirers—for some further correspondence ensued, but they do not appear to have met. At any rate, five years later, he was writing to explain that, as he was not then living in London, a meeting, which she had evidently requested,

---

[3] The late Lady Haggard kindly allowed me to use this letter.

would be impossible, though it would have given him the greatest pleasure.

It was not only to professed admirers that she sent her works in those early stages of her career. She followed the custom, which seems to have been a common one then, of dispatching copies to various celebrities, known or unknown to her, whom she herself admired. In the last century there was much more talk than we hear now about the brotherhood of artists, and one gathers the impression from biographies and correspondence that they were far readier to help one another with criticism, advice, and recommendation, their leisure not being wasted by the numberless disturbances which beset the lives of public figures to-day. Authors, too, even when successful, would freely write to "brother" authors personally unknown to them to express the pleasure inspired by their works—a very generous and delightful practice, but one which tends to die out under the influence of forms of advertisement by which such private tributes might be publicly exploited.

Edith would at all times eagerly approach other writers who had given her pleasure, and in her early days, as I have said, she frequently sent copies of her books to more notable poets in the hope of eliciting their favourable attention. In this it does not appear that she failed. Swinburne for one was sufficiently impressed by the *Lays and Legends* to write of them in these eulogistic terms to Philip Bourke Marston, the young poet who had been engaged many years before to Mary Nesbit:

> The Pines,
> Nov. 15. 86.
>
> My dear Philip,
>
> Some days ago I called Watts' attention to what struck me as the remarkable merit of some of the poems in a volume I had lately received from the author, poems which reminded me in some of their finer characteristics, rather of your own than of any other contemporary's. I am naturally much interested to hear of your connection with the author. I thought "Absolution" certainly a powerful poem, perhaps as much in the style of Lee Hamilton's

poems as of yours, very well conceived and constructed. I had read before (I forget where, but quite lately) "The Singing of the Magnificat" and it had struck me as something quite out of the common in conception. It is a pity the closing couplet should be so flat, but that might easily be remedied. "Baby's Birthday" is a charming little piece, and I am rather fastidiously exacting with respect to poetry on the great subject of "Baby."

The first part of "Children's Playgrounds in the City" I like very much, and the whole of the poem called "The Dead to the Living" is powerfully pathetic.

Come and see me if you can, on Friday next, and I will read you a lyric made near Beachy Head while returning from a long walk thither. I am very much in love with Eastbourne. Do you know it?

Ever sincerely yours,
A. C. Swinburne.

P.S.—I had forgotten to mention the poem called "Two Christmas Eves" which struck me as singularly powerful and original, the sort of poem that Charlotte Brontë might have written, if she had had more mastery of the instrument of verse.[4]

It is hardly likely that Marston omitted to let Mary's sister see a letter which must yield her so much satisfaction, and in any case Swinburne probably wrote to her himself; and what with his praises and those of many others whose opinions she valued, it is not astonishing that she was inclined to rate her poetry rather higher than we can think warrantable. It is said that she called on Swinburne, or was taken to see him, and found him less pleasant than she had expected.[5]

From Oscar Wilde, with whom, as the following letter indicates, she was personally acquainted, she heard nothing of her

---

[4] This letter is included here by kind permission of Messrs. William Heinemann, Ltd., and was first published in *Swinburne's Letters,* edited by Sir Edmund Gosse.

[5] Members of her family recollected that she sometimes referred to a meeting with Tennyson, whom she thought exceedingly disagreeable, but I have not been able to discover when and how she came into contact with him.

work but what was flattering. It cannot be said that his appro-
bation has the ring of perfect sincerity: nevertheless, she had so-
licited and must have been gladdened by it:

> 16, Tite Street,
> Chelsea, S.W.
> (? Nov. 1886)

Dear Mrs. Bland,

Thank you so much for sending me your volume of poems: I
have been turning over the leaves—tasting as one tastes wine—
and am fascinated by the sonnets on pages 64, 65, and 96, 97—but
I am keeping the book as a whole for study in the Clumber
woods next week. "The Last Envoy" seems a really beautiful
piece of work. You see I am getting to know you, petal by petal,
but I will not touch the longer poems just now.

Any advice I can give you is of course at your disposal. With
regard to your next volume—but you do not need to be taught
how to tune your many-chorded lyre, and you have already
caught the ear of all lovers of poetry. I hope, however, we may
meet again soon.

> Oscar Wilde.[6]

Impelled no less by poverty than by praise, she continued to
write with a vigour which, if we consider all her other activities,
we shall find very remarkable. Her circle was growing wider
and wider. She conducted what might be called a *salon*: her
parties increased in size and number until it seems as if at one
time or another almost all the younger men of letters and the
prominent Socialists of the day found their way to them.

In spite of all this work and pleasure she managed to make
time for fairly frequent holidays and also for a good deal of
theatre-going—an enthusiasm which, though keen, was apparently short-lived. The theatre, while it never left her quite indifferent, does not seem to have had any potent attraction for
her in later life; but throughout the eighties at least, she was an
eager playgoer, and went constantly to the Lyceum during

---

[6] Permission to print this letter was granted by Mr. Vyvyan Holland,
Oscar Wilde's son.

Irving's management. I had it from Alma Murray, one of the most notable actresses of that day, that she was critical and discriminating, and a lover of fine stagecraft.

In May, 1886, she was present at a performance which moved her greatly. It was an event of some importance in the theatrical world—the first rendering upon any stage of Shelley's tragedy, *The Cenci*.[7] The play was produced under the auspices of the Shelley Society, and owing to its being thought utterly unfit for public presentation, the audience consisted only of the Society's guests—an anticipation of a method of avoiding the censorship which has since become commonplace. Alma Murray, who took the part of Beatrice,[8] was described afterwards by Browning as "the Poetic Actress without a rival." She played, according to all contemporary accounts, with exquisite beauty, sensitiveness, and dignity; and her triumph at the fall of the curtain was hardly less thrilling to the spectators than to the actress herself.

Browning immediately wrote her a note containing these words: "After such a display of passion and pathos, what is impossible for you?" And E. Nesbit, never reluctant to do homage to a member of her own sex, expressed her admiration in verse:

> If he whom now for the first time we know
> Could have come back from nothing into being,
> He for the first time would have fully known
> How full a flame of genius was his own . . .
> Across all fairest leaves is writ "too late"!
> He cannot know of your supreme perfection,
> Nor know how you and he are best expressed
> Each through the other
>   . . . In a vision

[7] Amongst the audience were Robert Browning, George Meredith, J. Russell Lowell, Andrew Lang, and many other distinguished men of letters. Bernard Shaw was there in his capacity of professional critic.

[8] Mrs. Alma Murray Forman, sister-in-law of the zealous Shelley editor, H. Buxton Forman.

He may have seen you, and have so forecast
The triumph you should bring to him at last . . .
Whose undreamed dream you are, as he your Art's heart is.

Few women would have been so free from self-consciousness
in thus addressing their praises to another. It is a pity such well-
meant verses have not more merit.

The Blands were members of the Browning as well as the
Shelley Society, and attended its performances regularly. They
were ardent admirers of Browning, whose poetry Hubert Bland
is said to have read aloud in a manner that smoothed away all
its difficulties. Both of them read much, and with great catholic-
ity, and Edith would commit to memory all the passages which
pleased her best. Her energy of mind was unappeasable.

What is more curious is that her physical energy kept pace
with it. She was exceedingly lithe and athletic, and even after
the births of four children far more adept than the average Victorian woman in riding, swimming, and running. And she rode
one of the monstrous solid-tyred tricycles of the eighties! She
was proud of being able to do fancy skipping, and in appreciative company would perform a dancer's high kick, or bend
backwards across a gate until her head nearly touched the
ground. Her holidays, which occupy a particularly important
place in her life, were usually arranged so as to give her as
much scope as possible for physical activity. Hubert Bland, too,
who was a very well-built, muscular man, hardly less energetic
than his wife, shared her tastes in this matter; and they were
always entirely happy when they went away together.

As a rule they took their holidays in company, but sometimes
Edith would go to the country alone, or rather, only accompanied by one or more of her chlidren. On one of these occasions
she joined her sister and brother-in-law, Mr. and Mrs. John
Deakin, at a cottage near Hayfield in the Derbyshire Peak District. It was called the Three Chimneys—a lovely place standing
on a hilltop. Edith was delighted with her surroundings, and
felt eager to produce a novel in which they might be turned to
account. Her neighbours, who were also to supply material, in-

cluded the family of Woodcock, living at Aspenshaw, a large, rambling old house, where there were cheerful young people, big dogs, a pony for her to ride, and an atmosphere of peace and comfortable security which she had not known since leaving Halstead. Mrs. Vincent Taylor (once Miss Fanny Woodcock) gave me an interesting portrait of her as she was then—at the age of twenty-eight or twenty-nine. I transcribe it here, adding some details derived from other contemporary sources:

An exceptionally handsome, tall, slender, young woman, with a figure at once strong, graceful, and supple; eyes dark but bright and very watchful, beautiful eyebrows and a fine, broad forehead half-covered by a fringe of naturally curly brown hair; a narrow, delicate nose which faintly and most attractively misses perfect regularity; a firmly modelled mouth, rather thin, but sweet in its expression—the upper lip and the chin somewhat shorter than is common. All the forms of the face are definite to the point of sharpness, and this, with the alertness of her glance, and the quick movements of her head, suggests to almost everyone who sees her the epithet "bird-like."

At Aspenshaw, dressed in aesthetic clothes, daringly corsetless, she would lie at full length on the rug before the fire with the dogs beside her—so oblivious to the extreme unconventionality of her attitude that she charmed the young people, and disarmed the elderly. The men whom she met there frankly admired her, and she made little effort to hide her pleasure in being admired. Free from every suspicion of coquetry—as it was fit that an "advanced woman" should be—she was nevertheless a deeply feminine creature.

She never laid stress upon the fact of her successful authorship, or made the slightest effort to call attention to her literary or other talents. Nor did she give anyone cause to guess the many tribulations of the past five or six years. She was serious in discussing the social questions that interested her, but in general her manner was as gay and careless as a child's. Indeed, she had a child's flexibility almost all her life in recovering from every possible distress. Neither anger, nor worry, nor even grief itself, save in its direst extremity, could ever master her for long.

In consequence of this resilience she was one of those rare women who can really take a holiday. Her work, her money troubles, her conjugal problems, were all put behind her when she left London. She made a point, too, of having at least one holiday a year without her children. On these occasions she generally went boating on the Medway with her husband and two or three friends. She was skilful in handling a boat, and of all her pastimes she loved this and swimming best.

I am indebted to Mr. Noel Griffith [9] for my account of these Medway parties, of which he made one for several years. In about 1887 Mr. Griffith, travelling in a train, attracted Hubert Bland's attention by being intent upon a work of Herbert Spencer. A conversation on philosophy led to a conversation on Socialism, and Bland invited his companion to visit him at Lee for further talk. This was the beginning of one of the longest and most intimate of the many long and intimate friendships which the Blands enjoyed. In a year or so the young man joined them in one of the first of the Yalding parties.

The procedure was much the same as in successive years. They would leave London just before the hay harvest, when the Kentish fields and flowers were at their best, and hiring a double-sculling boat, start out from Maidstone for a week of sailing, bathing, and picnicking. Rowing up to East Peckham, near Yalding, they would put up at a little inn by the river for about a shilling a night each, and thence they would take out luncheon and pot of four-ale, and spend the whole of each day rowing, walking, and swimming. They learned, after much damage to their hands, to open the locks expertly with a crowbar—an accomplishment in which Edith took a lifelong pride. In the evenings she would play the guitar, and they would sing songs, some of which she had written herself. She would write poetry, both light and serious, and she had a happy facility in commemorating specially pleasant days or amusing adventures with verses of lively charm.

For a long while Yalding remained her favourite summer re-

[9] The late Noel Griffith, barrister-at-law, whose son, Hubert Griffith, a playwright and journalist, was E. Nesbit's godchild.

sort, but she was also in the habit of taking spring and winter holidays. She paid several visits to the South Downs, near Rottingdean, before that district had become hideous with the most inexcusable kind of building. Here she and her friends would spend their time walking or driving in a dog-cart over icy roads. And here she would meet that remarkable and tragical poet, John Davidson,[10] with whom she was on friendly terms for a long period. She used to describe how, playing cricket on the Downs, Davidson would take off his wig and carefully hang it on the stumps.

One summer Yalding was exchanged for Whitstable,[11] where the Blands gathered about them a larger party than usual of the young writers, critics, artists, and miscellaneous Bohemians who formed their milieu. Here W. S. de Mattos, a well-known Socialist, conspicuous in the Fabian Society, helped her to perfect her swimming, which became so good that some little time afterwards she was able to perform a rather extraordinary feat. In trying to open the sluice-gates of Yalding Lock, which is, I believe, the deepest on the river, Hubert Bland let the crowbar fall into the water. No one was in sight to be called to their assistance, and the occupants of the boat were wondering how many hours they might have to spend in imprisonment when Edith dived into the lock and—despite her dread of encountering an eel at the muddy bottom—managed to locate the crowbar, a particularly heavy one, and bring it to the surface.

It may seem surprising when we consider the expensiveness of holidays at the present time that this young couple, whose position was anything but secure, or even comfortable, should

[10] John Davidson (1857–1909) was the author of plays, poetry, and versified philosophy. His public, though respectful, was small. He committed suicide.

[11] This was in September, 1890. Prince Kropotkin was expected to join them, but wrote to say that it had been only "a castle in the air," as literary work obliged him to remain in London. I am deviating a little from chronological order but as these holidays of the late eighties and early nineties are not distinguished from each other by any major incidents, it seemed better to group them together here than to interrupt the narrative at several stages by separate references to them.

have been able to go away twice a year or oftener; but it was an era in which numbers of amenities we now take for granted were scarcely known except to the richest classes, and could therefore be forgone without any sense of privation. It was much easier to take a holiday on limited means when one was quite unconscious of the inconveniences of cottage quarters without bathroom, electric light, and running water; and before modern conditions had made it seem a hardship to be dependent for transport on a cart hired from the nearest farm or inn. The Blands and their circle never thought of staying at hotels.

But even allowing for this, there was unquestionably a certain mild degree of extravagance in all their doings. Neither of them was good at managing money, though both worked hard enough to earn it: they always lived up to their means with no margin of safety. Yet they indulged in few personal luxuries. Edith spent little on dress, even when her income was considerable; her jewellery was all of an aesthetic—that is to say, an inexpensive—character; and she never went in for fashionable amusements. But her generosity, like her hospitality, was far beyond what might have been expected of her means.

It is expedient to mention here that before the close of the decade Edith's relations with her husband were disturbed by a ruder shock than any that had yet befallen her, and one which affected the whole tenor of her domestic life from that time forward. She discovered that Miss Alice Hoatson with whom she was on terms of intimate companionship was expecting a child, the name of whose father she would not on any account reveal. Edith, quick in compassion as ever, and not discouraged by a secrecy which might well have aroused her suspicions, insisted on coming to the rescue in a manner nothing short of quixotic. She actually decided to adopt the baby as soon as it was born and pass it off as her own: for the plight of an unmarried mother and an illegitimate child was far more serious at that time than it is to-day, and only a step as drastic as this could have saved them both from many painful mortifications.

Edith was as good as her word, and soon added to her family of three young children a fourth of parentage only half known to her. Six months passed and then—I cannot say how—came the shattering discovery that the baby's father was her own husband.

The young wife would have been something more, or less, than human if her magnanimity had remained unshaken by this blow. She was passionately in love with her husband, and Alice, who had—perhaps from kindly motives—helped to delude her, was still an inmate of their house. There was, understandably, a violent quarrel, in the heat of which Edith suggested the departure of the child and its mother. Hubert Bland, in the difficult position of having unmistakable obligations to both women, took a course which may seem grotesquely strange to us, but in which he may have been more reasonable than appears. He protested that if his wife disowned her friend and the child, he would leave her.

She consented then to carry out her original plan and to bring up the baby Rosamund as her own (indeed, she was devotedly fond of it): but it remains an open question whether this consent was given under the pressure of her husband's threat and in terror of losing him, or whether—which accords better with her whole character—she would, after her first anger had subsided, have fulfilled her generous intention in any case. Certainly altruism prevailed in her subsequent behaviour, though, as might be expected, there were occasional lapses into resentment and dissatisfaction, and at such times there would be scenes and recriminations. But on the whole she kept to the course she had taken; and her nobility is even better evidenced by this than by her first impulsive act of kindness. For there are, I suppose, other women who, in the turmoil of a crisis, would have made the gesture, but where are those who would have continued to endure a situation so difficult long after it had lost its novelty and its dramatic elements?

To avoid any risk of over-colouring this matter, it is fair to say that she was not always able to conceal a preference for her own children from the adopted one, or so Rosamund believed when she discovered in early adolescence the secret of her parentage. Such a feeling was most natural and pardonable, but

Edith fought hard against it, and at times did really stifle it. In fact, she would emphatically have disclaimed that she either acted or felt less affectionately towards her younger "daughter" than towards her own children. In this her position was made easier by Rosamund's unusual attractiveness and prettiness.

But whether or not she did fail at times to repress her sense of the injustice of her position, and whether or not the primary motive of her conduct after disillusionment was the desire to keep her husband's love, it still remains that she undertook and carried out one of the most unselfish acts that has yet been recorded in the life of an eminent woman. It is an act which, were the adjective not supposed to be reserved for masculine honour, we might truthfully call chivalrous.

9 Further Work—Social, Literary, and Charitable

The Fabian Society grew constantly more influential and ambitious and its members more prominent; but Edith, though she never lost her interest in it or ceased to share the opinions it advanced, attended the meetings less frequently as they became larger and more official in character, and were translated from private drawing-rooms to public halls. Her husband, on the other hand, laboured with increased zeal in Fabian causes. He was one of the seven Essayists [1] who virtually governed the Society and shaped its policy, and though a certain ineradicable Tory spirit in him made the other six regard him at times as something of an obstructionist, his work was acknowledged to be of great value.

Edith, by temperament dramatic and inclined to enjoy attracting attention, found the business-like atmosphere of a public meeting uncongenial. She could shine more brightly in a drawing-room group, and that she did shine, though not always with a steady and serene light, has been attested by several who remember those days well.

[1] Mrs. Annie Besant, Hubert Bland, William Clarke, Sydney Olivier (later Lord Olivier), Bernard Shaw, Graham Wallas, and Sidney Webb (later Lord Passfield).

Shaw said that she was "pervasive of the whole society" and that this pervasiveness was due as much to her restlessness and her habit of making some small sensation at every meeting as to her charm.

At times when the others were serious, her little temperamental "tricks," as he called them—no doubt accurately—could be very trying. He would refuse to sit beside her until she promised categorically not to interrupt him in the middle of a discussion by asking for a glass of water, or "staging a faint." Nevertheless, she was much liked, as well by him as by the others.

Hubert Bland, though far more useful to the Society, was personally less popular. Touchy and at times excessively critical, he identified himself less closely than most of his fellow-Fabians with advanced views on general questions. He was, for instance, most severe and rigid in his attitude towards the ideas of sexual freedom then first beginning to be ventilated. He would take a violently condemnatory tone in denouncing everybody who aspired to rebellion against conventional morality. This was to be expected in one whose own position, as Shaw observed, was "fundamentally a little weak," and who was instinctively challenging potential attack on his personal conduct.

Bland was a conservative in everything but politics. He approved highly, as is evident from all his many writings on the subject, of the moral codes he flouted; and he approved of them the more, perhaps, because he was never able to flout them without enormous inconvenience. A man capable of these illogicalities and persistent in giving utterance to them, could not fail to arouse some antagonism in strong-minded associates. Shaw, whose polemics belonged only to his public character, and whose private inclinations tended always towards keeping the peace, would often tactfully intervene between Bland and those with whom he would otherwise have been in a state of friction.

By degrees he came to be recognized as "the Opposition," and it was even agreed that there was much to be said for his keeping a kind of Tory point of view in sight. He became known as "the Tory Socialist," and was perhaps the first of the species. Notwithstanding the occasional disharmony, his personal relations with his colleagues were happy enough for most of them to be guests at his house from time to time, and he and his wife at theirs.

At the end of the Fabian meetings the group to which Bland belonged would generally come together for more intimate conversation, and as a number of them—stimulated by the enthusiasm of Frank Podmore—were interested in psychical research, they often adjourned to experimental séances, at one of which a still famous exposure of Madame Blavatsky took place. Sometimes they would go to spend the night in a house reputed to be haunted.[2] E. Nesbit played no part in these investigations, but she must have taken a pleasure in hearing of them, for the supernatural always had a strong fascination for her.

The Fabians, when their official business was transacted, were in the habit of talking vigorously and at length on every conceivable aspect of those questions of sex, ethics, religion, and politics which were then beginning to be asked aloud for the first time in many decades. It was doubtless as a sequel to one of these discussions that Hubert Bland received from Bernard Shaw the letter which I am privileged to reproduce here. Although the references to the subject of this biography are only casual, they are apposite, as showing in some degree what sort of impression she made, at thirty-one, on a particularly shrewd observer. But even had she not been mentioned in it, I should scarcely have had strength of mind to omit as irrelevant a letter so likely to be read with interest for its own sake.

29 Fitzroy Square,
18th Nov. 1889.

What I said was that before a man gets to a consciousness of his spiritual self he has to pay a certain price. Of course such language is damnably unscientific; but then as we have not yet dis-

[2] Bernard Shaw recollected sleeping in a "haunted" house on one of these occasions, and having a queer dream which his companions took to be of occult significance, but he saw no ghosts.

covered the phraseology of the spirit of will, the thing cannot be
put scientifically. The ordinary man, leading the ordinary life,
never becomes conscious of the will or impulse in him that sets
his brain to work at devising ways and reasons. He supposes his
life to be a mere matter of logical consequences from a few bodily
appetites and externally appointed "duties" with their attendant
pains and penalties. If he believes in his soul, it turns out to be a
purely materialistic conception of some intangible organ in him
that will preserve his individual consciousness after death and
play a harp or roast eternally according to certain conditions fulfilled during his life. If such a man is to attain consciousness of
himself as a vessel of the Zeitgeist or will or whatever it may be,
he must pay the price of turning his back on the loaves and fishes,
the duties, the ready-made logic, the systems and the creeds. He
must do what he likes instead of doing what, on secondhand
principles, he ought.

And of course, there is a devil of a fight to acquire the power to
do what you like and to get fed and clothed for doing it. You and
I, according to the most sacred secondhand principles, should be
prosperous men of business, I for the sake of my poor dear
mother, who in her old age, has to live on a second floor and eke
out the domestic purse by teaching schoolgirls to sing, you for the
sake of your clever and interesting wife and pretty children. In
bygone days, when I had nothing to shew for myself except rejected MSS. and was reproached over and over again, more or less
directly, with being an idle, lazy, heartless, selfish scoundrel, and I
myself was too young to have my eyes quite open, I would absolutely go now and then to look after some opening which I had
no real intention of taking, but which I still thought it necessary
to find some external reason for not taking. No doubt you have
done the same thing in one form or another. Now I have no
faintest hesitation left. The secondhand system on which I
"ought" to have been a stockbroker has absolutely no validity for
me. My one line of progress is from writing stories, reviews, and
articles, more and more towards writing fully and exhaustively
what I like. And of course, my mother, the victim of my selfish-
ness, is a hearty, independent, and jolly person, instead of a miserable old woman dragged at the chariot wheels of her miserable
son, who had dutifully sacrificed himself for her comfort. Imagine
Mrs. Bland as the wife of a horrible city snob with a huge villa, a

carriage, and several thousand a year, which is exactly what, on moral principles, it was your duty to have made her. You and I have followed our original impulse, and our reward is that we have been conscious of its existence and can rejoice therein. The coming into clearer light of this consciousness has not occurred to me as a crisis. It has been gradual. I do not proceed by crises. My tendency is rather to overlook changes in myself, and proceed on absolute assumptions until the consequences pull me up with a short turn.

Wallas [3] made my blood run cold for a moment; but he really did not mean it. He was full of the meannesses of Kingsley and the profligacy of Bentinck; and it was about that he was speaking when, by what seemed like an intentional stroke, he made it appear for a moment that he was talking about you in the most personal way. This triumph of dialectics was quite unintended. I attacked him about it when he sat down and he was unmistakably taken aback and probably thought that I was giving an ingenious twist to what he said. Obviously, I think, it was too bad to have been done on purpose; you would have been justified in appealing to the exec. as a court of honour; for that sort of thing would make debating impossible on ordinary lines. However, you passed it off very happily; and the bulk of the audience did not catch the apparent innuendo.

There can be no doubt that the paper was a great success. The Coleridgian part was vital and very well done I think. You must have put a lot of elbow grease into it.

G. B. S.

With another emancipated personality already well-known and destined for celebrity, the Blands were on very friendly terms. Olive Schreiner, whose *Story of an African Farm* had been widely read ever since its appearance in 1883, went several times to their house at Lee during her various visits to England, and always entertained, so her friend Havelock Ellis told me, "a tender regard" for its mistress. That the two women had made a very deep impression on each other may be judged by striking

[3] Graham Wallas (1858–1932), professor of political science, was a schoolmaster at the time of the incident referred to in this paragraph—an incident which is sufficiently explained by the context.

passages from their letters during the year when they were most closely associated. While staying at Mrs. Charlotte Wilson's "idyllic cottage" in Hampstead, Edith wrote to Olive Schreiner thus:

> Thanks for your letter: it is very pleasant.
>
> I want to come and see you again, may I? You see I am partly on the way to you, here—and Hubert wants to come with me. If it's the least bit inconvenient please say so. You did me much good, the other day. You took me out of my world into another from which I came out with a sigh and a shiver, as the train took me away from you. But the remembrance of it does me good still.
>
> > Yours
> > Edith Bland.

And in a letter written to Havelock Ellis on her arrival at Alassio in October, 1888, Olive Schreiner made her own enthusiasm clear:

> Mrs. Bland ("E. Nesbit") was so kind to me before I left London. I don't think I should have got away without her. She came the last morning to finish packing my things and see me off. Do you know, she's one of the noblest women? I can't tell you about her life, because I mustn't, but it's grand. The last night she lay by me on the bed and drew me very close to her and pressed her face against mine, and do you know, I have felt it ever since.

Olive Schreiner was deeply concerned with the injustice of the prevailing moral code, and had evidently had some argument upon it with Hubert Bland, for in an undated note to Edith, written between 1887 and 1889, she refers to having sent him a long letter on this topic, and goes on to say:

> I thought I'd given Mr. Bland a wrong idea, from what he wrote, about my view of marriage, that it was the *legal* marriage I was so strongly in favour of and not simply the union of one man with one woman resting on their free will. I believe so firmly that this is the ideal after which the highest part of the race is feeling,

that I have no fear that freedom of sex union will lead the highest individuals to unite in any other form. That was all that was in the letter, and I asked you if you would send me your photograph.[4]

It is a pity that my information on the friendship of these two women, admirably suited to each other in temperament and outlook, is extremely meagre. Nothing further appears in my records but a postcard from Matjesfontein, South Africa, in 1890, saying: "I am sending this to Mrs. Wilson because I don't know your address. It's just to tell you that I never forget you. Please send me a line." [5]

The year 1888 must have been a particularly crowded one for E. Nesbit judged even by her own abnormal standards. Besides entertaining a good deal, writing stories and articles, and taking up charitable work on a somewhat extensive scale, another volume of poems was issued by Longman's, and no less than seven of the illustrated booklets which I have already described appeared under the imprints of other publishers. It is true that no great amount of time or trouble could have been involved in the preparation of the little gift-books. The work was generally done in company with Miss Hoatson (who as "Uncle Harry" —a pseudonym thrust upon her by her publishers—composed verses for children) on evenings when Hubert Bland went to visit his mother. The two ladies would write far into the night, inspired by draughts of weak gin and water. Their allowance for the session was supposed to be one tablespoonful of gin each, but sometimes Edith would claim an extra ration as absolutely necessary to fluency of thought. The poems thus pleasantly produced were of the most facile and unmemorable

[4] Mr. S. Cron Cronwright, husband of the late Olive Schreiner, cleared up the ambiguity of the passage above by stating that his wife favoured perfect "freedom of sex union" and thought the "highest individuals" would not unite in any other form.

[5] Apparently the Blands had once contemplated going to South Africa, for she continues: "Things in the business sense are very bad in the colony just now. I would not advise anyone to come out. There is a reaction after all the gold speculations."

kind; they reveal, indeed, certain rather maudlin tendencies—
which I hope may have been due to her sense of what the
prospective purchaser required. Only thus is it possible to account for some of the saccharine ill-polished verses which found
their place year after year in this series.

She was obliged very often to write to order on themes of
no consequence to her. In fact, she would sometimes receive
from a publisher or magazine editor a batch of pictures with
instructions to compose something to fit them: and her poverty
made her willing to accept this kind of commission. [6] It is a
most extraordinary thing that a writer who had done hack-
work without illusions for nearly twenty years should have created the Bastables: but E. Nesbit, in her work as in her private
life, was capable of unexampled deviations from the course one
might reasonably have looked to her to pursue.

Leaves of Life, the collection of her more sincere poems with
which she followed up *Lays and Legends,* was not as successful
as its predecessor. From the publisher's point of view it must
have been very definitely a failure, and a second series of the
Lays and Legends brought out three or four years later did little
better in the matter of sales. But until well on in the nineties she
was taken seriously as a poet by the group of admirers—several
of them better poets themselves—with whom she was in touch.
Without vanity, or at any rate without conceit, she, too, took
herself seriously, and hopefully awaited the day when her qualities would be recognized by a wider public than had yet ac-
claimed her.

Sheer need, however, forced her to continue with work which
was, and which she knew to be, ephemeral, and she left no
stone unturned to extend her market for it. Apparently she
wrote in January, 1888, to Walter Besant, then editing the journal of the People's Palace at Whitechapel, offering him material

[6] Something of the sort may have led, for example, to her publishing a
booklet called *The Lily and the Cross* in 1887, and another, quite different, called *Lilies Round the Cross,* in 1889. Both appear equally devoid
of personal inspiration and the similarity of the titles suggests that she
did not choose them herself.

for that paper. He replied telling her frankly what would be expected of her:

> . . . I send you a copy of the Palace Journal. You will understand that it is written *wholly* for the Members of the Palace who are young people between 15 and 25—4,000 in number. Everything that is put in is—or should be—considered with reference to them. Their literary standard is not high and what they like best is a story with a "bit of blood" i.e. a murder. We do not wish to gratify this passion for murder but we must make the paper interesting for them somehow or other. So if you have any *short* article—about a column and a half in length about *anything* that such readers would like to read—foreign travel—adventure— story in verse—short story—I should be very glad to look at it. Don't write down to our intelligence but consider what we like. We can give a guinea each for short stories. The Journal is not political or religious and must be very carefully kept out of the modern discussions and schools. . . .[7]

Perhaps deterred by the unattractive nature of these suggestions, perhaps by the lowness of the fee, she failed to make any contribution to the *Palace Journal,* but two months later she went by appointment to see its editor, having been recommended to him by her publisher. Whether her work proved unsuitable for Besant's requirements, or whether those requirements proved unsuitable to her, the only contribution which appeared under her name in his paper was a poem called *The Little Cobbler,* and it can hardly have fulfilled the editor's conception of what his public wanted. A few years later she wrote a number of stories on themes as sanguinary and violent as he or anyone else could have thought desirable.

In about 1888 Edith began to devote herself to social work for the poor of Deptford, for whose children she arranged year after year from that time forward, Christmas treats on a much more handsome scale than was then usual. An excellent organ-

---

[7] Major Philip Besant permitted me to print this extract. Sir Walter Besant (1836-1901), author of numerous novels, satirist of women's claims to political rights, one of the founders of the Society of Authors.

izer whenever she was given complete control (a bad one when obliged to occupy a subordinate position), she not only toiled arduously herself, but succeeded in making almost every one of her friends and acquaintances toil with her. The history of these treats reads like a sort of fable illustrating the very sad moral that too much benevolence defeats its own ends.

They began with a Christmas party of twenty poor children at Mrs. Bland's own home. This was such a success that the following year helpers were enlisted, and the number of children was increased. A year later it was increased again until it became necessary to hold the party at the Deptford Board School, the children being selected by their teachers on account of good conduct. There were tableaux, a lavish tea, and an equal distribution of apples, oranges, boxes of sweets, toys, and useful presents—generally made by the Bland family and their friends. Then Edith decided that it was unfair to provide only for the *good* children. The bad ones needed treats as much as these, or more, and they must all be invited. The number to be catered for rapidly rose to five hundred, and in a few years had reached a thousand! This was more than even her energy and resource could cope with, and so the parties had to be given up.

The preparations for present-giving and entertainment on such a scale were, as may be imagined, formidable, and were not without terrors for some of Edith's friends. In the three months preceding Christmas scarcely anyone entered her doors without being set to some useful labour. She had an engaging yet purposeful manner of making a request that only the boldest could withstand. But, on the whole, there was little difficulty in enlisting workers for the Deptford cause. Most of her visitors were delighted to have an opportunity of performing some immediate and practical service for the poor, and every Saturday there were working parties where she directed the making of innumerable garments—chiefly corduroy trousers.

And then there were rehearsals, for by 1892 the tableaux had developed into a quite elaborate pantomime, and the company met once a week for three months beforehand. Two performances were given, one for the children, one for their parents and other relations, and the standard is said to have been much higher than one expects of amateur productions. The first play they did was *Cinderella*—a novel version by E. Nesbit—and this was followed by *The Sleeping Beauty* and then *Aladdin.*

In *The Sleeping Beauty* the part of the King was taken by Laurence Housman, and the same actor played the Slave of the Lamp in *Aladdin.* Here is the letter in which Mr. Housman first consented to appear:

> 61 Marloes Road,
> Kensington W.

Dear Mrs. Bland,

I couldn't decide myself, so I asked the Holy Bible to come and help me. I shut my eyes and let my fingers go at random. This, when I looked, is what I read. "He made a pit, and digged it, and is fallen into the ditch which he made." Which means that I was fool enough to let you see me losing my head in a charade; and so now I am in for it. Like the parrot I am, when it is too late, "sorry I spoke."

. . . Hew me in pieces before the Deptford board-school children, and have done with me.

Songs? Two. One is "God Save the Queen" (on the night of the performance) and the other isn't. In vain moments I call myself a Baritone, my best note lies between F and B on the upper part of the bass clef. Songs I used to sing, and know part of, are "Conquering Kings their Titles take" and most hymns, "Peaceful Slumbering on the Ocean," "Drink to me Only," "The Minstrel Boy" (which I won't do on this occasion), " 'Twas on a night in the gay Spring-time," and no doubt others, but I will wade through anything you set me, only remember I have a bad ear, so don't give me any minors or accidentals to do. I shall simply hurdle-race them. Please as much as you can cut down the rehearsals. I will come part perfect, given time:

I feel in the attitude of Montgomery's dead warrior—lying on his stomach and gazing vacantly at the stars. It is a right and proper attitude for the surrender whether of one's body or one's soul at the demand whether of a deity or a charity organization.

> Ever yours sincerely,
> Laurence Housman.[8]

[8] Printed by permission of the writer. Laurence Housman (1865–1959), brother of A. E. Housman, artist and author of fiction and successful plays.

Housman was one of Edith's liveliest correspondents, and the only one, it would seem, whose letters she consistently preserved. She had met him, like several others amongst her closest friends, through her appreciation of his work. A poem of his, *The Corn-Keeper,* which appeared in *Atalanta* in 1892, was the occasion of her writing to tell him of her admiration; her letter resulted in a meeting and the meeting in a friendship which flourished for more than ten years.[9] Mr. Housman was a useful as well as a witty and entertaining companion, for he gave her many of her best ideas for her children's books, a matter on which I shall later speak more fully.

In about 1889 she had made another friend who was to become notable in the world of letters. This was Richard le Gallienne, who sent me the following brief but luminous memoir:

Though it is so many years since I last met her, my remembrance of Edith Bland is as keen and beautiful as ever, and I can still see her, as though it was yesterday, as I first saw her at Hampstead seated in an armchair with two little children at her side. It was a romantic moment for me, for she was the first poet I had ever seen, and, a youth first come up to London from the provinces, I looked on her with wonder, captivated by her beauty and the charm of her immediately sympathetic response. I fell head over ears in love with her in fact. She was quite unlike any woman I had ever seen, with her tall, lithe, boyish-girl figure, admirably set off by her plain "socialist" gown, her short hair, and her large, vivid eyes, curiously bird-like, and so full of intelligence and a certain half-mocking, yet friendly humour. She had too, a comradely frankness of manner, which made me at once feel that I had known her all my life; like a tom-boyish sister slightly older than myself. She suggested adventure, playing truant, robbing

[9] That it eventually lapsed was due to a certain uncongeniality between Housman and Hubert Bland which became too definite to ignore. Laurence Housman was actively sympathetic towards the Woman's Suffrage Movement. Bland was uncompromisingly against it, and such was his influence over his wife's political opinions that she, too, refused to support it. Housman was disappointed in her for being, as he felt, untrue to her own inward convictions, and while retaining their mutual goodwill, they drifted apart.

orchards, or even running away to sea. I was hers from that moment, and have been hers ever since.

At that time I would be about twenty-three, and she, I think, would be about eight years older. . . . I saw her frequently from then on for several years, and I owe her an enduring debt of gratitude for her sympathetic appreciation and criticism of my early work. For her own work I had an enthusiastic admiration. . . . But before long I left England for America, where till recently I have continued to live; and so, I am unhappy to say we saw no more of each other. But her memory has always remained one of my most treasured possessions. . . . I recall her as a beautiful and loved friend.

The writing of a biography is in many respects a melancholy sort of work, tending to produce in its author a sense of the impermanence of all good things. The endings of love affairs and friendships are perceived in the same moment as their beginnings. The sincerest of lovers fall apart, the warmest of friends are severed; and the biographer, his attention constantly directed towards the ravages of time and circumstance, comes at last to think that he sees the emblems of mortality lying heavy on every affection that is most precious. Were it not for such a tribute as that I have quoted, I know not where he would look for consolation.

10   *The Nineties*

In 1889 the Blands moved from Dorville Road, Lee, to 2 Birch Grove, a somewhat bigger house; and in 1894 they moved again, this time to Three Gables, Grove Park, their fourth home, and so far the most spacious and most comfortable. Their financial position was now fairly easy—or would have been if they had known better how to manage money and been less given to generosities in which a more prudent couple would not have felt the temptation to indulge. Hubert Bland wrote regularly for the London *Daily Chronicle,* the Manchester *Sunday Chronicle,* and other papers, and was making a name for his lightly philosophical essays on a wide variety of social and ethical questions; while Edith herself had as many commissions as she could well cope with. For all this, there was sometimes no small difficulty in settling the tradesmen's bills, and characteristically she took it amiss that butchers and bakers must be paid while the poor children of Deptford were half-starved. It is but justice to the butchers and bakers to acknowledge that when it was a question of priority, the Deptford poor children and Edith's copious collection of "down-and-outs" generally came first. The household bills would then run up to comparatively huge amounts, and would be paid off as soon as one of the two amassed a more substantial sum than usual. Though improvident they were scrupulous, and somehow or other they managed to fulfil their obligations.

From the time of becoming very definitely a professional writer, Edith had been assisted in her housekeeping by Miss Hoatson, who also shared the care of the children, for though she would be seized at times with a domestic fervour which engulfed all other enthusiasms, and would have moments when baking, or jam-making, or carpentering seemed the only things worth doing, her literary work, by which the house was largely kept going, made it difficult for her to attend systematically to its care. And while her knowledge of household economy was sound and her capabilities were great, in practice she lacked the steadiness, the sense of proportion, which distinguish the best exponents of the art.

Her larder was wholesomely and nourishingly stocked, but she went through phases when she would spend pounds to save shillings, and she was often absent-minded. On being asked once by Hubert Bland what had happened to the cold sirloin left from Sunday—it being now the middle of the week—she replied guiltily: "Why, I've never thought of it since! I'll go and see." At a later period she kept a gardener, "so as to obtain a cheap vegetable supply," and was surprised when it was pointed out to her that vegetables bought from a shop would not have cost her nearly so much as his wages.

Yet there was nothing of Mrs. Jellyby about her. Her children, though unconventionally dressed, and allowed more freedom than critical neighbours thought good for them, were very well cared for in all essentials. She had ideas on the rearing of children, widely accepted to-day, but then regarded with suspicion or even with strong disapproval. Barefooted, hatless, and gloveless they ran about at will; and this kind of upbringing was not thought a proper one by inhabitants of London suburbs in the nineties. But whatever they did to flout the middle-class standards then so firmly rooted, the Blands all had "a manner." Even when Fabian, the most irrepressible of the four, shocked the respectable neighbourhood by waylaying city gentlemen on their morning walk to the station and begging for pennies, he combined a certain grace with his disingenuous pathos.

A fond and well-meaning mother, yet erratic in maternal offices as in those of housekeeping, Edith was capable of causing discomfort to her children without realizing it herself—and this is very extraordinary when we consider that what has given her fame the promise of permanence is her fine insight into the secret places of the child's mind. When, for example, Rosamund was four or five years old, she would be made to go through an ordeal of nodding, smiling, and waving her hand before she was given anything she asked for. This was on account of a line from some poem they knew ("With a nod and a smile and a wave of the hand"), in being persuaded to act which the shy smile and gesture of the embarrassed child so amused the mother that she would stage the little scene for visitors.

Again, the girls, even when much older, were allowed no say in the choice of their clothes, and were dressed—as I have mentioned earlier—in a manner which, though admired by aesthetic adults, did them little credit with their school-friends. Edith would go to sales and buy large quantities of fabrics which the children were compelled to wear out; and so uncommon—though doubtless artistic according to the more advanced notions of the time—was their mother's taste, that they thought themselves very lucky if ever they were clad in ordinary-looking garments.

Her delight in the most graceful kind of charity sometimes caused her to forget where charity is supposed to begin. She had needy relations whom she would assist at the cost, indirectly, of her own household; and she was rebuked once by Rosamund for buying clothes for one of her nieces when Rosamund's own underwear was, as the child herself put it, "in such a state that she couldn't elope even if she wanted to." But these thoughtlessnesses were a small matter in comparison with those many qualities of hers which must often have made her children unconsciously the envy of their fellows. She played with them seldom, it is true, but when she did play she was both earnest and inventive; she loved to give presents and agreeable surprises, and made a particular point of keeping up birthdays handsomely. If in the heat of temper—and she had a quick temper—she acted unfairly, she would admit herself wrong afterwards, and behave with penitence. And overworked as she was, she would celebrate special occasions with topical verses as well written as those she intended for publication—just as she had painted elaborate Christmas cards for her friends in the days when this sort of work had meant part of her livelihood.

These rhymes afford almost the first clear prophecy of what was to be her real province as a writer. It is true that she was already contributing numerous verses and stories to children's gift books; but in these she did not let herself go; they contain little that sets them apart from what a hundred other efficient writers were producing for the same purposes. It will hardly be denied that the most shining charm of her first great success, *The Treasure Seekers,* lay in its apparent ease of manner, its ingenuous fluency. Like Jane Austen, she learned ease of manner by experimenting in her family circle, where all artificial restraints might be abandoned.

Her daughter, Iris, coming downstairs for the first time after the affliction of measles, is welcomed with five stanzas of jubilation in which the delight of all the household pets is fancied in such terms as these:

> The tortoise rejoices to know you are well,
> Though he veils his delight in the depths of his shell.
> And pigeons, forgetting their family cares,
> Coo: "Let us be joyful! She's coming downstairs!" . . .
> Sing Guineas, sing pigeons, sing bold black-and-tan!
> Sing tortoise and Kerry—as well as you can!
> Shout tadpoles and newts, let the greenhouse resound,
> While the hose makes a hissing and rapturous sound,
> Till the busman remarks, as he gathers his fares,
> "They're cheering for Iris, who's coming downstairs."

She admonishes the same daughter for carelessness in an impressive yet disarming strain:

> What have you done with the pencil I lent you?
> In what shade does my pen lie hid?

What did you do when on errands I send you?
Dropped the money—you know you did!

("Years ago, it is true, but the principle is the same," says a characteristic footnote.)

What of poor Collins who asked you plainly
To bring the money to pay his bill?
Picture him waiting and watching vainly,
    Eagerly watching—and hoping still.

Bad little Rabbit! Dear little Rabbit!
    Do grow careful as old you grow.
Carelessness is a dreadful habit—
    I'm old and careless, and so I know.

The family must have been at this time a lively and happy, though not a peaceful one. As Edith grew older, she tended more and more to give way to moods of irritation and resentment over very small matters, and was not always careful to repress them in the presence of her children. At mealtimes there were often stormy outbursts which ended in her rushing from the table and violently slamming the doors as she retired to her study. The children would be left staring uncomfortably at their pudding plates, and Hubert Bland—himself by no means mild of temper—would get up and make for *his* study, invoking Heaven and slamming doors with equal violence. But he was the only person who could make his wife see reason when she gave way to these tantrums, and after a short time he would be heard at the door of her room begging to be let in. Then there would be an affectionate reconciliation and they would call each other again by the nickname "Cat," which was always the gauge of mutual good humour. "There, Cat dearest, kiss your old Cat and come and eat your pudding," he would coax her; and they would walk downstairs arm in arm, and she would penitently kiss everyone all round and tackle the pudding obediently.

A mother who will apologize may be exasperating, but she is not likely to be depressing to her family, and there were many compensations for her lapses from tranquil and logical conduct. The young parents kept the sort of house that children love; there was always something "going on," and their freedom, though likely to be restricted suddenly and unexpectedly, was much wider than was usual in those days. Their mother's beauty and talent they took, of course, entirely for granted, but her physical dexterity must have been a source of pleasure. What child would fail to appreciate a tomboy mother who could run and climb, row and swim, and make really interesting things with her hands, and ride bicycles when cycling was a new and thrilling craze?

There were neighbours, however, who looked with mistrustful eyes upon these activities—especially the cycling, for which she actually wore serge bloomers. It was known, too, that she smoked cigarettes and sometimes took a puff at a cigar; and her slim, uncorseted figure, clad in aesthetic gowns which showed more of her neck than the ordinary mode allowed, was not the sort of figure that seemed modest to wasp-waisted ladies. Besides, she had a little court of "clever" young men who were devoted to her; her house was always full of people. It was suspected, and rightly, that one or other of them might be on terms that went beyond friendship. They could not know how overwhelming her provocations to seek compensation had been. Unheeding, if not unconscious of disapproval, she continued to cycle, smoke, and receive her young men; and never returned the compliment of her hostile critics by taking the least interest in *their* affairs. She was too busy. She had too much work to do, and too many interesting people to talk to.

For these she kept almost open house, both she and her husband devoting themselves entirely to entertaining on Sundays, while during the rest of the week there would be a great many casual callers. Sometimes there were informal dances, Edith or Miss Breakell playing the piano in turns, or together. Edith had an excellent ear and as she could give a sufficiently dashing, if not perfectly accurate version of any tune she had heard two or three times, her repertoire was extensive. Very often there would be charades; these were always a favourite amusement of

hers, for she welcomed any opportunity of dressing up and acting. But chiefly the hours passed in talk—talk on every conceivable subject generally led by Hubert Bland, his strong personality dominating over almost every other in the room.

Only Shaw, so one observer has recorded, could ever succeed
in eclipsing him. Indeed, so vivid and compelling was his
manner, so forceful his mind, that his failure to achieve some
great public position was always considered a mystery by his
friends. Edith, vivid and forceful as she was herself, was content
to let him shape her opinions, if not her personality. Whether
she alone, brilliant but in many ways unstable, could have collected and kept about her as much distinguished company as
she became accustomed to receiving, is thought doubtful by
some of those who knew them both. On the other hand there
were members of that company who liked her very much more
than they liked her husband.

Richard Whiteing, then famous as the author of *The Island*
and *No. 5 John Street,* Adeline Sergeant, a very popular novelist of the day and one of the first to encourage E. Nesbit to
write prose, Graham Wallas, not yet, of course, laden with his
academic honours, Laurence Housman, equally gifted as artist
and writer and versatile in both vocations, and Richard le Gallienne, soon to be one of the leaders of the *fin de siècle*
movement—all these were intimate and most of them frequent
visitors in the early nineties. Bernard Shaw and the other
prominent Fabians were also to be seen at Lee from time to
time, and Sydney Olivier more often; Mr. Shaw, wearing the
light woollen clothes which were then considered very singular,
and Mr. Olivier in a smoking jacket of chocolate-coloured velvet
which, on one occasion, had to be mended by Edith on his arrival, as the sleeve was hanging by a thread.

Sometimes Edith would induce her husband and Shaw to put
on gloves and spar together. Hubert Bland was fond of boxing
(he had once beaten a powerful gipsy boxer in a stand-up fight
at a race-meeting) and, but for the handicap of bad eyesight,[1]

---

[1] Hubert Bland wore a monocle, which in those days of his youth was
sometimes considered an affectation in him. This was very far from the

would probably have excelled in sports. Trials of strength and agility occasionally varied the evenings of literary or political discussion. Bland, who was a volunteer, could rest his Army rifle along the table on its heel and muzzle, and lift it with one hand by its grip to the perpendicular—a feat which it was not easy to emulate without risking a sprained wrist. Edith, who had an almost boyish admiration of physical prowess, took no little pride in his dexterity.

She herself, in Shaw's phrase, "was always full of fun." We shall see that at a later period of her life, she was inclined to stand on her dignity; she remained lively, whimsical, humorous, but—and this is not inconsistent with her childlike qualities —she grew to be the sort of person with whom one takes no liberties. In the nineties dignity had not yet become a settled characteristic. She would suddenly and rather charmingly relapse into boyishness, as when walking one day in Regent's Park on Mr. Shaw's arm, chatting in a particularly elegant and ladylike manner, she suddenly astonished him by exclaiming: "Shaw, I do believe it's going to rain like Hell!"

It is a curious fact to be noted in reading the lives of authors that those most given to play seem to be also the hardest or, at any rate, the most prolific workers. E. Nesbit, whose time was so largely occupied with hobbies, holidays, and amusements, yet managed, in her own erratic, unsystematic way to fulfil all her engagements to editors and publishers.

On weekdays, when under pressure from one of these, she would depute someone else to receive whoever might happen to call and lock herself in a room at the top of the house with a notice forbidding disturbance on the door. Like almost all writers, she found it difficult to set about her work, and was easily diverted from it by every attractive scheme that presented itself; but she had one fortunate and enviable capacity—when the task became urgent she could shut herself off from interruption and bring a most powerful concentration to bear upon it.

truth, for he could scarcely see without it. Crossing Holborn with Bernard Shaw one day he let his monocle fall and it was broken, and he became so helpless in the traffic that Shaw had to take him by the arm and steer him almost as if he were blind—as, indeed, he eventually became.

In about 1890 the Blands and some of their neighbours and literary friends formed a debating society called "It," which met periodically at various houses in Lee, Eltham, and Blackheath. Several interesting papers were read and discussed by a company which included most of the eminent figures I have mentioned. Shaw occasionally joined the debaters, and argument was spirited and eloquent. But the society collapsed suddenly at the end of a brief and brilliant career. The unintentional cause of its downfall was a journalist member, Harold Cox, future editor of the very conservative *Morning Post,* who, being a young man in advance of his time, decided to read a paper in advocacy of nakedness. It was entitled, I believe, *Nudity in Art and Life;* and the speaker, waxing enthusiastic over a subject we should now think ordinary enough, instanced the charm of a lovely young woman lying naked on a tiger skin. This was altogether too much for Blackheath decency in the nineties, and the society never recovered from the shock. Whether the supposed impropriety annoyed her or merely the result of it, Edith herself was extremely angry with the speaker.

Hubert Bland was so much at his best as an orator that it is not surprising to find that both he and his admiring wife enjoyed a debate as much as any pleasure that came their way. The topics were not always serious or seriously treated. There was, for example, a mock trial for Breach of Promise of Marriage, held at somebody's chambers in the Temple.

> I was put up [says Laurence Housman] to conduct an impromptu case against Oswald Cox (brother of Harold), who came dressed as a baby in bare legs with his hair tied up in ribbon—his defence being that he was an infant under the age of consent. I was quite incapable in those days of speaking; and I hated the job and did it badly. Alfred Sutro was defending counsel; Oswald Barron was the judge.[2]

[2] Alfred Sutro, O.B.E. (1863–1933) was author or part-author of many successful plays. Oswald Barron, F.S.A. (1868–1939) was an expert on medals, heraldry, and genealogy. He became Maltravers Herald Extraordinary.

On another occasion Mrs. Bland took me to a debate in the Temple, where G.B.S. and Belfort Bax spoke: Bax read a paper and the rest commented. Somewhere else she took me to hear James Frazer of "Golden Bough" fame read a paper on the marriage customs of Indian and Burmese tribes. . . . At that time there was an annual "Crab and Cream" supper . . . in the Temple. Crabs were laid all down the table. Everybody ate at least one—most of us tried two. After this came Devonshire cream and strawberry jam; wine permeated the feast, and Benedictine crowned it. At the end, all the unseasoned innocents, like myself, were—if not drunk—quite incapable.

For all their many festivities, most of the Blands' friends were poor, some of them to beyond the degree where poverty can be carried off lightly. The only man of leisure and affluence in the circle was Darcy Reeve, one of those rare beings capable of using their money in a manner that seems satisfactory to those who have none. He did two very good deeds for Edith. The first, from which their friendship sprang, was inspired by his admiration of her *Lays and Legends*. He discovered that the volume was out of print, and thereupon approached the publishers—while he was still a stranger to the poet herself— with the suggestion that they should bring out a new edition. On being told that the sales of the last had not been sufficient to warrant a reprint, he offered to pay the expenses of publication, and soon laid his altruistic scheme before E. Nesbit. He financed not only the new issue of *Lays and Legends* in 1892, but also the "Second Series" of poems under the same title.

When he went to visit the Blands at Lee he found Edith suffering from bronchitis, and altogether in a very poor state of health, and begged her to go and recuperate in the south of France with her companion, assuring her, as she protested that she could not afford to act on such advice, that he intended her to have the holiday at his expense. She felt that, since he had already undertaken to finance her poetry, she ought not to tax his generosity further; but he was persistent, and succeeded in pressing no less than £300 upon her.

The resort chosen was Antibes, then a small and remote village, and Edith with Alice Hoatson set off in high delight to be joined after a week or so by Hubert Bland and two or three friends. But the holiday did not begin propitiously. Edith was ill on the journey, and by the time they reached Dijon she had lost her voice and could scarcely utter an audible word. At this station, to their dismay, they were asked to leave the train, although they had been asssured in Paris that it went straight through to Marseilles, and under that impression had ordered sleeping accommodation, and had undressed and retired for the night. In choking, whispered tones, Edith protested to the guard who had awakened them that there must be some mistake; the train was surely going to Marseilles. Her only reply from him and every official she approached was that she must make haste to prepare her luggage for removal. While the two travellers were hurriedly trying to gather together clothes and valuables, the light was put out and they could do nothing but grope desperately about their compartment. Edith sent for the stationmaster to get the lights turned on, but when she whispered close to his ear in the darkness, he started back as if he suspected some sinister design, and made no effort to help her; so they were obliged to seek the platform with their arms full of clothes and such other effects as they could manage to retrieve in the dark.

They were hustled into a second train, with no consolation but an admission that they had been misinformed in Paris, and soon discovered that they had lost their watches, their purses, and many other possessions, and had only a few francs between them. When they reached Marseilles at seven in the morning, after a journey full of distresses, Edith declared that she could go no further, but must see the Consul and a doctor at once. She was told that the Consulate was two miles out of the town, and would not be open for some hours, nor would it be easy to get a doctor immediately. They went into a café for breakfast, but by this time Edith was very ill indeed, and sat shivering, unable to eat anything. The hour was a difficult one at which to get a conveyance, and the Consul was not traced without further discomforts. He turned out to be a Frenchman, and apparently of a careless Southern temperament, for it was by no means easy to make him see the urgency of their case. He recommended them to catch the next train, not to Antibes, which he said was too cold at that season, but to Toulon, advising them to talk to the Consul about their losses when they got there, as he could do nothing for them.

Toulon was not in those days a meeting-ground of English pleasure-seekers, and the best accommodation Edith and her friend could find was in a dirty and dilapidated hotel with a generally depressing atmosphere. Here they spent four dreary days, and, having after great exertion recovered some of their property, they proceeded at last to Antibes, where by degrees the ill-effects of the journey were shaken off. Miss May Bowley, one of the party that met them there later, gave me a description of their activities.

"Mrs. Bland," she wrote, "hired a guitar and went about with it slung round her shoulders. She and Miss Hoatson provided rather extreme examples of the aesthetic dress then in vogue for literary and artistic people, and we were regarded as something in the nature of a free show by the inhabitants of Antibes, who turned out to stare at us wherever we went. Mrs. Bland, who had been very ill, sometimes needed support when walking, and Mr. Bland did not at all mind her strolling about with the arm of a French officer round her waist. (We had made the acquaintance of some officers quartered in the town.)

"Some of the journalists at Nice invited our party to a local dance. An officer who had rooms there lent them for the ladies to change their dresses. The room was so intolerably stuffy that Mrs. Bland insisted on forcing the window open, though it had been painted while shut! While she and the other ladies were actually leaning their heads out of the windows to get a little air, they were horribly embarrassed by the return of the astonished owner of the room, who had come back to fetch something. At this dance, one of Mrs. Bland's partners trod so much on her toes that she told him it was the custom in England to dance side by side!"

"Her packing," the same informant writes, "was equal to her housekeeping. She bought a very beautiful green tea service at Antibes, but as she *would* pack it flat on the bottom of a tin trunk every article was found smashed when we arrived in England." [3]

During this holiday the Blands saw a good deal of Grant Allen,[4] who was staying at Cap Martin, and they appear to have liked one another, though I find no evidence that the association was continued when the holiday was over. The only record I have is from a member of the party, who says that when he came from his large and luxurious hotel to dine with them in their much humbler surroundings, he made a great fuss on account of his fear of getting typhoid in that place, and later he held forth to a largely feminine audience on the inferiority of women, a thing which may seem curious to those who recollect that a couple of years later his novel, *The Woman Who Did,* was looked upon as a feminist tract.

At Antibes Edith, reviving an old hobby, did a little outdoor painting in water-colours. Both she and her husband prided themselves on possessing something of the artist's vision, and it was impossible to be out with them for long before one or the other would see something which aroused the exclamation: "Oh, isn't that paintable?"

The Blands were now confirmed in their habit of taking as many holidays as they could muster time and money for. In 1891, for instance, there had been first a trip to Oxford, where they met Professor David Ritchie, widely known at the time as a political author and lecturer; then, one month afterwards, a journey to Telscombe in Sussex (here some time later they sent their son Fabian to a private boarding-school); again, at short intervals, two little holidays on the Medway and one at Rottingdean. No doubt it was these brief but complete respites from the crowded life in London that enabled them to work and entertain incessantly when they returned to it.

[3] E. Nesbit's daughter, Iris, told me this story is by no means to be taken as typical, for she was usually most adroit.

[4] Grant Allen (1848–99), journalist, scientist, and prolific author of novels, some of which made a considerable stir. He attacked various social conventions and championed women against the unfairnesses of the moral code accepted in his time.

Edith continued to go away alone from time to time, some-times staying with her half-sister, Mrs. Deakin, who was living near Worsley, in Lancashire. It was a coal-mining district, and, at the period of Edith's visit in 1893, there was considerable distress there, owing to a strike. She at once interested herself in the local soup kitchens and relief funds, and threw all her energy into alleviating suffering. She gave parties, too, for the village school children, one of whom carried through forty intervening years a recollection of "her tall, fine presence, her expressive, sensitive face and sparkling eyes," and the feeling of distinction that this splendid lady imparted when, in playing a round game, she bent down to bestow a kiss.

Within a few weeks or months of this journey to Lancashire, there were not only two more trips to the Medway, but another holiday on which E. Nesbit made, in a thoroughly characteristic manner, a discovery that was to have important consequences for her. The summer was an exceptionally hot one and, anxious to escape from the intolerable closeness of London, she went with her two eldest children "to explore Hythe." In carrying out this intention, she lighted upon a four-horse char-à-banc about to start on an excursion. With scarcely an enquiry as to where it was going, she mounted into it with Paul and Iris, and was driven thus unawares to the beautiful seaside village of Dym-church, then quite secluded and almost unknown to the outside world. Its attractions so delighted her that she decided to exchange those of Hythe for them. She took rooms immediately, and sent to London for the rest of the family.

She was devoted to Dymchurch from this time forward, and returned there year after year, eventually furnishing a house which she kept as a permanent holiday resort, entertaining numbers of her London friends there. It was at Jesson St. Mary's, two or three miles away, that she died thirty-one years afterwards.

Almost every holiday and friendly reunion produced its little affectionate records in the shape of verses. Mr. Basil de Sélin-court, for example, regretting, on a dull day in October, the last vanished traces of summer, addressed some lines to Edith and her daughter Iris in which he fancied them as able to keep the summer's gladness about them at all seasons. She, ever willing to devote to friendship the time that might have been spent in fulfilling more material needs, responded at once:

> You think the Summer lingers here?
>   We dreamed that she had fled with you,
> Since, yesterday, the leaves fell sere
>   And skies forgot their blue.
>
> But when this morning broke we knew
>   Not ruined was the golden gear,
> The smiles, the tears, the sun, the dew,
>   That crowned June Queen o' the Year.
>
> We will not weep by Summer's bier
>   More than some sad sweet tear or two.
> She is not dead but sleeps the drear
>   And sighing season through.
>
> And when December comes to woo
>   The quiet hearth with firelit cheer,
> Meeting, we three shall find anew
>   Our happy Summer, dear!

Laurence Housman was also ready to "drop into poetry" on suitable occasions. Here is the curious impromptu by which he signified acceptance of an invitation to tea:

> As a tired hired steed
> Fares fired to his feed,
> As a shell pell mell
> From a one-ton gun
>   Takes its run,
> As the flight of a kite
> Out of sight into height,
> As the speed led by greed
> Of an eagle or a seagull,

So shall my speed be,
So aspire my desire
Till the train stops and stands
And lands me at Lee
In time for tea (D.V.),
At the hands of the Blands.

L. H.

But Mr. Housman's favourite method of communication was to send hasty but delightful sketches which said as much as a whole letter. A postcard reproaching E. Nesbit for having failed to keep an appointment shows him seated forlornly at a tea-table under a clock. A sketch accepting an invitation to play Badminton is a visual reminiscence of an occasion when, in the course of strenuous play, he had accidentally hit Edith with his racket and made a deep cut on her nose. At the time when these drawings and many others in the same style were done, he was, with Aubrey Beardsley, William Morris, Walter Crane, and Charles Ricketts, a leader of what may be called the Book Decoration Movement, and one of the foremost of those black-and-white artists whom the nineties produced so lavishly. He had helped to create the *fin de siècle* mode, and E. Nesbit had written an amusing skit on his style in her book *A Pomander of Verse*, published in 1895.

A lady whose lover has a passion for art has changed the fashion of her dress again and again in order to keep up with his perpetually advancing tastes. "The formless form and tone-less tones" of Madox Brown and Morris, the soft frills of Marcus Stone, the shining silks of Sargent—all these she has adopted to gratify his eye: she has even consented to appear "as vague as Mr. Whistler's ladies are." But there is a point at which she must draw the line:

. . . Now at last you sue in vain,
    For here a life's submission ends:
Not even for you will I grow plain
    As Aubrey Beardsley's "lady friends".

> Here I renounce your hand—unless
>   You find your Art-ideal elsewhere;
> I *will not* wear the kind of dress
>   That Laurence Housman's people wear!

I have mentioned that E. Nesbit made a practice of writing to other authors whose work gave her pleasure. One of these was Rudyard Kipling, for whom she had an almost impassioned admiration, which, were no other evidence of it in existence, might still be guessed by the appreciative references scattered throughout her own works. She opened correspondence with him in about 1896, and for some years sent him copies of whatever she wrote that was likely to appeal to him. He in his turn thought highly of her talents, and when she attained a genuine celebrity at last with her books for children, she had the delight of knowing that she had earned the praises which of all others she thought most worth having.

It was not only to authors of acknowledged reputation that she addressed her applause: the young and still unknown claimed, on the whole, far more of her attention. Early in 1896 Henry W. Nevinson, later to win international fame as a war correspondent but at that time quite obscure, brought out his second book, a volume of short stories about the nailers and miners of South Staffordshire. A few days after its publication he was surprised and gratified to receive this letter:

Dear Sir,

Your book "In the Valley of Tophet" has come here for review. I have read it, and after some hesitation, I yield to the temptation to write to you about it. The desire to write to a stranger about his work has only twice before come to me.[5] To write of your stories in detail would be to bore you—let me then briefly say that their strength and pathos seem to me equally notable. Both in

[5] This statement is doubtless more accurate than at first it seems, for it was rather about *her* work than their own that she had written to "strangers" while her career was still uncertain and her talents in need of encouragement. From this time forward she seldom if ever approached any author without some notion of being of service to him.

sentiment and in treatment your stories seem far above anything else of the kind that I have read. They appeal so strongly both to heart and judgement that I find it hard to write about them without seeming fulsome—and no doubt in my desire to avoid that pitfall I am falling into one on the opposite side. I have tried to write of the poor—and I have not succeeded well. Had I been able to do what I long to do, I should have written such stories as yours.

Are you in the mood for making new acquaintances? If you are, will you come and see us? I fancy we should have many tastes and feelings in common. If we found that this was not so —I mean if you did not like us—you need not come twice.

The main points are, I hope clear: that we admire your book extremely—and that we should like you to come and see us. Will you?

Yours faithfully,
Edith Bland
(E. Nesbit).

Mr. Nevinson sent back an answer that must have made her vividly aware of her power to give pleasure:

May 27 1896

Dear Madam,

. . . I cannot say how pleased and encouraged I am by what you write of my little book. Such praise from an authoress and poetess of your reputation and position in literature is as welcome as unexpected; all the more because it comes from a leader in a movement with which I have unfortunately had no personal connection, though I have long admired it from a distance.

As to my bits of writing, I seriously think very little of them. For nearly twenty years I have been trying to learn how to write, but I perceive that I shall never succeed in learning that art in this life. For what others do so easily day by day, still costs me endless distress, and gives me no satisfaction when it is done. So I have to follow my business, which takes me most of my time, and I can only practise at learning how to write in my odd moments. You may imagine then with what a sense of reward such praise as yours comes to me.

It is very kind of you to ask me to Grove Park. I will come as soon as I possibly can.

. . . I must thank you once more very heartily for the great kindness and generosity of your letter.

Yours faithfully,
Henry W. Nevinson.[6]

Some further correspondence ensued, and after a little delay it was arranged that they should meet—at breakfast for some reason—at the house of friends. This was one of the few occasions on which Edith failed to achieve an almost immediate friendship with someone whose friendship she had sought. Henry Nevinson, though intrepid in scenes of danger, was at this time painfully shy and reserved in private life, and he was a little overwhelmed, perhaps, by a personality then the very antithesis of his own. "Breakfast," as he has written, "is a bad time for me as for most other people, and the object of showing myself to a famous writer was still worse. So I had nothing to say to E. Nesbit or anyone else." A little later he joined the staff of the paper for which her husband also worked, and she must have been surprised when she heard, year after year, of the nervous young man's knack of turning up in the thick of wars and revolutions all over the earth.

Few writers have had a wider range of literary tastes than E. Nesbit or cultivated friendships with other writers so different in outlook and in accomplishments. A fervent Ibsen enthusiast (she had attended the first performance of *Ghosts* in 1893 and talked Ibsen for weeks afterwards), she could shed tears over *Jessica's First Prayer;* a disciple of Kipling, she still perceived all the charm and delicacy of Henry James; she read the most advanced and challenging literature of the nineties and managed to appreciate it without any infidelity to her earlier loves —Dickens, Thackeray, George Eliot, and Charles Reade; fairy stories, adventure stories, contemplative poetry, political and religious works, anything that was good of its kind was capable of providing entertainment for her. And when there was noth-

[6] I was enabled to print this letter through the courtesy of the writer. He died in 1941, aged 85.

ing better to be had, she was glad enough even of what was not good of its kind. As she once told a friend, she would sooner at any time in her life have read a railway timetable than nothing. As for her friendships, she seemed as she grew older to become rather more than less sensitive to the attractions of new intimacies, and the interesting possibilities of strangers.

Among those diverse, almost incongruous, groups of novelists, poets, journalists, and propagandists, which were to be found on Saturdays and Sundays at Three Gables, was Edgar Jepson, a favourite visitor at the Blands' home for several years, both in London and at Dymchurch, and of whom it is recorded that no one else had a better gift for cajoling Edith into good humour after a day of small adversities.

He had written and published two or three novels when they met, and so cannot be counted as one of "that brood of authors which she hatched," as H. G. Wells has put it, "in much the same way as a hen hatches chickens"; but her interest in his work encouraged him, and there was something generally inspiriting in mixing, under such kindly auspices, with a large circle of young writers all at different stages of promise or achievement.

It was not only towards her friends and protégés that her heart overflowed with a desire to be helpful. With quixotic eagerness to rescue even the least attractive distressed, she took up all kinds of hopeless causes, and there was always some temporary "pensioner" whom she was trying to settle in life. She was too zealous to be quite discriminating in her benevolent schemes, and occasionally her friends as well as herself suffered the consequences. Among these victims were Mr. Jepson and two bachelor companions who were persuaded to take on a housekeeper for whom she had been seeking a place.

Mrs. Tanner, duly installed in Mr. Jepson's home in Grove Park near the Blands, soon turned out to bear a close resemblance to Copperfield's Mrs. Crupp. She was tolerated, however, for the sake of her patroness, and the discomfort of her presence might have been borne indefinitely had it not been for a lucky accident. Edith had called on the bachelor household accompanied by a woman friend, and they were all pleasantly conversing in the drawing-room when Mrs. Tanner suddenly entered and, in a state of intoxication which made it necessary for her to lean against the doorpost for support, addressed to the company in general a long and vehement speech, from which it appeared that she was unwilling or unable to cook the dinner. Everyone tried politely not to notice that she was drunk, but when she was persuaded to leave them at last, Edith was obliged to admit between laughter and distress that her "deserving case" had been an error of judgment, and the establishment was relieved of its burden.

In August, 1898, she turned forty. Writing to her mother a few days later she said: "I had a very nice birthday. Fabian made a bonfire in the evening and decorated the garden with Chinese lanterns. I had some pretty presents. A moss agate brooch—a gold ring (fifteenth century), gloves, table centres, a silver watch chain, a book, a pair of little old flint-lock pistols, and some beautiful flowers. I *am* forty, as you say: but I don't feel forty. When I am ill I feel 90 and when I am happy I feel 19."

In spirit she was as near nineteen as any woman with a substantial family and numerous responsibilities can be. In some aspects of her character she was still the "loving child, Daisy," whose name she signed to this letter—still irrepressible, adventurous, humoursome, and incautious, as when she had puzzled the nuns of the Dinan convent. But while she had retained in miraculous integrity, not only her memories of childhood, but also many of the faults and virtues of a child, her capacities had matured almost out of recognition.

The true flower of her genius suddenly broke into blossom, and that habit of seeing things rather as an intelligent and emotional adolescent than as a ripe-thinking adult, which until now had made some of her work crude and some vapid, became the most precious of her assets. From this time forward she wrote—or, more accurately, she was able when she pleased to write—with the graceful ease of one who is sure of her ground and knows what lies within her power.

11   *The Nineties—Work*

E. Nesbit being by now a prolific writer, it will be well to deal separately with her work, and the matters directly connected with it, and to do so I must turn back a few years.

In 1890, besides bringing out one or two of the little foreign-printed booklets I have described, she formed an association both pleasant and productive with the house of Raphael Tuck. This firm had already purchased a number of her designs and verses for Christmas cards (it was not, however, that for which she had done so many "hand-painted greetings" at the beginning of her married life), and now it brought out, in a guinea edition, her first book for children. It was *The Voyage of Columbus,* a narrative in verse, profusely illustrated.

She was making occasional contributions to such an enormous number of newspapers and magazines, many of which are now extinct, that it is beyond the powers of the most meticulous biographer to discover precisely when and where her earliest tales for children appeared. But Raphael Tuck was the first publisher to print them between covers, he encouraged her to write them, and found a place for almost everything of the kind that she offered him. The children's miscellanies issued by him during the nineties were liberally supplied with verses and very simple little stories from her pen.

Her personal relations with the members of the firm were of the happiest: Mr. Gustave Tuck, the founder's son, and several of his assistants retained a lively recollection of the handsome young woman, high-spirited, charming, whimsical, who would sweep into the office and compose verses impromptu on any subject that appealed to her—a photograph of Mr. Tuck's little daughter, a private jest with one of the staff; or tell their fortunes by palmistry, gleefully promising three husbands to an unmarried secretary and apportioning long journeys and unexpected legacies as generously as a professional clairvoyante.

In 1895 she was one of the judges of a literary competition organized by the firm. Clifton Bingham,[1] with whom she later brought out a little book of verses, was also on the committee, and Sir Walter Besant was the chairman of it. Always genuinely anxious to be helpful to beginners, E. Nesbit gave herself wholeheartedly to the task of reading some hundreds of manuscripts, and her visits to the publishing house became yet more frequent and informal than before.

Her relations with other publishers were not always so friendly. To anticipate, she was associated with something near thirty in all, and although repeated changes must have been due very largely to the diversity of her work—for she attempted almost every possible species of fiction and poetry—it is not to be denied that in business dealings she tended to be irritable. This is not very astonishing when we consider how many evils used to be rampant in the publishing trade. And she had the misfortune to make more than one bad bargain.

Her versatility was in many respects a great drawback to her. She took the better part of twenty years to find her level, and even then did not realize that she had found it. Her letters and the conversations remembered by her friends, even to the end of her life, abound with regrets that she had been obliged to write prose for money instead of writing poetry for love. She knew that her books for children were good books; she was thor-

[1] Clifton Bingham (1859?–1913): a popular and prolific writer of songs, children's poems, etc.

oughly conscientious and thoroughly conscious in her artistry while she worked at them; but she never imagined that they were the highest manifestation of her literary capacities. It was because those capacities were numerous and unequal that her efforts to win fame—for she did want fame—were long protracted, and not at best as successful as the efforts of several greatly inferior writers in the same field.

The perpetual changing of one style of work for another is not only an obstacle to steady improvement in the style for which one is best fitted; it is also a hindrance to the building up of a reputation. Except when the author is already renowned, each change of work involves a change of public; and in the meantime one may lose the following acquired before. Most writers have two or three styles, but E. Nesbit experimented in about a dozen. She wrote horror stories, sentimental love stories, and stories in dialect; she wrote poetry for public recitation, poetry for the nursery, Socialist propaganda poetry, and what, for want of a better term, I can describe only as serious personal poetry. Then there was the work for children, and even here we find immense diversity—tales for the child upwards of nine or ten, and tales almost in words of one syllable for infants; episodes from history and from Shakespeare's plays retold in simple language, long romances brimming over with pure invention. And besides all this there were productions almost impossible to classify—birthday books, an instructive volume on dogs, little plays, stories written in collaboration, book reviews.

We must assume that a simple willingness to undertake any task that would be speedily paid for was the cause of all this varied activity, and not sheer restiveness and instability. E. Nesbit looked upon herself first and foremost as a poet. No one can say that it was necessity alone which compelled her to write prose—indeed, it is hardly likely that she would have been able to suppress a talent so lively and abundant; but it is very improbable that she would have written prose as often and as diversely without the ever-present need of money to spur her on. It is very improbable, in short, that she would have attempted those simple, rudimentary forms of juvenile fiction from which, after some ten years of practice, she rose to the creation of a magic world.

In 1891, to continue in detail the history of her career as author, she brought out nothing on her own account, but attained the distinction of seeing her work in an anthology of *The Poets and Poetry of the Century*. In 1892 the "Second Series" of *Lays and Legends*[2] was published at Mr. Darcy Reeve's expense, but failed to excite the attention that might have been expected from the reception given to the earlier volume. Discouraged, perhaps, by its unsuccess, she turned with redoubled energy to lighter tasks more certain of reward, and in 1893, contributed to half a dozen of Raphael Tuck's books, and began writing *In Homespun,* a special group of short stories—all set in Kentish scenes and done in a sort of mild dialect. They are what they were intended to be, pleasant light reading from a pen that now moved with great facility. And the plots, somewhat to their detriment, are as facile as the writing; she used the same ingredients several times—the favourite theme being the rivalry of two girl cousins in love with the same man. There is no serious attempt to achieve probability in the action or conviction in the delineation of character, though in every story there are excellent, shrewd touches, and the economy of the style is very striking. The collection proved attractive enough to justify the publishers, Messrs. John Lane, in printing it in their famous Keynote Series three years later.

With the firm of John Lane, as with that of Raphael Tuck, her relations were pleasant. It was at a dinner party given by Mr. Lane in 1892 that she first met John Davidson, and she was among the company of "distinguished and beautiful women,

[2] This book contained a complimentary rondeau to Austin Dobson (1840–1921), then the favourite exponent of what he himself called *vers de société*. She evidently sent a copy of it to him, and asked his advice on this and on certain questions of versification in general. He replied with a polite letter in which he pointed out "a minor blemish in her otherwise charming verses," and answered the points she had raised; but he addressed her as a stranger and her admiration did not lead, as so frequently happened, to friendship.

dowagers, socialists, poets, and artists" which Mr. Richard le Gallienne has described as frequenting his (Lane's) tea parties.[3]

In 1893 E. Nesbit produced two more volumes of short stories, with yet another publisher. *Something Wrong* and *Grim Tales,* which appeared under the imprint of A. D. Innes, were collections of tales from the several periodicals for which she was then working—*Longman's Magazine, Temple Bar,* the *Sketch,* the *Victorian,* the *Sunday Chronicle,* and others.

In the following year she collaborated with Oswald Barron, an intimate friend, in further short stories, which, after duly appearing in magazines, came out in book form under the title of *The Butler in Bohemia.* Another half-dozen of Raphael Tuck's books contained tales and verses from her pen, which, far from wearying, became constantly more ingenious with practice; while a "birthday book" of quotations from her own work, compiled for another publisher, may be counted as evidence of growing popularity. (*Poet's Whispers,* a second birthday book arranged by her a year later, is made up of quotations from the works of other poets, and shows that she was familiar with a very large number.)

The year 1895 marked a notable advance in her career both as poet and prose-writer. In this year she published *A Pomander of Verse* with The Bodley Head; two collections of children's stories with Marcus Ward, whose delightful Walter Crane books are eagerly sought by collectors at the present time; and *Holly and Mistletoe,* a book of Christmas poems, some of which were the work of Norman Gale and Richard le Gallienne. Her contributions to this volume were merely a selection from verses she had written for Christmas cards some time before, and therefore call for no special comment.

The poems in *A Pomander of Verse* betray all those influences of the nineties which Holbrook Jackson analysed in his

---

[3] "I particularly recall," he says in *The Romantic '90's,* "the Rossetti-like head of Mrs. Graham R. Tomson, the boyish, bird-like charm of 'E. Nesbit,' the flower-like loveliness of Olive Custance—since Lady Alfred Douglas—and the noble silent beauty of Ethel Reed, whose early death robbed the world of a great decorative artist."

well-known survey.[4] E. Nesbit was not one of the Decadents, but she admired some of them and was too interested in the movement to be entirely out of it. In 1895 she was deeply under the spell of the *Yellow Book,* in which some of her own work appeared, and her poetry at this time reflects—though perhaps only half-consciously—the pallid glitter, the luxuriously artificial sensuousness, the emotions symbolized and conventionalized, which were summed up in the term *fin de siècle*. She laughed gently at the Decadents in one of the poems in this very book, but she was influenced in spite of herself.

And so she writes of "death-white nights," of "death-strong" nets, of "flame-flowers" and "white roses paled with love"; and divides the poems into sections headed *Ambergris, Myrrh, Bergamot,* and other flavours of the period. A certain fragrance of her own pervades them, but the scent of the exotic spices is obviously novel and pleasurable to her. The battle-cry of the anti-sentimentalists, "Art for Art's sake," seems to have had its effect upon her; she has conquered the tendency to be maudlin, while the long dramatic lyrics which she prided herself upon writing very well, but which were sometimes no more than mere recitation pieces, are not to be found in this fashionable book—and "fashionable" here has no deprecatory significance.

The Marcus Ward productions present so different an aspect of their author's personality, that it is hard to see how she could have turned so lightly and gracefully from one species of work to the other. In the *Pussy Tales* and *Doggy Tales,* admirably illustrated by Lucy Kemp-Welch, we have a clearer presage of the E. Nesbit whom we know and love to this day. These short stories, though much slighter than her subsequent achievements in the same field, abound with touches of humour and delicate pathos peculiarly her own. It is the real, the best E. Nesbit, who

---

[4] *The Eighteen Nineties,* reprinted by Messrs. Jonathan Cape in their *Life and Letters* series. Jackson mentions E. Nesbit as one of those poets, who, "though lacking nothing in individuality, sing with an accent so much in tune with the 'divine average' of culture and experience that some sort of permanence is assured to their work in special fanes of poesy, if not in the broader avenues of popular acceptance."

E. Nesbit in 1905, aged forty-seven,
photographed for the *Strand Magazine*.

John Collis Nesbit,
Edith's father.

Sarah Nesbit,
her mother.

Edith, aged eighteen.

Mary Nesbit, her sister.

E. Nesbit, aged three, when she was known as "Daisy."

"Daisy" at six years of age.

E. Nesbit at the age of
twenty-nine.

Well Hall, Eltham
E. Nesbit's home for
twenty-three years.

E. Nesbit, aged forty-five, at the prime of her career.

Hubert Bland at the age of forty-five.

The "Magic City" made by E. Nesbit and exhibited at the Children's Welfare Exhibition, 1912. (Above) Panorama of the whole city. (Right) The Temple of Flora.

T. T. Tucker, "The Skipper,"
E. Nesbit's second husband.

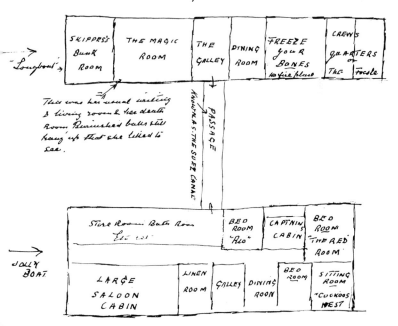

Romney Marsh

| SKIPPER'S BUNK ROOM | THE MAGIC ROOM | THE GALLEY | DINING ROOM | FREEZE YOUR BONES No fire place | CREW'S QUARTERS THE Focsle |

"Longboat" →

This was her usual writing & living room & her death Room. Reviewshed balls still hang up that she liked to see.

KNOWN AS THE SUEZ CANAL PASSAGE

| Store Room Bath Room Etc etc | BED ROOM "Rio" | CAPTAIN'S CABIN | BED ROOM THE RED ROOM |

JOLLY BOAT →

| LARGE SALOON CABIN | LINEN ROOM | GALLEY | DINING ROOM | BED ROOM | SITTING ROOM "CUCKOOS NEST" |

Floor plan drawn by T. T. Tucker for the author, showing the arrangement
of the bungalows at Romney Marsh, where E. Nesbit spent her last years.

E. Nesbit's grave, with "The Skipper's" simple memorial.

speaks in such a passage as this, where the kitten which tells the story is being taught by his mother "such little accomplishments as she thought necessary for my station in life":

". . . If you practise the little tricks I show you now with the ball of worsted and the tips of our tails, then, when the great hour comes, and a career is open to you, and you see before you the glorious prize—the MOUSE—you will be quick enough and clever enough to satisfy the highest needs of your nature."

"And supposing we don't play with our tails and the balls of worsted?" I said.

"Then," said my mother bitterly, "you may as well lie down for the mice to run over you."

The deftness with which in the fewest possible words she gives to the most fantastic animal conversations an air of perfect reality, must be hardly less wonderful to the adult reader than it is entrancing to the child. There is a goodness that defies analysis in this effortless description of a fond mother-cat's attempt to glorify her kittens by washing them, like human children, in a bath of water:

Mrs. Tabby White waited till she heard the last of Nurse's steps on the stairs below, and then she put both her cat-children into the tub, and washed them with rose-scented soap and a Turkey sponge. At first they thought it very good fun, but presently the soap got in their eyes and they were frightened of the sponge, and they cried, mewing piteously, to be taken out. . . . When she took them out, Mrs. Tabby tried to dry them with the soft towel, but somehow catskin is not so easy to dry as child-skin, and the little cats began to shiver and moan: "Oh mother, we were so nice and warm, and now we are so cold! Why is it? What have we done? Were we naughty?"

One forgets that cats never do try to wash their kittens with soap and Turkey sponge. The absurdity of the situation is overlooked in the verisimilitude of the picture, and when, after one of the kittens has caught a chill and narrowly escaped from death, Mrs. Tabby White says to them: "My darlings, I was

wrong, I was a silly old cat," and they reply, "No, . . . darling
mother, you were always the best of cats," one feels a little glow
of kindliness towards the whole feline race, as if one's knowledge of its nature had really been enlarged.

In 1896 the only work of hers to appear in book form was *As
Happy as a King,* a children's story in verse. She had plenty of
other work on hand, however, for besides her miscellaneous
writing and the first three chapters of *My Schooldays* in *The
Girl's Own,* she had become one of the poetry critics for the
Athenæum, and continued in this position for some years. It
would be interesting to learn her ideas about the contemporaries
whose work she reviewed, but unfortunately the notices were
unsigned and cannot be identified. Mr. Vernon Rendall, who
was sub-editor at the time, remembered her as a competent
critic with a bright and pointed style and a gift for compres-
sion.

With several years of experience as a writer for children and a
steadily increasing demand for her juvenile work to encourage
her, she now conceived the idea of producing a magazine entirely for children, there being little or nothing of the kind in
existence at that time; and she wrote to various eminent authors
for the promise of material. Among them was Rudyard Kipling, who replied expressing his willingness to help, but warning her that a list of "star" names would be of no avail unless
she could get enough good matter to keep the paper going for
fully twelve months. Whether she attempted to follow this advice I cannot say, for the scheme came to nothing in the end.
The publishers whom she had in mind rejected it, and when a
children's magazine was successfully launched a little while
later by Arthur Mee, E. Nesbit, somewhat resentful, was not
one of its contributors.

Notwithstanding the various activities of 1896 that I have
mentioned, she managed to devote several months of that year
to the making of her first novel—the first, at any rate, since *The
Prophet's Mantle* written with her husband as collaborator
eleven years before. Early in 1897 she sent the MS to Adeline
Sergeant, then at the height of her popularity, for an opinion.

The older novelist (born in 1851) wrote back in terms of unalloyed eulogy. She thought that the book was "certain to achieve success," that it possessed every possible requisite for a serial story, and that it was strong in characterization, thrilling in incident, and clever in conception. "Your name," she said, "is so well known as a writer of lovely verse and striking short stories, that you will indeed be made welcome in the ranks of novelists!"

Miss Sergeant, who had already published over seventy books of her own, should have been a good judge, at least of commercial prospects; but her generous optimism was misplaced. *The Secret of Kyriels,* a commonplace and unconvincing mystery story, was a good while finding a publisher, and it added little to its author's reputation and probably not much to her exchequer. By the time it appeared, however, nearly two years later, *The Treasure Seekers* was in the press, and she could afford to smile at a failure.

The year 1897 was spent in covering one or two more stages of her strangely vacillating approach towards that high level of excellence which began with *The Treasure Seekers* and was maintained with scarcely a lapse—so far as children's books were concerned—for fifteen years. She continued her series *My Schooldays,* and did three books for Raphael Tuck: *Tales Told in the Twilight, Royal Children of English History,* and *The Children's Shakespeare;* the first a collection of very short stories, the two others, as their titles suggest, a simplified relation of historical incidents and the plots of some of Shakespeare's plays, all very efficiently done. One cannot but suspect that she was startled when she saw the last-named work in its printed form,[5] for the highly-coloured illustrations represented all the characters from Romeo and Juliet to Petruchio and even Pericles, as tiny children, and King Lear himself seems merely to be a little boy with an immense cotton-wool beard.

At the beginning of the following year she was engaged with the first set of Bastable stories, most of which appeared at irreg-

[5] It was later re-issued in a completely different guise.

ular intervals throughout 1898 in the *Pall Mall* and *Windsor* magazines. Superior though it was to anything she had ever done before, she seems to have taken this work entirely in her usual stride. The only mention of it that I have found in her correspondence is one bald statement, casually slipped in among references to her incessant toil at stories, articles, verses, and reviews. "I am writing a children's book," she says to her mother, "called 'The Treasure Seekers.'"

If she suddenly attained any new consciousness of brilliant powers as a humorist, of unflagging ingenuity, and a limpid fluency in providing those "constant slight surprises" which are said to be the secret of good style, she kept the joy of the discovery to herself. At any rate, there are no records of her elation in the memory of her friends: she continued to regret that her financial position did not allow her to devote herself solely to poetry.

It was occasionally said by those critics whose pleasure lies in tracing every literary work to its supposed sources, that E. Nesbit had drawn her inspiration from Kenneth Grahame's *Golden Age,* which made its first appearance two or three years before. No blame could attach to her if this assumption were true, yet it is just to state that it was false—so false, indeed, that E. Nesbit herself, who detested plagiarism and thought it a stigma to be accused of it, never felt it worth while to defend herself on a charge so groundless.

It will be apparent to any reader familiar with both authors that *The Treasure Seekers* resembles the *Golden Age* only inasmuch as both books are concerned with a family of imaginative children, and both are written with exceptional insight and conviction. That the two families play the same sorts of games and enjoy the same sorts of pretences is no evidence that the later creation is an imitation of the earlier, for these games and pretences are the common property of all imaginative children. Edith drew them from memories of her own young days strengthened by discussion and comparison. Oswald Barron, to whom she dedicated the book, had conversed with her often and at length on their respective childhoods, "identical," she said, "but for the accidents of time and space." She had been working towards the achievement of the Bastables for years. She had studied children's literature extensively—George Mac-Donald, Mrs. Ewing, and Mrs. Molesworth, for instance, were writers whom she admired fervently; but she owed few direct debts to any precursor.

One of these few was the ingenious device of half-concealing the identity of the supposed narrator, Oswald—of letting it be guessed only when in boyish egotism he gives himself away. It is one of the happiest things in children's fiction, and she had found it in Dickens, whose works she knew extensively and revered. He had used it in *A Holiday Romance,* but there is not a page of *The Treasure Seekers* that lacks the magic vividness only to be imparted by an original mind. The plausibility of the manner is remarkable. Take, for example, Oswald's explanation of the reason why the book is more exciting than real life:

> The best part of books is when things are happening. . . . This is why I shall not tell you in this story about all the days when nothing happened. You will not catch me saying, "thus the sad days passed slowly by"—or "the years rolled on their weary course," or "time went on"—because it is silly; of course time goes on—whether you say so or not. So I shall just tell you the nice, interesting parts—and in between you will understand that we had our meals and got up and went to bed, and dull things like that. It would be sickening to write all that down, though of course it happens. I said so to Albert-next-door's uncle, who writes books, and he said "Quite right, that's what we call selection, a necessity of true art." And he is very clever indeed.

Virtue after virtue unfolds itself as the book proceeds. There is not a dull paragraph. No woman writer, surely, has ever been able to induce laughter so often and so wholesomely!

I have touched before on the wonderful verisimilitude of these stories: over and over again some slight but deft touch recalls to us exactly what it felt like to be children, the way we talked amongst ourselves, the things we noticed. The Bastables are perhaps nicer than most real children are—purer, more honourable, less greedy; ruinously destructive, terrifyingly adventurous though they are, they yet provide for the child-reader a "good example," for they despise all forms of meanness and are never consciously cruel. Yet the moral is implied, not preached. Occasionally a pretty plain hint as to right conduct is dropped in, but only where it is apt or even entertaining.

What sound admonition could be couched less priggishly than Noel's passage on quarrelling and Oswald's comment on it?

> "Quarrelling is an evil thing,
>   It fills with gall life's cup;
> For when once you begin
>   It takes such a long time to make it up."

. . . Noel is very funny with his poetry. But that piece happened to come out quite true. You begin to quarrel, and then you can't stop; often, long before the others are ready to cry and make it up, I see how silly it is, and I want to laugh; but it doesn't do to say so—for it only makes the others crosser than they were before.

Or this passing reference to the desirability of apologizing?

I do like a person to say they're sorry when they ought to be—especially a grown-up. They do it so seldom.

It cannot really be said, however, that E. Nesbit's own grown-ups are slow to apologize. A more tolerant, obliging, sympathetic set of people it would be difficult to imagine. If there is any lack of fidelity to nature in the Bastable books, it is, alas! in the galaxy of charming adult characters. Even when they begin by being gruff and cantankerous, they generally end by melting into kindness. They are not like the people we met in our childhood, yet somehow they convince us even as we protest. And some of them convince us unprotesting. There is Z. Rosenbaum, for instance, the money-lender whom the children visit under the impression that he is a Generous Benefactor of the poor and needy. He, like the others, melts, and decides to give them a pound, but when it comes to parting with the money, his business instincts become too strong for him:

> And all the time he was stroking the sovereign and looking at it as if he thought it very beautiful. And so it was, for it was a new one. Then at last he held it out to Dicky, and when Dicky put out his hand for it the G. B. suddenly put the sovereign back into his pocket.
>
> "No," he said, "I won't give you the sovereign. I'll give you fifteen shillings, and this nice bottle of scent. It's worth far more than the five shillings I'm charging you for it. And, when you can, you shall pay me back the pound, and sixty per cent interest—sixty per cent, sixty per cent——"
>
> "What's that?" said H. O.
>
> The G. B. said he'd tell us that when we paid back the sovereign, but sixty per cent was nothing to be afraid of.

Such a touch as this can, of course, only be appreciated by the adult reader. Yet although all these books abound with ironical humour and wisdom too subtle for a child's comprehension, they mysteriously succeed in remaining children's books *par excellence*. She never patronizes, never appears to be insinuating as—say—Charles Kingsley does: "Now I know this is just a trifle above your head." And neither does she go to the other and still more objectionable extreme. Describing her method to her friend, Berta Ruck, years later, she said: "I make it a point of honour never to *write down* to a child. Sometimes I deliberately introduce a word that it won't know, so that it will ask a grown-up the meaning and learn something by it." When she conveyed instruction overtly, it was always in some new and interesting way.

Altogether *The Treasure Seekers* and its sequels are as free from flaws as anything of their kind that has ever been done.

In the year when the first set of stories was appearing serially, she brought out *Songs of Love and Empire,* a volume of poetry published by Constable, and *A Book of Dogs,* containing a large amount of anecdotal material and illustrated with excellent pencil drawings by Winifred Austin. This brief but probably laborious work was done for J. M. Dent—her eleventh or twelfth publisher, counting those who produced the illustrated booklets.

The *Songs of Love and Empire* were Edith's expression of the imperial patriotism which had found voice at the time of Queen Victoria's jubilee in 1897, with Rudyard Kipling as the very articulate leader of the chorus. The book was dedicated to her husband in a manner that showed how little eighteen years of married life had served to diminish the admiration in which she held him:

> To you the harvest of my toil has come
> Because of all that lies its sheaves between;
> You taught me first what Love and Empire mean,
> And to your hands I bring my harvest home.

At the time when this book was being prepared for the press, she sent some of her poetry to W. E. Henley, with whom, judging by their correspondence, she was on terms of moderately intimate friendship. His letter of reply [6] is unfortunately more mysterious than I could wish, since I neither know which were the verses he praised, nor what was the trouble which he thought "the true motive" of her poetry. Her conjugal problems were always fairly urgent, and there is reason to believe that they were more so at this time than at most others; this is the only solution I can offer.

> Stanley Lodge
> Muswell Hill, N.
> 13.3.98.

Dear Mrs. Bland,

These are quite the best verses of yours which I have ever read. Had I a journal I should be pleased indeed to print them. I do not

---

[6] W. E. Henley (1849–1903), poet and man of letters. Collaborated in writing plays with R. L. Stevenson. His most famous poem is *Invictus*. Many of his phrases have passed into the language. Mrs. Maude Henley enabled me to reproduce the quoted letters.

think them faultless—far from it. But they are *vécus*—they have heart and passion; and I congratulate you. What you told me about your latest trouble makes me rather wonder if it be not their true motive, and (if I be right) why you do it wrong by turning it to other issues. But of this I have scarce the right to speak. And I hope you will believe me when I say that my first thought is always for the verses.

My scheme of coming to London has fallen through. So that we shall be glad to know that you can and will come to us.

Yours very sincerely,
W. E. H.

Henley always took a great interest in her poetry, and often spoke highly in its praise,[7] but he was not unconscious of her weaknesses, and in another letter written a year later he laid a shrewd finger on the worst of them—her dangerous facility:

> I liked the verses. If you can keep up to the level of them, by all means go in for a sequence. I believe that, if you write them with all your heart—above all, if you do not run the risk of breathlessly making too many—you will do a piece of notable work. Think, if ever you feel disposed to settle down into the market-woman's canter—think to yourself this stage-direction: —"*Enter the ghost of The National Observer.*" [8] And then say to yourself: "No, I *won't*. I'll make these verses for myself and two or three friends," as Mozart made *Don Juan*. The idea is so good, and you are so full of sympathy and insight and knowledge, that—*if* you look out for the ghost—I am sure you will do an excellent piece of work. And if you do, you may look for as excellent a hand from me.

One further letter from W. E. Henley, though it only touches lightly on E. Nesbit's work, will be of interest to his admirers. He writes to thank her for a copy of *The Shropshire Lad* and some short stories of her own, which I cannot identify with certainty.

[7] She was proud of the gift of a book from him inscribed to her as "Frater in Arte."
[8] *The National Observer* was a paper edited by Henley.

9, Park Crescent,
Worthing.
23.2.99.

Dear Mrs. Bland,

Very many thanks indeed. I didn't think you meant to give me
the Shropshire Lad: which I bought with my own money last
year. But, being away from books, I thought I'd like to see him
again, so I didn't protest against his dispatch. Now I find my
name and yours in a second copy of his works, and very glad I am
to find them. And my own copy will serve to bestow elsewhere.

I like him well enough, here and there, to wish I'd written him.
But I find him very monotonous. I think if I had written him, I
should have burned at least two thirds of my work, and stood to
win in what was left. But that doesn't prevent him from being a
man with something to say and a very distinguished way of saying it.

Some of your own stories I like. Some—as the wraith one—I
like less. But I am glad to know that they and their like are getting written. For I think our own back gardens are as interesting
and as beautiful (at least) as any kailyard that ever was run.

We have taken a house here for two years, and we shall hope to
see you there soon. 'Tis a quiet, pleasant, sea-scented old place,
with any amount of sunshine: and I shouldn't wonder if it presently put me even more on my legs.

My wife (in the agonies of moving) sends her love.

Yours always sincerely,
W. E. Henley.

In 1899 *The Story of the Treasure Seekers* came out in book
form, and from that time forward for many years was reissued
almost annually. She had been in the habit of selling the full
copyright of her tales for children before publication, but with
The Treasure Seekers a new era began both in her private and
her public life. She had now a really handsome source of income which it was in her power to increase almost at will. The
Strand Magazine commissioned a series of tales, for each one of
which she received £30, a fee equivalent to fully six times as
much in these days. Every set of stories was afterwards collected
and turned into a book, and considerable sums were paid to her

in royalties. Hubert Bland was also doing very well, and they were able, on the strength of an excellent income which showed no sign of being likely to diminish, to move from Three Gables to the large, rambling house at Well Hall which was to be her home for the next twenty-three years.

12   *The First Years at Well Hall*

The house known as Well Hall at Eltham, Kent, is familiar to many of E. Nesbit's readers as the Red House, which figures in her novel of that name—the only novel of hers which might be called a popular success—and as the Moat House in many of the Bastable stories. In fact, it crept into her work, if I may use the expression, at intervals throughout the rest of her writing life. She loved it; it might be said to have become part of her personality. It had all the faults she could forgive, and all the virtues that most delighted her.

It stood on an historical site which has often been the subject of research by antiquaries. The house itself was a red-brick eighteenth century structure, but, besides an ancient moat still filled with water, there was also a little range of Tudor buildings. These had suffered many alterations in the seventeenth century and later, and were in use as cottages, but a long out-building dated 1568, though in a poor state of repair, could still boast brick arcading, mullioned windows and panelling, and moulded chimneys and gable ends of authentic Tudor origin.

Before the house lay a spacious lawn, supposed to be the site of an earlier mansion which is known to have been the property of the Ropers, Sheriffs of Kent, a family rendered illustrious by alliance with that of Sir Thomas More, Henry VIII's ill-destined

Lord Chancellor. Margaret Roper, his devoted daughter, lived at Well Hall for many years, and it is said that she brought his severed head to her home so as to ensure it decent burial. Whether this story be apocryphal or not, it goes without saying that Well Hall was supposed to be haunted.

Edith was charmed with everything she saw of the house, the outbuildings, and the adjoining grounds, which were fragrant with sweet briars, gilliflowers, and many old-fashioned herbs seldom found in gardens more recently planted. There was an orchard, too, with ancient, gnarled apple-trees, and a promising half-acre or so laid out for vegetables. The condition of the whole domain was somewhat discouraging, and would have caused any woman of prosaic mind to think twice before taking on the responsibility of its upkeep, but she was blind to everything but its beauties, and her husband was not less favourably impressed. Early in 1899 they embarked upon the toils and excitements of removing a fairly numerous household.

The Red House, though the dramatis personae and the circumstances of the case are changed for the purposes of fiction, contains a recognizable if somewhat idealized account of the manner in which they first installed themselves. There were actually more discomforts and unlooked for expenses to be faced than she thought fit to describe. A staircase collapsed almost at the beginning of their tenancy, and it was a long time before they were able to cope successfully with all the dilapidations. She compared notes on her many woes with W. E. Henley, and his letter of reply suggests that she was undergoing the reaction of depression and disappointment which would necessarily follow upon the first elation at her discovery.

St. George's Lodge,
Chesswont Road,
Worthing.
17.4.99.

Dear Mrs. Bland,
    You are indeed unfortunate! and I hope you'll like the new house better than you expect to like it. I hope, too, that it isn't

very far, and that the toils and miseries of removal will leave you as young as you were when you started in for them. My wife is broken down by them, and just now, when she should be resting on her labours, our maid has taken typhoid—God knows how or where or why—and she's once more up to the neck in cares. 'Tis a hard case, so of course we've a nurse; but the Chatelaine is none the less shriven and driven. For, on my part, I find the work of getting stronger terribly slow; and also am a part of her burden, and I don't get very much lighter as the days go by . . .

Yours always, dear Mrs. Bland,
W. E. H.

At last the worst problems were disposed of; the house became presentable, and there was the delightful housewarming party without which neither of the Blands could have felt their residence to be properly inaugurated. But the augury, had they known it, was anything but propitious. Material success is said often to come attended by sorrow and disaster, and Edith was not spared a full realization of the irony with which providence will give with one hand and take with the other. The first few years of residence at Well Hall, though they brought increasing fame and prosperity, contained griefs which were among the greatest she ever endured.

At some time in 1899, probably shortly after leaving Three Gables, she gave birth to a child which died immediately or was stillborn. She had mourned over another child, or children, who had died in infancy, but this was the bitterest loss of all, for she was now forty-one years of age, and she knew intuitively that her child-bearing days were over. This blow was heavy, but there was another in store for her.

Thirteen years before, as I have told, she had adopted a child of Hubert Bland's borne by another woman, and had brought it up as her own. And now—at this of all times—she was called upon to play the same part again, and for the same seduced friend. In October, 1899, she took upon herself the care of her husband's son, to whom—as to his daughter—she kept up the pretence of motherhood until it could no longer be maintained. In what spirit she began this second adventure in magnanimous deception it is difficult to conjecture, for one cannot know how far the pleasure she derived from carrying off a dramatic situation reconciled her to its undeniable pangs. But, whatever she felt at the beginning, she was neither resentful nor regretful later. Indeed, she followed the course to which she had pledged herself more unswervingly than in the days of her tempestuous youth. She was calmer now and almost resigned. She still loved her husband, and passionately, but his ruthless self-gratifications no longer had any power to astonish her.

"It was my own fault," she was able to say afterwards, speaking to a friend of the *liaison* with Alice, to whom she remained attached. "I might have prevented the opportunity. I didn't, and I deserved the consequences." True or false as this statement may be, it seems to have summed up her attitude. She denied all feelings of jealousy.

In the month of John Bland's birth, her half-sister, Saretta Deakin, died. Edith was fourteen years younger than Saretta, but she had enjoyed a warm and intimate friendship with her, and had, in fact, referred to her as a second mother. For all the success of *The Treasure Seekers,* and Hubert Bland's growing fame, there must have been many gloomy days. The family was scattering and diminishing. Her brother Alfred had died five years before at the age of forty; Henry had settled long ago in Australia never to return; her mother was eighty-one years old, and her failing health was an object of anxiety to the daughter, who, writing in this very year, still called herself "Your own loving child."

For the brighter aspects of this period—from March to September charming and ingenious stories, later to be published as *The Book of Dragons* by Harpers, were appearing in the *Strand Magazine,* and Dents re-issued the *Pussy and Doggy Tales* with additions and alterations in one volume. There were holidays now that did not have to be planned with rigid economy; there was the eldest son, Paul, practically grown up and about to earn his own living, according to his father's wish, and there was Iris showing artistic capabilities very sympathetic to her mother, and able to look forward to a training at the Slade

School; Rosamund, handsome and promising, still a schoolgirl; and last Fabian, mischievous, generous, incorrigible, lovable, the male counterpart of the child who had been known as Daisy.

But Edith was in poor health, and like many people of enormous vitality and courage, she had a paradoxical tendency to "work herself up" about illnesses, and—while behaving admirably in crises—to be rather an alarmist where lesser spirits might have been less perturbed. As if she were not inclined to attribute a sufficient gravity to her rare physical disorders on her own account, she had the misfortune to consult a doctor who must have been at once the most tactless and the most incompetent member of his profession.

She had been confined to her bed for some days with a severe attack of lumbago when a new pain obliged her to send for the doctor. He examined her and informed her without mincing words that she was suffering from cancer, and must prepare for an immediate operation, adding, with a brutality happily rare in medical practitioners, that the chances of her recovery were remote. The shock, terrible as it must have been, had one happy effect upon her. The lumbago, probably a displacement, was cured in an instant: she was up and dressed in half an hour. Her daughter Iris happened to be making some dressing-gowns for her, and remarking from time to time that one of them would doubtless serve her for a shroud, she set about putting her affairs in order.

The news of her supposed disease had been broken to her on a Saturday: the following Monday she was to see a specialist with a view to the operation. On Sunday evening the usual gathering of visitors was expected at Well Hall, and she did not put them off. Laurence Housman was one of the company, and gave me an illuminating description of her behaviour:

> Some—but I think not all of us—were told that she was about to face a serious operation, and . . . that things might go very wrong indeed. Whatever her own apprehensions were in the matter, she carried us through the evening with colours flying, apparently in the happiest spirits possible. And of course we all played up to her example to the best of our ability.

One of the diversions was "thought-reading." I was sent out of the room; and in my absence problems were devised. When I was re-admitted, E. Nesbit took me in hand, and acting as medium, galloped me to success. It is the only time in my life that I have been able to "read" thoughts by this sort of process; and I ascribe my success (which was surprisingly rapid and to the point) to her jubilant will power. She was quite determined that she and I together should convince the sceptics that thought-transference was a fact. That night it certainly was.

This was pretty good for a woman who believed herself to be in imminent danger of death. The following day, the specialist fortunately discovered that there was no sign whatever of cancer or any other disease. The next time she met Mr. Housman she announced: "Well, anyway, I found out that I wasn't afraid of death!"

"The discovery," he writes, "gave her great satisfaction. But I am quite sure that what also pleased her was the way she had 'played up' while possible doom hung over her. She had a dramatic nature, and loved not only writing plays for amateurs to act; but acting the play of her life in her own person—a little theatrically. Indeed, she had so much of a 'presence' that a certain amount of 'pose' came naturally to her, and that without any insincerity."

This estimate has been widely confirmed by friends of long standing and acute perception. The love of "dramatizing" undoubtedly caused her to overstress some of her minor trials, but she had others fraught with a misery it would be hardly possible to exaggerate. The greatest of them was to follow soon upon the disasters already recorded in this chapter.

In October, 1900, Fabian, who had been suffering from a series of colds, was ordered to have his tonsils removed—an operation regarded at the time as absolutely trivial. The surgeon and the anaesthetist came to Well Hall to perform it, and so slight were the after-effects anticipated that the maid, in laying the table for the midday meal, did not think it necessary to omit Fabian's cover. But—whether through the anaesthetist's incompetence, as has generally been thought, or whether on account of some physical disability unguessed at—Fabian lost consciousness never to regain it. All efforts to restore the faintest breath of life were unavailing: he died three months before his sixteenth birthday, in the full vigour and promise of adolescence.

Although Miss Hoatson, Hubert, and Edith herself had tried for two hours after the departure of the doctors to produce some sign of recovery in him, she would not believe that he was really dead. When her husband went to take the news of the disaster to his sister, she ran frenzied about the house collecting hot-water bottles, under the impression that she might warm her son's body back to life. Miss Hoatson implored her not to stake the least hope on a measure so certainly destined to prove worse than futile, but she was desperate and would not be gainsaid. About his bed she set the sixteen candles which should have been used to celebrate his approaching birthday and left them burning around him all night in the pitiful belief that warmth and love would work some miracle. But when she went to his room in the morning she saw for the first time upon his face the painful, indisputable evidence of death.

Grief had darkened the house, and darkened for a time the mother's mind. *Her* child was dead—the wayward and affectionate boy so like herself—and under her roof were two children irrevocably bound to her, yet unrelated. Distractedly she poured out her sense of the unfairness, the bitterness of this, and her lamentation reached the very ears for whom it was least intended. Rosamund heard the words and realized their import, while yet too young to realize the agony that inspired them. She, too, suffered, and thus shock succeeded shock.

By degrees the family resumed its normal courses, the parents took up the broken threads of work and pleasure, and angry sorrow at what could appear only as a wanton waste of young and flourishing life subsided. But Fabian was remembered. The anniversary of his death brought tears and remorse for every punishment he had ever suffered, every hasty word addressed to him, and seven years later E. Nesbit's most pathetic short story, *The Criminal*, revealed how haunting a melancholy still obsessed her.

"My son; my little son," she writes to this lost child, miserably recalling how he had been locked in a room to repent of one of his mischiefs, "the house is very quiet, because all the other children grew up long ago, and went out into the world. The lamp has just been lighted, but the blinds are not drawn down now. Outside the winter dusk is deepening the shadows in the garden where, in the days when the sun shone, you used to shout and play. Do you remember, understand, forgive? I do not think that you forgive or do not forgive. I do not believe that you remember now that quiet room which was your prison. . . . But you remember, perhaps, hours when your mother was not your gaoler; when she held you not in prison, but in her arms that loved you—hours when you were not alone. These other things . . . it is your mother who has them to remember."

After 1900 Edith appeared no more at Fabian meetings, though her husband took as active a part in them as ever. Public lectures and debates, too, ceased to interest her much, unless someone as good as Bernard Shaw were to be listened to, in which case she and Hubert Bland would round up their friends and form an appreciative party. But private debates were still a favourite amusement, and on one evening a week Well Hall was devoted to polemics, the audience usually consisting of thirty-five to forty guests, seated as in a public hall. Many and brilliant were the speakers, who numbered not only most of the famous Socialists whom I have already named, but several newcomers whom I shall have occasion to mention later.

The days were largely made over to work, but not in any very systematic manner. Despite the pressing demands of the editors for whom she was engaged in serial writing, there would be long barren stretches when, utterly unable to concentrate on her task, she would potter about the house and garden, make clothes, talk with friends, or play truant to town. Then, becoming aware with horror how soon the next instalment of her story was due, and with what painful agitation the illustrator was awaiting it, she would set to work in a state of desperate concentration. The mornings and the later part of the afternoons would be spent in filling sheet after sheet of the glossy,

coloured paper on which she habitually wrote. As each sheet
was completed it was flung on the floor, until she seemed to sit
on an island in a little sea of papers. At the end of the session
she gathered them together and revised them, but she never
paused to correct in the heat of inspiration.

This was as near as she approached to routine. When under
pressure even more urgent than usual, the belated work, instead
of being accomplished in a few days after the fashion described,
would be disposed of almost in a single sitting—a sitting of
about thirty hours broken only by the briefest possible night's
rest. It was, in one sense, fortunate for her that, once her composition was launched, she could proceed with a facility such as
few writers of her merit have been able to boast. But it was a facility which, while it lent swiftness, colour, and an attractive
semblance of naïveté to her stories for children, was ruinous to
much of her other work. "She wrote too easily ever to have been
a great poet," one of the friends who saw her at work has said,
and another: "Her verses cost too little effort"—an obvious want
of which she never at any time appears to have been conscious.

Such defects as are apparent in her novels are not difficult to
account for when we learn that, having a commission to write
a serial for a magazine and not having devised any material for
it to within a few days of its being due, she said to an enquirer:
"Never mind, I'll write a non-committal chapter in an hour or
two!"

In 1901 she published three books and one of her illustrated
gift booklets, and made more money than in any other single
year of her life. Her royalties on *The Wouldbegoods,* the first
sequel to *The Treasure Seekers,* came to no less than £1,100
within twelve months, apart from what she had already received for it as a serial (at least £350). *The Treasure Seekers*
reached its third impression, which was quickly sold out, bringing her a further substantial sum. *Nine Unlikely Tales,* reprinted from the *Strand* and other magazines, was another—
though less handsome—source of income; so also *Thirteen
Ways Home,* a book of short stories for adults, brought out by
Anthony Treherne. For almost all the short stories published in

book form she first received magazine fees. There were also fees and royalties from America.

In the same year a series of delightful tales was appearing in the *Strand,* under the title of "The Psammead"—later to be changed to *Five Children and It*—illustrated, like the Dragon stories published a little earlier, by H. R. Millar, an artist so entirely congenial that even (or especially) her warmest admirers must be willing to acknowledge her indebtedness to him. E. Nesbit had many illustrators—some of them, like Lucy Kemp-Welch and Spencer Pryse, artists of very high attainments—but there will be few, I think, ready to dispute H. R. Millar's pre-eminence as the interpreter of her invention. He fulfilled to something near perfection the exacting demands she made upon him; one has only to compare the books containing his pictures with those in which the work of other draughtsmen was used to perceive at once how marvelously sensitive he was to her requirements. She herself shared this view, and was so surprised at the skill with which he had expressed the very essence of her ideas that she frequently insisted there must be some sort of telepathy between them. Mr. Millar was not of this opinion; she forgot, he said, her power to suggest in a few words as much as most writers would take a page to describe. But she, who had known how far astray an artist can go even with a full description before him, maintained that telepathy was the basis of their co-operation.

He had many obstacles to contend with, and trials in which at times only his personal regard for E. Nesbit supported him. She was nearly always behind-hand with her MSS, and would expect him to make five or six elaborate and detailed pictures in a couple of days. Reminded of the immense amount of work in these drawings and the close application to the text which they required, she would be humbly apologetic and would assure him that if, through her delays, the drawings did not fit the text, she would alter her story to fit the drawings. Sometimes she left matters so late that she could not send the text at all, and he was obliged to work only from a *précis* of the chapter in question. I have seen two or three of these *précis* in her own not very legible hand, and they have increased my astonishment that he was able to produce a series of illustrations so graphic and so accurate.

Her correspondence with him abounds with apologies: "I am sorry I am so late . . . I will try to do better next month." "I am very much behind-hand with this number, and I think it best to write and suggest subjects for two or three drawings so that you can be getting on with them. . . . I will let you have the full chapter as soon as I can. If any little details in your pictures don't agree with the story I can make that right." And so forth. Every note ends with "Yours in great haste," or some equivalent expression. Through all the delays and anxieties he worked placidly on, and it speaks much for his amiability that he never quarrelled with her, a thing not very easy to avoid with so temperamental a writer.

Besides the difficulties I have touched upon, there was another to be coped with. The utmost ingenuity had to be exercised in bringing the same three or four children into each picture without incessant repetition of design. If, for the sake of variety, he left one of them out, young readers would send in letters of complaint: a character omitted was invariably some enthusiast's favourite. There was a constant demand, too, for the originals of the drawings, and although six or seven pictures were produced every month, the generous artist seldom had one original in his own possession.

Mr. Millar had illustrated a good many of E. Nesbit's stories before he ever saw her face to face. It was in 1901 that she arranged a party at which he was to meet a contingent of juvenile admirers invited to Well Hall.

"I have a vivid remembrance of our first meeting," he wrote in reference to this occasion. "Mrs. Bland walked into the room carrying a long cardboard box under her arm. It was, in fact, a corset box: and probably in answer to my look of apprehension, she laughed and said, 'Don't be alarmed! It's not so bad as you imagine.' She opened the box and the contents proved to be tobacco, cigarette papers, and some enormously long cigarette holders, which anticipated those used by Edgar Wallace by

many years and inches, too, I imagine. She was very complimentary about my illustrations, and keenly cross-examined me
as to how I did them. She was especially intrigued by the
Psammead itself (it was at the time when the Psammead
stories were first appearing) because, as she said, it was exactly
like the creature she had in her own imagination—and 'How
did I come to imagine it, too?'" The party was a great success,
and effectually cemented a collaboration that was to last for
thirteen years.

With their successors, the tales of the Phoenix and of the
Amulet, and later on the Arden books, the Psammead stories
represented something entirely new in the realm of children's
fiction: no such curious and unheard-of fairies had ever been
portrayed before in contact with a family of hearty English
children. Each of the supernatural characters has its own vivid,
convincing personality. The traditional fairy queen, gracefully
waving her wand and uttering noble sentiments in a silvery
voice, is a pale, meaningless cipher to those who have known
the cantankerous Psammead, the lovable but outrageously con-
ceited Phoenix, and the Mouldiwarp who talks in dialect. They
are neither "good fairies" who moralize, nor fiendish ones who,
without motive, work evil spells; they belong to the rarer and
much more engaging species of fairies who, while lacking nothing of magical power, are yet made credible and familiar by
human weaknesses and vanities. In ordinary fairy-tales, it is the
magic and its consequences alone that excite interest; here we
have not only magic most wonderful and denouements queerer
than have often been conceived, but subtle distinction of character in mortals and immortals alike, and a humour so lively that
eagerness to unravel the plot is repeatedly forgotten in laughter,
even when the reader is a child.

Five Children and It was the first of a series of books in
which the waking dreams of children are realized and crystallized as their sleeping dreams are crystallized in *Alice in
Wonderland*. No one has ever been able to imitate them,
though several have tried. They were the production of a mind
capable of throwing off in an instant all the shackles of adult-

hood while yet retaining all the skill of experience. In their own sphere they were without parallel, and no parallel in any other sphere suggests itself—unless it be in the works of F. Anstey,[1] to whom she owed one of those indirect debts which are at the same time payments of tribute. *The Brass Bottle, The Tinted Venus,* and F. Anstey's other fantasies are the only pre-Psammead novels in which the wildest extravagances are rendered at once plausible and delightfully humorous by being given a realistic setting and a dramatis personae of perfectly normal individuals.

E. Nesbit's unconcealed admiration for F. Anstey was reciprocated; the author of *Vice Versa* read and enjoyed her books and considered that they never achieved success proportionate to their deserts.

Of direct debts E. Nesbit owed not a few, for though humour, a sense of character, and a clear, economical style were hers unfailingly when children were to be her audience, her ingenuity was often heavily taxed to provide new dilemmas and dispose of old ones. Her plots were frequently discussed with inventive friends, whose advice she did not hesitate to take and to acknowledge by a dedication or some other courtesy. Laurence Housman was frequently consulted and his ideas put into effect. One of the best of her strange supernatural creatures was a conception of his own, as I shall show in the appropriate place.

His willingness to be of service is the more remarkable in that he was himself working with a passionate intensity, both as draughtsman and writer, during the whole period of his friendship with her. His numerous letters treat of incessant labours, and of the horrors and joys of creation, the fears, the worries, and the hard-won triumphs, and would make—if I were engaged upon his biography instead of E. Nesbit's—a species of reading very disillusioning to the amateur. No greater contrast can be imagined than his self-immolating fervour, his readiness to shut himself up for weeks at a time "in the clutches of his

[1] Pen name of Thomas Anstey Guthrie (1856–1934), probably the greatest of the late Victorian humorists.

last ten thousand words," and E. Nesbit's casual attitude towards her own productions. It is not to be wondered at that the friend who allowed his work to take so much out of him should have been somewhat suspicious of the merits of tales accomplished in the midst of a hundred other activities, and should occasionally have felt embarrassed when called upon to offer praises he did not feel she had earned.

In 1902 E. Nesbit turned forty-four, but nothing in her conduct or outlook yet appeared to indicate the decay of youth. She had lost her lissom slenderness, and her prettiness had given place to a gracious mellow charm of feature and expression, but her zest for life was as keen as ever, her moral courage still undaunted, her impulsiveness, her joy in play-acting, her quickness to take offence and to forgive—all were as they had been twenty, or even thirty years before. To glide along the Medway playing her guitar and singing, to picnic on bread and cheese and ham under the flowering elders, to write spontaneous verses commemorating such excursions when she should have been preparing manuscript for some justifiably impatient publisher or artist; none of these delights had shed their glamour for her.

Nothing could better express how fully, how miraculously almost, she had retained the gusto and the sensibility of youth than these extracts from two poems addressed to the companions of a Medway holiday in 1902:

> Shall we remember in some time far off,
> When youth is gone, and life has lost its sweetness,
> What scents and sounds this day was woven of,
> Whose memory flaming in our life's December
> Shall melt its snows with June's divine completeness.
> Shall we remember? . . .

> What save the memory of days like these
> That shall light all sad days that may come after,
> The memory of pansies, dreams, and cheese,
> Of empty matchboxes and peace and pleasure,
> Of silence rare, of leisure, love, and laughter—
> These are the gain time cannot take away,

Flowers blooming from the seed of this good day,
An endless treasure.

These verses were presented to Iris's friend, Douglas Kennedy, a young man who seems to have come to court the daughter and remained to fall in love with the mother. The second poem, in which there is a disrespectful reference to the Psammead, will come as a painful surprise to those who like to believe that good authors invariably rejoice in their work and do it without thought of gain:

How can I work? The stupid task
That heartless publishers may ask
Is all too hard for me to do,
Dear Medway, since to you, to you,
My thought flies, falling like an arrow,
Amid your meadowsweet and yarrow.

Dear Medway, on the breast of you
Shall float the boat and the canoe,
And underneath your grey-green willows
We'll spread soft appin and soft pillows.
Oh, happy five that there shall lie
And watch the wood and stream and sky . . .

But ah, this joy that we were made for
Must in hard coin be duly paid for—
So I must whet my wits, and add
A chapter to the Psammead,
While Douglas labours to acquire
Gold from th' illusive wheel and tyre.

Dear Douglas—work like billy-oh
That to the Medway we may go.
The Medway calls us with her flowers,
Her dreamy stream, and full-dowered hours.
And I will earn, working like mad,
The Medway, with the Psammead.

In December, 1902, E. Nesbit's mother died at the age of eighty-four, having survived all but two of her six children—and one of these two had long been at the other side of the world. Edith, who had been bound to her by ties of affection closer than usually exist between a very aged mother and a daughter with numerous private and public interests, must have been deeply distressed; but correspondence is not voluminous for this period, and Mrs. Nesbit's only obituary in my records is contained in these words from Laurence Housman's consolatory letter:

> I am most sorry to think of your loss and what it means. It recalls to me the quiet charm of that dear old lady as I saw her at your house some years ago. She left on me the impression then of a sweet and beautiful character, and I have always felt sad at hearing that her increasing infirmities did not make the last years of her old age happy ones. One can quite understand that along with the great sense of loss comes a feeling of consent that it should be so.

This death, sad but less pitiful than the others which had cast their shadows across the first four years at Well Hall, was the last that was destined to touch Edith nearly for more than a decade to come. Uninterrupted by major calamities, the parties, holidays, and varied enterprises of work and recreation crowded faster and faster upon each other's heels, all a little heightened in colour and importance, at least externally, by reason of the Blands' being no longer poor and struggling rebels, but people of acknowledged substance and success.

13 *The Edwardian Years—I*

E. Nesbit's publications in book form during 1902 were *Five Children and It,* which appeared very shortly after its last instalment in the *Strand,* and *The Revolt of the Toys,* a small work done for her early publisher, Ernest Nister. In the meantime, she was occupied with her second and, in many opinions, her best novel. *The Red House* is a pretty and attractively unpretentious piece of work, distinguished by a larger share of the Nesbit humour than is evident in the other books for adults, but yet rather wanting in any other distinction. It has one extraordinarily amusing chapter into which, in the happiest and most natural manner, the Bastable children make an entrance and are seen through the eyes of grown-ups. (In *The New Treasure Seekers,* written some time later, Oswald describes the Red House and its inhabitants from the point of view of the children—an excellent trick and skilfully accomplished.)

This novel, issued by Methuen at the beginning of 1903, was reprinted three times within as many months, and enjoyed fairly substantial sales for several years afterwards. She herself was exceedingly pleased with it, and sent copies to numerous friends in the profession of letters. W. E. Henley, writing shortly before his death, acknowledged the gift gratefully, but doubted whether he would have the pleasure of reading it until he had got off his hands "a bulky, insistent, and very damnable copy of verses: to say nothing of *Troilus and Cressida* (the text) in my new edition, *The Edinburgh Folio* of Shakespeare." But he expressed a hope that she would visit him at his home whether he had first read the novel or not.

Andrew Lang *did* read the book, but not with much enjoyment.

> Dear Mrs. Bland [he wrote in February, 1903],
>   Many thanks for your book, and still more for the children in the Treasure Seekers, and the other tales. Their chivalry reminds me of the Great Montrose.
>   I fear that of all forms of the passion of Love, from the possibly Platonic to the boisterously illegal, the Connubial is least adapted to Art.[1] It was after seeing "two young lovers newly wed" that the Lady of Shalott said "I am truly sick of shadows." The effect is to make me feel painfully shy, but I have only begun the book, and I hope there is a genuine ghost. In my own recent fiction, I have remarked that "the author is unwilling to intrude on the licence of a privileged affection." I think Mr. Henry Fielding has a similar phrase. But this bashfulness may be peculiar to a few finely tempered souls, and I am sure that the rest is very interesting.
>
> Sincerely yours,
> A. Lang.[2]

In a second letter on the same subject he again expresses his feeling that the book "intrudes on the licence of a privileged affection." "I was a little alarmed," he says, referring to a passage in it, "by a salute of XXV kisses. I thought that people should kiss and not tell. I observed," he adds by way of mitigation, "that too much was not made of the baby."

Nevertheless, he thought highly of her gifts, and some three years later he wrote: "If your Red House was not my sort, the others were very much so, and the balance is largely in your

---

[1] *The Red House* is concerned with the adventures of a recently married couple.

[2] In the same communication he answers a question of hers about the indications of a ghost in the garden at Well Hall: "The ghost in the garden is usually the ghost in the house. Possibly if you tried a planchette he might communicate."

favour." And in yet another letter: "I hope that before *you* die, the public will know the worth of your work as I do," which was much from an extremely frank, uncompromising critic.

But if the author of *The Red House* was disappointed at its failure with Andrew Lang, she was, perhaps, consoled by the praises of Richard Whiteing, whose own reputation as a novelist then stood high. His view is worth quoting if only for the revelation of how different an impression the same work can produce upon minds of different tendency:

February 9th, 1903.

Dear Mrs. Bland,

Thank you for sending me The Red House. . . . It is so very much yours, so very much in what one might now call your style that one would know it as yours without any help from the title page. I think that is a great thing for a writer to have, especially when it goes deeper than mere manner, but right round to the whole point of view. The bantering playfulness of the love scenes, for such they are from first to last, though they are post marital, is not to be surpassed. This is another fresh and distinctive note. The way in which the love making usually ends with marriage in romance, as it is said to do in real life, is sometimes quite disheartening. Now what I like in your book is that you begin with a marriage. I have sometimes thought that every novel should begin in that way now, for of course it is the starting point of the whole problem, the rest is more or less matter of convention, but the game really begins with the rice and the slipper. I wish I had your lightness of touch, but that is only a greedy way of saying that I wish I had everything. For you know what it is, every writer has his distinctive something, and as one reads one envies him that something, like the fat boy who wants to have his plate heaped with five times as much as he can manage. Of course the one quality that one envies often quite precludes the other, so it is a silly way of going on at best, and one has to learn to take oneself for just what one is. . . .

With good wishes for you and yours,

Very sincerely yours,
Richard Whiteing.[3]

[3] Richard Whiteing (1840–1928) worked on various newspapers in Europe and America besides writing books. He lived to see *No. 5 John Street*

E. Nesbit continued to regard this novel with satisfaction. More than four years after its publication she sent a copy of it to William de Morgan, a writer whose work she held in high esteem, and must have been gratified by the opinion expressed in his letter of acknowledgment:

> Bay of Biscay.
> 12.6.07.
>
> Dear Mrs. Bland,
>
> Your very kind present of books reached me in Florence just before I came away. The two children's books I had only time to glance at, and had to leave them behind—but the Red House I brought with me to read on the voyage, and have just finished it. It is charmingly idyllic and original in structure—and what an accumulation of photographic detail!
>
> A sea-voyage is really the time for reading, and your book was a book in the right place—With many thanks to you,
> Believe me, dear Mrs. Bland,
>
> Yours very truly,
> Wm de Morgan.[4]

When an author sends unsolicited copies of his works to other authors who happen not to be his intimate friends, it may generally be concluded that he seeks praise—or, at any rate criticism, and as Edith was seldom a good subject for criticism, except where her books for children were concerned, one must needs believe that she sought praise. She was more easily wounded by an adverse opinion than one would have expected any writer of such capacities to be. Her friends record a quite alarming sensitiveness in this respect, and her letters themselves occasionally contain a hint of it. Mr. Housman remembered with embarrassment after long years how hurt she was when she wanted him to say that, of modern woman poets, she came about next to Christina Rossetti, and he insisted that Alice Mey-

filmed. Mr. R. S. Garnett, Richard Whiteing's executor, gave the sanction which enables me to use his letter.
[4] W. F. de Morgan (1839-1917), celebrated associate of William Morris as stained glass artist and potter, began writing successful novels when over sixty. For permission to print his letters, I am indebted to Miss de Morgan.

nell and Mrs. Marriott-Watson, to name no others, were her betters.

I have not seen any letters of hers—except, it is well to repeat, those referring to her children's books—in which she accepted or prepared for a criticism without some attempt to justify herself. The most good-humoured answer to one which has come my way is contained in a letter to H. G. Wells, written just after reading his *Modern Utopia* in 1905. He had complained that the stories in *Thirteen Ways Home* were over-sentimental.

"Thirteen Ways Home are fairy tales," she wrote, evidently quoting a statement of his to this effect. "Yes: so's the Red House: but in the same sense that your Utopia is a fairy tale. Love is not always the detestable disintegration that you pretend to think it. Sometimes, and much oftener than you admit, it is 'nice straight cricket.' Anyhow one wishes it to be that— you do, too—anyway why should you have a monopoly of Utopias? All the same, I'm not very proud of Thirteen Ways Home, though I have a sneaking regard for George's Monument, and the Question of Conscience, and Darkening Counsel. I'll grant that they're too sentimental. But it's a dreadful thing, and one of the curses of middle age to forget how to be sentimental."

Not only is it plainly to be seen that she received all outside criticism of her work with reservations, but she was hardly ever self-critical—or, at any rate, openly so. I have not before me a single instance of her making apology for any piece of work whatever, although I have examined a good deal of correspondence in which she refers to books that were distinctly inferior to her best, so inferior, indeed, that one would think even their author must have been conscious of their weaknesses. It is true that in a letter addressed to her brother she does ask him not to be too severe with a novel she had written in thirty days (and which decidedly needed the clemency she invoked), but she did not appear to find any cause for regret in such misuse of her own genius.

It is difficult to reconcile her almost childish eagerness for applause with her undeniable modesty. In no circle that she en-

tered did she ever trade upon her reputation as a brilliant and
sought-after woman; she never patronized, never made any
pronouncement as if she had earned the right to make pro-
nouncements; and if her behaviour generally suggested a certain self-consciousness, the self of whom she was conscious and
whom she proudly lived up to was the generous, erratic, open-
hearted Bohemian, not the versatile woman of letters who could
boast twenty-odd years of fruitful toil. No one of all those
whose impressions have gone towards the making of this book
has ventured to describe her as a vain woman, yet almost every
one of them saw her as eager for praise and seriously perturbed
if it was not given to her. The explanation is, perhaps, that to
one whose own judgments are intensely personal, as hers were,
appreciation is synonymous with affection—and she wanted
affection passionately.

The number of her friends was enormously large, but it
seemed to her that she could never have enough or do too much
for them. Her husband was equally lavish of his time and of his
means, not only in entertaining those who were congenial, but
in helping and encouraging many who could personally be of
little interest to him. Had the Blands been tainted with the least
trace of snobbery, Well Hall might have been the resort of
celebrities exclusively; as it was, perfectly obscure and perfectly
insignificant people found place in every gathering and were
not less welcome than guests of famous achievements. H. G.
Wells has spoken of the house as "a place to which one rushed
down from town at the week-end to snatch one's bed before
anyone else got it."

To Dymchurch, too, where Edith now had a cottage furnished
with second-hand bargains picked up in the village itself,
all sorts and conditions of visitors came down to work, to play,
to talk, to rest. Everyone who proved acceptable at Well Hall
was invited to a Dymchurch week-end sooner or later, and no
one ever stayed there without enjoyment or returned without
a little store of beguiling memories. Several families whose
names are associated with art and letters had seaside houses
in that district. There were the Sterndale Bennetts and the

Thorndikes, the Jepsons, and the Griffiths—whose son Hubert
Griffith, later well known as writer and traveller, was then a
little boy and a great favourite with E. Nesbit, his godmother.
(*The Phoenix and the Carpet* contains an admirable little
dedicatory poem addressed to him.) Sybil and Russell Thorndike were among the dearest of her young companions, their
mother an affectionate friend for nearly twenty years.

At Sandgate, a few miles along the coast, H. G. Wells was in
possession of Spade House, and as the two families were intimate,
mutual invitations were issued and accepted, and an informal
and exceedingly charming correspondence still exists to bear
testimony to the happiness of those flourishing years.

Wells had read some of E. Nesbit's work long before he met
her, and had never doubted that she was a man (a delusion
which she always found flattering, and did her best to confirm
by writing all first-person stories in the masculine character).
Under this impression, he attributed a male Christian name to
her in his fancy, hitting upon "Ernest" as the one that would be
most appropriate; and when on meeting her, in 1902, he discovered his mistake, he continued to call her Ernest until by degrees he dropped this nickname for two more generally favoured—"Duchess" and "Madam." To her, he was usually "My
Dear Sir."

In the very early days of their acquaintanceship he won her
heart by doing the thing which of all others was best calculated
to kindle a glow in her. He turned up suddenly one day at Well
Hall carrying a valise, and greeted her with a single sentence:
"Ernest, I've come to stay!" Nothing could have gratified her
more than this frank confidence in her Bohemianism, this demand simple and direct for the hospitality she took such pleasure in giving. His bedroom was delightedly prepared, and an
entertainment devised for him in the form of charades based
upon the titles of his own works, acted by the whole Bland
family.[5] After this his visits were frequent and joyfully looked

[5] H. G. Wells has described the Blands' household from his own point of
view in his *Experiment in Autobiography*. The full story of this friendship and its ending, however, has not yet been told.

forward to, although he was one of the few people who had sufficient moral courage to refuse to play Edith's "intellectual" games—and these were, after charades and dancing, her favourite evening pastime.

She loved all games, and would compete as eagerly as a child, firing her companions—even those who had joined reluctantly—with enthusiasm. Her admirers might like to know some of the games that found favour with the gatherings at Well Hall or the Dymchurch cottage. One was called Subjects and Adjectives. For this, difficult and outlandish nouns were written on pieces of paper and put into a hat, and in another hat were placed slips inscribed with adjectives: each player then took two adjectives and one noun, and had to write a verse in which these words were introduced as reasonably as possible. Rhyming games were very much to her taste, and she played them with great skill. A rather difficult one consisted of writing verses of complete nonsense but yet as perfect as possible in their assonances and cadences. One evening they played at parodying well-known literary styles in a completely meaningless context. Edith produced an instantly recognizable parody of the language known as Journalese.

But it was not in literary games alone that she found enjoyment. She could become engrossed for hours with whist, piquet, or patience, and she liked chess and other board games. Nor was it until she had left her fiftieth birthday a good way behind her that she became impervious to the charm of hide-and-seek, devil-in-the-dark, and other amusements of the same strenuous family.

Mrs. Noel Griffith, who was in close touch with the Bland household for many years, wrote me a lively description of Well Hall hospitality, of which I shall gratefully quote all but the few passages which have been anticipated in earlier chapters:

"The Blands' parties were large and frequent, and played an important part in their lives. Many notabilities attended them. Often ten or more of us would band together for the tiresome journey from town to join the seven or eight inhabitants of the house for an evening's amusement which was usually kept up until the small hours. It seemed a long and tedious way to go, and on a foggy night, after waiting perhaps an hour for a train from Cannon Street, and then being shot out to wait again on the chilly platform at Blackheath to catch the Well Hall train, one wondered why on earth one had accepted one's invitation so readily.

"One arrived late without a qualm (for meals were invariably late there) to be greeted by a large placard at the principal entrance saying briefly 'The Front Door is at the Back!' This was because the front door opened directly into the long hall where we dined when there were a lot of us, and it was therefore undesirable to let in the cold air. Or the notice might imply that there was more chance of being let in at the back: with any luck a gardener's boy, a child, or even a maid might hear us. Generally, even when we had made our entrance the prospect of dinner seemed to be remote, and we wandered about feeling forlorn and neglected, and still wondering why we had come. Mrs. Bland would be finishing a chapter, and Hubert his article for the *Chronicle,* and we knew that nothing could happen until their work was done.

"Then at last Mrs. Bland would appear on the stairway, radiant—in riotous spirits, perhaps, because she had just escaped premature death by not falling over a dustpan left on the stairs; and that was, of course, an omen that it would be a good party. She always wore the same kind of dress, a long flowery silk one, probably with Turkish slippers, and certainly with many silver bangles. These reached nearly to her elbow and were never removed. They were presents and she prized them as an Indian prizes his scalps.[6] She bathed in them, and they got in her way often, but I never saw her freckled arms without them until I went down to Romney Marsh at the very last, and she showed me that her hands were so thin that she could slip them off easily.

"Her companion, Miss Hoatson, wore the same flowing dresses, but hers had more form about them, and a waist line.

[6] These bangles were tributes from her husband, who added one to her collection each time she published a book.

"Hubert would at last crawl lazily out of his den in 'immaculate evening dress' with velvet coat and a monocle worn on a black watered-silk ribbon which hinted at foppishness, though the glass was a necessity.

"The dinners themselves were always 'chancy.' If poems, articles, and books were going well, they were quite grand. At one time two Swiss lads did the cooking and were full of surprises. I remember once they made little châlets of white sugar with real lights inside as a sweet. In leaner times we had a huge soup-tureen of haricot beans, doled out graciously and gaily, without comment by Madame, a large block of cheese to follow, and delicious apples from the garden. There was always plenty of red and white wine in beautiful Venetian bottles and the table looked lovely. Hubert had passion and skill as a rose grower. In summer we (the guests) used to gather a wicker clothes-basket full of roses, picking them off short to save the remaining buds. We would make a thick mat of them from one end of the long table to another, setting in at intervals the silver branch candle-sticks that Mrs. Bland adored.

"The party never flagged once the Blands had appeared. A friendly atmosphere hung about them, an atmosphere of festivity. They were intensely *lovable;* and we were gay because we knew that our hostess was enjoying the large company, and thinking how lucky she was to have got so many 'darlings' together. The conversation was good, and everyone was given a chance to express his own ideas. Hubert was a brilliant talker, but he was also eager to listen, especially to youth. 'Remember the respect due to youth,' was one of his favourite sayings. Edith herself would wind on for hours if she was in the mood, while the children of the house were never shut away, and gave their opinions as definitely and dogmatically as the rest of us.

"Invariably, in the midst of the most distinguished gathering, one would find some weak or wounded creature who was taking shelter at Well Hall—a baby rescued from poverty or illness (who surprisingly appeared at late dinner), a poor relation waiting for a job, a painter seeking recognition, a timid girl whom someone there believed in and encouraged to write stories. No one who knew the Blands could resist seeking their comfort and their counsels in distress.

"After dinner we danced in the cleared drawing-room, and there were games and more talk. Devil-in-the-dark caused the destruction of so much good furniture all over the house that it had to be stopped. Mrs. Bland collected old glass lustres long before there was a craze for them, and there were fine chandeliers in the drawing-room, which contained many beautiful pieces. . . .

"The dinner and dancing and talk lasted so long that most of us missed last trains and slept where we could, the men usually finding accommodation in the garden cottages. Next morning it was considered in the best taste to depart by an early train without seeing our hosts. The house would be in an incredible muddle, and the most tactful procedure was to breakfast with Paul, the eldest son, who left early for the City, and then vanish unheeded."

To parties such as these came a strange assortment of artists, writers, and politicians, among whom were H. G. Wells, Graham Wallas, Sydney Olivier, Laurence Housman, Arthur Watts, Berta Ruck, Gerald Gould, Cecil and G. K. Chesterton, Oswald Barron, Edgar Jepson, Horace Horsnell,[7] Alfred Sutro, and many others whose friendship with the Blands belongs to a later period. There was also to be seen from time to time a little group of priests and Catholic propagandists of whom Monseigneur Benson [8] was the chief: an oratory had been specially fitted up for him in a tiny room leading off the bedroom he usually occupied.

And the extraordinarily eccentric author known sometimes as Baron Corvo and sometimes as Frederick Rolfe came and went—in a comparatively peaceable frame of mind. At any rate, there is no record of his quarrelling with the Blands, though his

[7] The late Horace Horsnell was H.H. of the *Observer*. He acted for a time in his youth as E. Nesbit's secretary and was greatly assisted by her, but refused to make any contribution to this book.
[8] Robert Hugh Benson (1871-1914), Catholic priest, formerly a clergyman in the Church of England; author of many historical novels.

quarrels with almost everybody else were violent and spectacular. Corvo was the most singular of all their acquaintances even including the young anarchists with whom they had been familiar in the eighties.

He had come into the Well Hall circle, partly through his interest in the work of the Fabian Society and partly through his hope of getting Hubert Bland to find someone who would finance him while he worked on "a very large amount of absolutely unique historical material about the Borgias," or who would buy that material from him; and he remained intimate with the Bland family in his incalculable, erratic way until he left England for the last time, even writing very agreeable letters—he who had written some of the most disagreeable letters ever conveyed by the post!—to John Bland, then a child. His first communication to the Fabian Society, written in a handwriting that might have served for the text of an illuminated devotional book, must have provoked something approaching amazement:

> Mr. Rolfe (v. Literary Year-Book) encloses a subscription of Five Shillings. He is not a Socialist; and his experience of socialists is entirely disagreeable. He is a Roman Catholic; and finds the Faith comfortable and the faithful intolerable: consequently he is not even on speaking terms with Roman Catholics. But he is a student; and, as such he is not anxious to confuse the goodness of a cause with the badness of its agents. And so, begging pardon for these explanations, he ventures to ask the Secretary of the Fabian Society to supply him with the "Credo" of the Fabians, for purposes of study.
>
> He is led to make this request by his immensely excited admiration of Mr. G. B. Shaw's article in the Clarion for 11 Feb. Jesus Coll. Oxford.
>
> "XV Feb. 1906.[9]

Two or three months later he wrote to Hubert Bland, with whom he was still unacquainted, proposing a meeting at his solicitors' office to talk over the Borgia question. "It is a big

[9] This letter is published by kind permission of Miss Katherine E. Rolfe.

affair," he said, "involving two or four thousand pounds or there about: for I can't consent to waste the thing for less. It is not a matter for publishers, or for scholars, but for men of the world. I know none of the last: but R. H. Benson of Cambridge read your *With the Eyes of a Man* [10] with me during the vacation, and we examined your picture; and we decided that you were as man-of-the-worldly as possible. So I should like to have you in this Borgia scheme if it is likely to be in your line."

Hubert Bland was certainly not able to find either four thousand pounds or two to finance Rolfe's work, but he gave him what assistance lay within his personal means, and both he and Edith seem to have enjoyed his company, difficult though he made himself. He was not only a professed Catholic, but he had been a candidate for Holy Orders. His rejection had filled him with a virulent hatred of the church, or rather with its temporal body; and with *Hadrian the Seventh* and other works, some of which were too libellous to be published, he became a bright and dangerous firebrand. From the study of Baron Corvo [11] by A. J. A. Symons, to whom I was indebted for most of these particulars, I have taken a description of his peculiarities at the time when the Blands knew him best:

"He astonished his hosts in country houses by appearing in a mole-velvet dinner jacket, and by uttering incantations in the moonlight that brought to his legs mysterious and unknown cats. Though restrained in dress, he developed a passion for rings, and wore ten on his fingers, and an equal number strung round his neck. . . . On each hand he wore one ring in which was mounted the rowel of a spur, and he explained that when the Jesuits made, as they would, their inevitable attempt at abduction, he would smite them on their foreheads and the lines thus excoriated would blind the assailants with blood while he escaped." In aspect he was "tall, priestly-visaged, eagle-nosed, clean-shaven . . . reticent, unsmiling." What sort of figure he

[10] A collection of Hubert Bland's essays published in 1905.
[11] Published in *Life and Letters*, July, 1928, and later incorporated in A. J. A. Symons' famous book, *The Quest for Corvo*.

cut among the genial young Bohemians who frequented Well
Hall it is difficult to imagine.

As it was impossible for Rolfe to know anyone for long without venting his many grievances against contemporary Catholics, and as it was equally impossible for Hubert Bland to listen
to opinions he did not share without courteously attempting to
refute them, it is not extravagant to conjecture that they had arguments which would have been worth listening to—for Bland
was extremely skilful in marshalling his points, and the author
of *Hadrian* was gifted with a most pungent eloquence. And it
happened that Bland was at that time a loyal member of the
Church—which later received his wife, who probably derived
her religion, as her politics, from him.

He was generally understood by his friends to be a *convert* to
Catholicism. Here, however, it appears that they were in error,
for there is reason to believe that he was brought up in the
Catholic faith, had renounced it in his youth in favour of ag-
nosticism, and had adopted it again in early middle age. It was
seldom that he discussed religion, but on one of the rare occasions when he did so, he explained that his return to the Church
had been due to his interest in the philosophy of Hegel, which
had convinced him of the validity of Catholic dogma.[12] Cecil
Chesterton, writing of Bland after his death, said: "He was a
Catholic because he felt that if one were to have a religion, it
must be a religion at once traditional and dogmatic."

Though loyal to the dogma, as I have said, he was quite irregular in his observances, attending Mass rarely and making
no attempt whatever to influence his children; and his wife was
equally undevout judged by orthodox standards. Indeed, most
of the Catholic believers of their acquaintance thought their

[12] The late Gerald Gould, to whom this information was addressed,
gave me the following note upon it: "The statement seemed to me at the
time to be nonsense, but he was not in the habit of talking nonsense,
and apparently believed what he said. The only sense I can attach to
the saying is some sort of symbolical relation between the Hegelian conflict and synthesis, on the one hand, and the mystical doctrine of the
Trinity on the other; but apart from the fact that each gives us three
points, I can see no real connection.

formal profession of faith somewhat mysterious, since they cared little about being in what is technically called "a state of grace." Their conversion had never been made public (for the obvious reason, in Hubert Bland's case, that he was not a convert but a reformed apostate), and the Catholic community in general—or such of it as knew the Blands by repute—was undecided whether to consider them as outside or inside the fold. They looked upon themselves as Catholics, and continued to describe themselves as such—Hubert until his death, Edith until, during the War, she decided that the Pope had failed to exercise the powers she attributed to him. And even after that, she did not wholly throw off her avowed allegiance.

In 1903 the *Strand Magazine* published the first installments of a new Psammead story under the title of *The Phoenix and the Carpet*. It was in no way inferior to the earlier work, and contained some episodes even more boldly original. The magic bird's visit to the Phœnix Fire Office, which he insists upon regarding as a temple erected in his honour, is among the most brilliant of all her fantastic conceptions. The Phœnix himself was invented by Laurence Housman, and the following passage from a letter written by him in acknowledgment of a gift of the book, which was published a year later, shows how little he regretted having given her an idea which he had first intended to use himself:

> The Carpet and the Phoenix have alighted on my hearth. I have dipped and am continuing to dip into the entertainment they afford. It is delightful to find how fruitful small suggestions—mere pegs or stems on which to hang a story—become under the genial breath of your invention. It is so long ago since I proposed the carpet and the phoenix as properties for a magic plot to be woven around, that I had forgotten all about them. I can't decide whether the artist has been drawing Mr. Lamert [13] or me as the father of the family—but I hope it is me. There is a smartness and

---

[13] Mr. Sidney Lamert, who rented one of the Well Hall cottages while he was managing editor of *The Sun*. On his recommendation Fabian was sent to Loretto School shortly before his death.

a smugness which suggests careful study of the libellous portrait you have of me. . . .

I hope this book will be as great a success as all its predecessors—I know already that I like it better than the Book of Dragons, and I don't think that complete reading will diminish the impression.

Rudyard Kipling,[14] too, wrote in terms of unequivocal praise, and H. G. Wells was not less charmed. He permitted me to publish the letter he sent her on receiving his copy:

> Spade House,
> Sandgate.
> 17.12.04.

'Steamed Lady

I never told you how we like the Phoenix and the Carpet and how extraordinarily more than the late Mrs. Ewing who was once first we now esteem you. The Phoenix is a great creation; he is the best character you ever invented—or anybody ever invented in this line. It is the best larking I ever saw. Your destiny is plain. You go on every Xmas never missing a Xmas, with a book like this; and you will become a British Institution in six years from now. Nothing can stop it. Every self respecting family will buy you automatically and you will be rich beyond the dreams of avarice, and I knock my forehead on the ground at your feet in the vigour of my admiration of your easy artistry.

Our best wishes to you for a picturesque and various Xmas.

> Yours ever
> H. G. Wells.

While the Phoenix serial was still appearing in the *Strand,* another set of tales was issued by their author. These were combined in a volume called *The Literary Sense,* a title which, as she later decided, was a very regrettable choice. It gave the impression that the work was a sort of critical study, whereas it was actually a collection of entertaining short stories, among the best she ever wrote, each one of which relied for its denouement

[14] Kipling, unfortunately, would not allow any of his letters to E. Nesbit to be reproduced.

upon the chief actor's *instinct for drama.* She herself had such a strong sense of dramatic effect, and was so unable to resist the temptation of playing up to it, that she could portray other characters of the same tendency with fidelity. The book was published by Methuen's, who had made a great success of *The Red House,* but—owing, she thought, to its misleading title—it did not do well, though the vogue for short stories was then in full swing and her own reputation considerable.

Mr. Wells expressed his opinion of the new tales thus:

September. 17.1903.

Dear Mrs. Bland,

The stories are good and gay and I've liked the book immensely. They are a game and a very pretty game and all sorts of people will do their little talks more carefully on account of them, and with little plagiarisms more or less carefully handled. They hang queerly and pleasantly between the illusions of the schoolgirl and the blood and racket of this sensual life. They are not the heady stuff of Romance nor that reality that cuts to the bone, but they are quite delightful Young Fancies.

Yours ever,
H. G. Wells.

The same year saw the publication of another small work for Raphael Tuck, *The Rainbow Queen,* and in the meantime, incredible as it may seem, *The New Treasure Seekers* was making its appearance in the *London Magazine.* How so prolific a writer managed to crowd parties and holidays of all kinds into these already crowded years it is not easy to understand. She stated the case without explaining it in describing the character of one of her own heroines:

"Her passionate energy was of the kind that makes days elastic and stretches them till they include one's duties as well as one's pleasures." In the same book [15] she touched upon another capacity of her own which stood her in good stead through all the years of her career: "This gift of being able to put aside, at will, the troubling things of life, laying them apart till a more

[15] *Daphne in Fitzroy Street.*

convenient season, not, cowardly, shrinking from them, but bravely holding them at arm's length. . . . It is a gift that stamps its owner brave, and keeps him young."

For all the need she had imposed upon herself to turn out a certain minimum of work, she seldom seems to have made any attempt to simplify it by engaging a resident secretary to deal with her correspondence and relieve her of such tasks as could be done by an assistant. She did employ secretaries from time to time, but only fitfully and in a rather vague and indeterminate way. Some young friend in need of a temporary occupation would be installed at Well Hall as a kind of companion-amanuensis, but her letters almost always appear to have been handwritten, and her stories were sent to the publishers as often as not in handwritten form.

During the years of her zenith she received a very large number of letters from unknown admirers—usually children, and she always made a point of answering them, though she was seldom able to do so within two or three weeks of their receipt. Often her son Paul would be called upon to assist her in coping with an enormous arrears of correspondence, disposing of as many as thirty letters under her direction in a single evening. But as a rule she wrote in her own hand—a hand deceptively simple in appearance, but difficult to read and given to rather confusing abbreviations. She signed her name to all intimates with a peculiar rebus, representing at a casual glance a clover leaf, but exhibiting on closer inspection her initials, E. B.

Intermittently she kept in touch with her numerous relations settled abroad. Most of them were in Australia, but there was one, a pupil of her long-dead grandfather, who was Parish Clerk to St. Andrew's Church at Rochester, in the State of New York. This was Thomas Nesbit, who appears to have been a second or third cousin, and whom it is improbable that she had ever seen since her childhood. Some kindly impulse, or some desire to keep what hold she could upon the family ties loosened by time and distance, prompted her to write to him and tell him her news. She received back a letter of such formal courtesy and Victorian innocence that it might have been composed fifty years before at the Commercial and Scientific Academy in Kennington Lane:

"I am aware that you are quite an authoress seeing your stories in the magazines. I would respectfully say that the Nesbits seem to have had quite a literary turn of mind. When old Mr. Anthony Nesbit of Kennington Lane was living, he was a great author of scholastic works. I as a boy scholar at the school used to read his proof sheets. He wrote his Arithmetic and Key to the same, Grammar, Geometry, Trigonometry and Land Surveying. . . .

"Your stories in Harper's [16] and others seem to be generally written for children, and I should suppose your own family would be greatly interested therein. I presume dear Madam you are aware of the death of my eldest sister . . . and recently my other sister . . . departed this life also, so that I am the only one of our family left. When I look around me and remember Mr. and Mrs. Anthony Nesbit, Mr. John Nesbit, your father, Mr. Edward his brother who died in Australia and Miss Mary Ann and Miss Julia their sisters also gone, it certainly does remind one of the shortness of life, which at the most is but a passing shadow, and soon we are gone.

"I hope your family is all well. As for myself I am happy to say I am quite well, the Gracious Father blessing me with most beautiful health that I think ever man was blest with, seeing that I am now writing this without lines or glasses in my 75th year.

"I ask your pardon for trenching upon your very valuable time, and shall be glad to hear from you, if it be agreeable so to do."

E. Nesbit could well afford an indulgent smile for the phrase

[16] The children's serials were usually published in America in *Harper's Magazine*.

"quite an authoress." Between fifty and sixty books of verse and prose now bore her name as author or part-author upon their title pages; more than twenty of them were entirely her own and of substantial length. And nearly thirty others were to follow in the future.

There can be little doubt that it would have been better both for her health and her fame, and for her purse, too, in the long run, if she had written less, or at least been more careful in disposing of her work. Even when she was at the height of her success, she would sometimes accept trivial commissions unworthy of her talents or her reputation. Had she restricted her output so that only her best was published, and that in a manner not destructive to her prestige, she would not, I imagine, have failed to fulfil H. G. Wells's genial prophecy in a letter recently quoted. But she could not husband her art: she scattered it far and wide. The desirability of earning money was constantly before her, and in getting and spending she did, alas! lay waste her powers.

It is not good policy—considering the material aspects of the question alone—for an author of high standing to bring out two or three books a year. The most devoted admirer flinches before so reiterant a demand for his attention. The author is deemed to be "writing himself out," he is "commercial," he has "ghosts" to help him.

The New Treasure Seekers, though not less excellent than its predecessors, did not enjoy so large and instantaneous a success on being issued in book form in 1904. It was competing against *The Phoenix and the Carpet.* And there was another book, too— *Cat Tales,* done in collaboration with Rosamund Bland, who was already showing a literary ability worth encouraging. Short stories were appearing in magazines; there was a volume of serious poetry in preparation. From almost every point of view such prodigality was a mistake, but no power on earth could have convinced E. Nesbit that her career was being mismanaged.

"As if art that was worth its salt couldn't take care of itself without being kept in cotton wool!" she made a character say in one of her novels. "As if art wasn't strong enough to live out of doors!" She was right if she was thinking of what survives for posterity, but if she had in mind the artist's career in his own lifetime it would appear that she was wrong.

14 *The Edwardian Years–II*

Although Edith had reached the high-water mark of her prosperity during the period I have described, several years of success still lay before her. There were worries, setbacks, weeks of overwork, weeks of irritability because she was not working when she knew she should have been, but on the whole life went on gaily and even radiantly. New friends were made almost every week—real friends, too, who loved her and remained devoted to her, not mere amiable companions; and these did not oust out the old friends. The circle simply widened or divided into smaller circles. There was room for multitudes of loves.

It will, I think, be interesting here to quote two typical first impressions of her vital and compelling personality. One was recorded by an observer whose whole acquaintance with her lasted, perhaps, a matter of twenty minutes: the other is the first glimpse by a stranger who afterwards became a friend. Both meetings took place in about the same year, and they show, better than any portraiture I could attempt, the curious variability of her aspect, behind which lay a radical good feeling that did not vary.

"It was a Saturday afternoon," wrote my first informant,[1]

---

[1] Mr. Albert Coumber.

"and an artist friend and I were wandering round what was then the comparatively rural district of Well Hall in search of a likely subject for a picture, when we alighted upon a plot of ground near an interesting block of old red-brick buildings. We decided to make these our subject, and, spreading out our sketching materials, proceeded to work. We were quite absorbed and oblivious of everything but our drawings when we were suddenly startled by a deep female voice, demanding whether we knew that we were *trespassing,* and on looking round we were confronted by a very stately lady dressed in a sweeping robe, who repeated the question in somewhat sepulchral tones. A little annoyed by the lady's manner, I explained that we had not been aware that the land was under her jurisdiction, and suggested that we should withdraw at once, but in a modified tone she intimated that this was unnecessary. 'Only,' she said, 'we like to be asked.'

"I handed her my card, a short conversation followed, and Mrs. Bland—of whose identity, of course, I was unaware—examined our sketches and said she would like another young artist to see them. She went away and returned shortly afterwards with her daughter. Further conversation followed, and then the lady who had at first been so alarming said in quite a friendly, sociable way, 'I shall send you out some tea.' She courteously withdrew, and in a little while a servant brought us tea on a silver salver."

It was thus that the middle-aged E. Nesbit appeared at a casual encounter—aloof, majestic, awe-inspiring almost, and then suddenly likely to perform some quite unlooked-for act of kindness. And now my second correspondent [2] reveals her in another guise:

"I was a girl from a conventional home, just finished with school-life and returned from abroad, not having struck out in any particular direction either in thought or act. An uncle of mine, who had run away to Australia as a boy, came home with a fortune, and was horrified at the amount of distress and

[2] Miss Kathleen Waters at the time of the incident recorded; afterwards Mrs. P. T. Heady.

poverty in London. He wanted nothing but to pour out his money to help the underdog, and he had no idea how to start, being utterly out of touch with English political life. Someone said 'Go to see the Blands,' and so one winter afternoon, he bundled me into his early open Ford car and we drove to Well Hall.

"He told me it was a business visit and that I was to wait in the car. I did wait, but not for long. Through the dusk I heard a fine warm voice, and soon there stood beside the car a stranger whom I could not see clearly, but I got an immediate impression of well-being, happiness, welcome, and romance. She dragged me out and swept me into the house—into a great place full of people, mostly young and all laughing and talking in the bright light. She unpeeled my wrappings, which, according to the fashion of the time, were fairly voluminous, and exclaimed to everyone, 'Fancy leaving anything so charming to sit alone in the dark!' At once I was made to feel at home. I tasted for the first time the joy of real talk, the charm of gay, debonair, colourful life. I thought the girls lovely and Hubert Bland marvellous, but it was only when we were lumbering home in the car that I grasped that I had been having tea with *E. Nesbit*.

"The Blands put my uncle in touch with the people who could use his money and his goodwill, but they didn't make him into a socialist. *I* was ripe for conversion, however, for when Mrs. Bland gathered me in that day I thought: 'If these are socialists, what a glorious faith it must be!' and when she gave me the Fabian Essays with a dedication in her handwriting expressing 'a fervent hope' for my salvation and autographed by herself and all who were at that party (notable names they were too) I began to read everything I could get hold of on Socialism and . . . the movement owes at least my feeble efforts on its behalf to her. She was so generous, so vital, that I imagine she swept most of her young friends up, as she did me, into the warmth of her heart, and gave them a vision to carry them through life."

Many such tributes as this have reached me; but it would be misleading to let it be imagined that the spell with which she held so many young girls in bonds of affection never broken was founded upon any psychological understanding of the needs and longings of girlhood. The unhappy fact is that such understanding was in her a missing quantity. Both her daughter and her adopted daughter were of the opinion that she neither liked nor made the slightest attempt to comprehend young girls. Girlhood figures largely in her novels, but in an artificial style which can only confirm this judgment. She fascinated because she was a fascinating creature who set out to be liked by as many people as possible, not because she had a particular interest in young women. In family life she was often out of touch. She could only sympathize actively with distresses she had herself experienced, and she had been a boyish child and a boyish girl. Feminine adolescence was outside the range of her enlightenment: masculine adolescence she understood and loved.

She was not a masculine woman, but neither was she, in the full sense of the term, a feminine one. Strange paradoxes were everywhere apparent in her. She gloried in material independence, but spiritually, as her relations with Hubert Bland must show, she exemplified dependent womanhood. She loved children, but was not, as I have explained much earlier, maternal. She enjoyed masculine occupations and hobbies—plumbing, carpentering, handling a boat; and yet she could take a delight in needlework or cooking. Dress mattered little to her except inasmuch as it was an expression of her individuality: the whims of fashion moved her not at all. She never had an extensive wardrobe even when her income was considerable; she made no attempt to achieve the variety in dress aimed at by the typically feminine woman; she had disliked frills and furbelows even when they were at the height of their vogue and she herself a slender, pretty girl. Nevertheless, with the inconsistency we perceive in every aspect of her personality, she was fond of jewellery and wore so many bangles, beads, and other trinkets, that they were one of the most vividly remembered features of her appearance.

She had no trait more strikingly unusual in a woman than

her indifference to advancing years. She never seems to have been secretive about her age nor to have regretted the decay of her youthful appearance. She once told Berta Ruck how an old suitor had come to see her after a parting of several years during which she had been married and borne children. He had looked at her with obvious distress, and had suddenly blurted out with more candour than tact: "But what has become of all your good looks—your pretty hair, your lovely eyes, your little soft hands?" Edith told this story laughing, not bitterly nor wistfully, but with real amusement, as if her admirer's surprise and disappointment had been a sort of joke to her. Yet her feminine passion for admiration was in no way diminished as she grew older—nor did she find it less easy to obtain.[3]

The same sets of opposing characteristics are very evident in her incalculable *manner*. Described by Mr. Noel Coward (who was speaking of her, too, as he saw her in her last years) as "the most genuine Bohemian I ever met," she was still capable of a quite rigid formality. She drew a fine line of demarcation between intimacy, at which she was adept, and familiarity, which she would not tolerate. There were certain infringements of etiquette which, tacitly or volubly, she always rebuked. Anyone who was unfortunate enough to mistake her ease of manner for a permission to take liberties was quickly shown his error.

"She was all for a certain *tenue,*" Miss Ruck has written (and few of Edith's friends were more alive to her delicately balanced sensibilities), and she confesses to having been reproved more than once for a slangy and casual address, and pulled up sharply when, on a certain visit to Well Hall, she plunged into conversation with another guest concerning friends not known to the hostess. This was in the days when Berta Ruck, a young girl in the very earliest stages of a novelist's career, "sat literally at E. Nesbit's feet" learning all that the older woman could impart about the craft of fiction.

"Next to my husband, Oliver Onions," she has recorded, "she

[3] Writing to Berta Ruck a fortnight before her death, she said: "When I was alive I never wished to change the outward appearance, or rather the selfness of my body with all its defects."

took more trouble over me than anybody. It is impossible to say which of the two was the more helpful, but *I* think that she, being a woman, had a better idea of my limitations (as well as a more practical idea of the limitations of my reading public)! I am ashamed, now, when I remember the hours of her precious time that I then unthinkingly and unblushingly took up, sitting in the study at Well Hall—a bare, upper room, furnished only with necessities, and, invariably, a big jar of flowers—reading aloud reams of my perfectly hopeless young writings. Hopeless from the selling point of view, hopeless from the point of view of entertainment . . . I wish I could convey to you her patience in listening to my efforts, her generosity in praising any phrase or bit of description that she could approve —her unconquerable frankness over anything that she considered beneath my powers as far as they went. 'Won't do, Berta! Won't *do!*' she would exclaim suddenly and would stop me to show how various details of the story were not consistent, pointing out the faults kindly but quite firmly. She gave me advice and help of which I shall feel the benefit throughout my life."

Berta Ruck had studied with the Blands' daughter, Iris, at the Slade School, and was one of the group of friends who surrounded E. Nesbit when, in the spring of 1904,[4] she took a flat in Paris for three months, and lived there with Iris and Rosamund and her niece, Dorothea Deakin,[5] Saretta's daughter. Other members of the group were Arthur Watts, who later became a famous *Punch* artist, but who was then an art student with means stringently limited, and Justus Miles Forman, the

[4] It was in April at the beginning of this holiday that she attended the first performance of Isadora Duncan, who danced to the Andante of Beethoven's Seventh Symphony. Before leaving she wrote to Wells and Housman asking for introductions. Wells suggested that she might see Arnold Bennett, "who's rather a lark in an irritating way." "Shall I send you a sort of testimonial," he asked, "telling them what a thoroughly respectable person you are, or what?" She seems, however, to have missed meeting Bennett through indisposition, as an entry in his published journal indicates.

[5] Dorothea Deakin was a novelist whose books were widely read in the Edwardian period. She died in 1924. E. Nesbit was much attached to her.

young American author who met his death in the disaster of
the *Lusitania* some years later.

The summer began early, and by May the heat in the city was
such that, much as she loved the cafés and the boulevards,
Edith conceived a passionate desire to get into some country village. Within a few hours she had organized a trip to Grez-sur-
Marne, and had spirited Arthur Watts away from his lodgings,
disposing of all the difficulties he was obliged to urge by a positive command that he was to be her guest for the three or four
days of their absence from Paris. The party, depleted by
Rosamund and Miss Deakin, who had returned to England,
was made up to a round half-dozen by a new member, initiated
a little while before.

One evening in Paris they were all sitting in a public room of
their hotel, when they heard somebody strumming agreeably on
a mandoline. "Now *that* sounds like a nice person," said Edith,
and commissioned Rosamund to go and borrow some matches
from the player and report on his eligibility. She thus had an
excuse for addressing him next day. He was, by one of those
strokes of good luck which so often fell to her lot, both young
and attractive—an American artist named Hermann Webster—
who turned out to be an acquisition worth the little plot she
had laid to secure him.

In the daytime at Grez-sur-Marne "they played about," in the
words of Commander Watts, "with boats and barges," always
her best-loved outdoor pastime, or went for rides in a donkey
cart, taking all their meals in the open air. In the evenings there
were talk, games, and music, enjoyed while they sat on a terrace
overlooking the picturesque river. Almost every moment of this
holiday within a holiday was pure pleasure. E. Nesbit has testi-
fied as much in mock-heroic couplets describing the activities
and characteristics of all the party; three of her companions
bear witness here.

There was only one incident of discomfort unrelieved by
amusement. On the second evening, when they were gathered
round a lamplit table on the terrace, they saw a man making a
drunken, lurching advance towards the steps, and a face hideous with dissipation appeared in the circle of light surrounding

them. Such a sight was repugnant in the extreme to Edith, who, notwithstanding her ability to write blood-curdling stories, was painfully sensitive to any sort of squalor in real life. Hermann Webster immediately rose and drew the man away into the hotel, where he happened to be lodging. The weather next day was bad and they were obliged to spend the morning indoors, where, to their embarrassment, the intruder of the night before suddenly appeared among them. He was sober now, however, and had discovered E. Nesbit's identity. She, too, had learned something of him; he was an English musician, once celebrated, now half-forgotten and drinking himself to death with absinthe.

Going up to the ancient piano in the salon, he asked her: "Do you remember when I set such-and-such a poem of yours to music?"

"Yes," she said; and he sat down and played on cracked tuneless notes an air that sounded thin and strange. She looked miserably round at her companions, so much moved that it took her some time, volatile though she was, to recover her gaiety.

I should, perhaps, have made reference before to her popularity as a writer of songs. Some of them were a fairly substantial source of income to her. The well-known verses beginning "Little brown brother, Oh! little brown brother," were set to music again and again—most notably by Liza Lehmann shortly before her death—and were described by E. Nesbit herself as the most profitable work she had ever done, taking into consideration the little effort they had cost her. No other poem of hers has found its way into so many anthologies.

She was several times obliged to deal with attempts at "piracy," not only in connection with this song but with others. On one such occasion the offence led to her making two new friendships. In 1904 Alphonse Courlander [6] had published a story in which one of his characters sang a song about a blue

[6] Alphonse Courlander (1881–1914), author and journalist, wrote his first book, *The Taskmaster*, when he was twenty. Special correspondent to *Daily Express* and *Daily Chronicle*. War correspondent in Balkan Wars, 1912–13. *Mightier than the Sword*, his last novel, was very widely read.

bird. Edith read it and recognized the lyric as her own. She wrote to the author telling him that she had not been aware that these words had been set to music, and enquiring the name of the publishers. This being furnished, she was able to persuade them to give her a cheque for £20, and so, highly gratified, she sent Mr. Courlander her thanks and an invitation to come to tea with her. After this she took a friendly interest in his career, and when he married drew his wife into the Well Hall circle.

In 1905 E. Nesbit's name appeared on two prose books and one of verse, *The Rainbow and the Rose,* brought out by the firm of Longman, who had published *Lays and Legends.* It was dedicated to Iris and Rosamund, whose names were symbolized in the title, and was the first volume of "serious" poetry she had done for seven years. Although there is much in it that one cannot but wonder at her caring to see in print (including a sort of rhapsody on Queen Victoria's death, beginning

> The Queen is dead. God save the King,
> In this his hour of grief),

it maintained a higher level than any of its precursors except *A Pomander of Verse.* Nevertheless, it is difficult to see how she could treasure for a lifetime the illusion of having betrayed her true destiny by writing prose.

The fact that she could read her verse aloud in a voice so beautiful and delicately modulated that her listeners were carried away for the moment into praising it for melody and subtlety, which were actually qualities of her rendering rather than her writing, may have confirmed her in a view which her astuter critics never shared. The weakness of her poetry she herself indicated—half-consciously it seems—in an autobiographical article: [7]

"Right or wrong I could never bring myself to lay my soul naked before the public. My published poems are nearly all *dramatic lyrics.*"

[7] In *John o' London's Weekly,* 15th Nov., 1919.

Great poetry is seldom written by poets who set out with the principle that they must conceal the truth about their souls. A very large proportion of E. Nesbit's lyrical work is palpably *insincere*—a fault not less grave in a poet than a want of technical efficiency. No one can suspect that she had any marked partiality for her own sex; she seldom attempted to conceal her preference for the other; yet, again and again, she wrote love poems as if addressed by a man to a woman. Her motives, it may be assumed, were connected with the shrinking from reality which she has described; she wanted to write love poetry, but not to expose her heart. Needless to say, these verses —produced in disguise—rang false, but she never realized it.

The youthfulness of her mind, which was the greatest charm of her personality and the fountainhead of her success as an author for children, shows itself in her poetry as mere immaturity. It is a generally recognized characteristic of those verses which nearly all literary people turn out in adolescence that they are concerned with extraneous themes and experiences imagined rather than tasted by the writers: although the emotion which inspires them is sincere, and passionately so, the sentiments expressed are often extravagantly artificial. E. Nesbit did not outgrow the habit of uttering sentiments that she had plainly never felt, in poetry meant to be taken seriously. If anyone is inclined to dispute this criticism then he must believe that she was stricken down with grief by the death of a very aged sovereign whom she had never met, and that she spent twenty or thirty years falling desperately in and out of love with beautiful red-lipped enchantresses—than which nothing could be more unlikely.

Happily it continued to be expedient for her to write prose. The two children's books published in 1905 were *Pug Peter,* a dog story illustrated by Harry Rountree and John Hassall, and *Oswald Bastable and Others,* a collection of tales reprinted from magazines. Four of them are Bastable adventures—the last records of that cherished family. But the other series, in which the Psammead and the Phoenix had made their welcome appearance, was still continuing in the *Strand Magazine.*

The Story of the Amulet has an inner story of its own as the work on which E. Nesbit expended more time and energy than on any other of her creations. It is dedicated "to Dr. Wallis Budge of the British Museum . . . as a small token of gratitude for his unfailing kindness and help in the making of it." Upon this dedication hangs the complete history of the conception and construction of the book. I am indebted for it to the famous Egyptologist himself.[8]

During the thirty-one years of his tenure as one of the keepers at the British Museum, Sir Ernest (then Dr. Wallis Budge) was accustomed to interview about two thousand visitors a year, coming to him with every conceivable sort of question upon the subjects in which he was expert. On her return from Paris in 1905 Edith made one of the two thousand. He asked her to explain the nature of her enquiry, and was surprised to be told that "she didn't know exactly"; she was a writer of books for children, and must begin a new story at once. She found the ordinary materials for children's tales rather hackneyed and exhausted, and wanted to explore some different avenue. Was there any of *his* work that might prove suitable for her purpose?

Dr. Wallis Budge had never been asked to supply material for juvenile fiction before, but there was no resisting the Nesbit charm, and he cast about for some way of satisfying her demand.

"The literature of Egypt," he said, "might be of some use to you. The Egyptian people loved stories, and many of the kings and great potentates employed story-tellers as members of their households."

She asked what sort of stories they had favoured. He explained that the tales dealt largely with sex and were interspersed with a good deal of magic.

"You get," he explained, "the moon-faced maiden and the violent and passionate lover, with everybody taking advantage

[8] The late Sir E. A. Wallis Budge, D.Litt., Litt.D., D.Lit., F.S.A., Keeper of the Egyptian and Assyrian Antiquities at the British Museum (1893-1924), and author of numerous celebrated works on Oriental subjects.

of everybody else, and the moral comment—*nil*. Very attractive no doubt, but also rather improper. An entirely magical story would probably be more in your line."

She questioned him as to the character of Egyptian magic, and he described the use of amulets and Words of Power. He ended by recommending her to go away and think the matter over, and to come back to him if she decided to write on the themes he had suggested. A few days later she returned, acquired further knowledge, and wrote the first instalment of her book. She brought each chapter to him, and he devoted many hours of his time to giving her authentic material for the Egyptian and Babylonian adventures of the children, impressed more forcibly at each meeting with the quickness of her intelligence and the infectious quality of her enthusiasm. He read her portions of Babylonian texts so that her banquet scene might have an authentic foundation, and translated from hieroglyphics passages throwing light on the Egyptian customs at various periods. She listened avidly, and going away, would return to the Museum a week or so later with her gleanings gathered into tales through which thousands of children have seen their first vivid glimpse of past civilizations.

Her gratitude to Dr. Wallis Budge is revealed not only in the dedication of the book, but in a little portrait of him contained in it. He is represented as "the nicest gentleman" in the group of British Museum officials who witnessed the "impertinent miracle" of the Queen of Babylon.

E. Nesbit was delighted with H. R. Millar's illustrations to this story. She had the original of one of them framed, and it hung in the house she last lived in.

Between the days of writing and the visits to the Museum, she continued to take holidays at Dymchurch and on the Medway. H. G. Wells joined her party for a few days at Yalding. In a note reminding him that they would be found at the "George," and that "it would be dreadful if he were to seek them vainly at the 'Bull' or the 'Anchor,'" she made reference again to *A Modern Utopia,* the book of which she had spoken in a letter quoted earlier:

I've read your Utopia again. I don't disagree as much as I thought. And I think it's a splendid book. I wish I could write books like that. You must be very very glad of yourself when you think of that book.

She paid him a dexterous compliment, too, in *The Story of the Amulet,* showing him as she imagines him seen by people of a future age:

. . . The great reformer—surely you've heard of *him?* He lived in the dark ages, and he saw that what you ought to do is to find out what you want and then try to get it. Up to then people had always tried to tinker up what they'd got.

Wells, in his turn, could pay compliments, as this letter inviting the Well Hall party to visit Spade House will show:

Spade House,
Sandgate.
13.8.05.

Dear Lady,

This fickle Heart is still distributed in palpitating portions among the inhabitants of Well Hall and Jane [Mrs. Wells] joins with me as ever in such regards. We want to get a lot out of you all when you come to Dymchurch. We want you all to come over in ones and twos and threes and be affectionate, first some of you and then others and play the pianola too and even it may be read at times. Who are coming and when? We have appointed one room with two beds in it for all September (except the 9th when Edward Clodd is here and one occasion of Garnetts) as the Well Hall Room, and other accomodation can be arranged for. Jane says *you* are coming, you personally, on your way. Is that so? Bland might like to come over when Clodd is here, and help me put the fear of God into him. But for Bland and me there is always philosophy. With Rosamund I have really to go thoroughly into the sorrows of an incipient literary career. Iris—I never *have* talked to Iris. Gyp ever values the riper experience of a man like John. Miss Hoatson has never even so much as looked at Spade House. I hope you begin to see the advantage of regarding Dymchurch as a sort of circulating library of you; and me coming

over to change you. For them as likes games it is proposed to erect
a sort of badminton, but there we are open to advice.

Yours ever,

H. G. Wells.

Good accommodation for Bicycles—TEAS,
I have also a very high-class game of soldiers that is not to be
sniffed at even by Paul.
Miss Ruck and Enid and Reynolds count as *Blands*.

In the late autumn of this same eventful year Edith went to
Wales for a short holiday with Berta Ruck's parents. Colonel
Ruck, who was Chief Constable of Carnarvonshire, was able to
arrange for her to be taken over one of the Welsh prisons, an
experience which interested and—judging by the unfavourable
references to prisons in some of her later work—depressed her.
The officials with whom she went round never forgot her voice
as she turned back to a convict with whom she had exchanged
some conversation, and said quietly and earnestly: "I wish you
well."

She could speak very cruelly when she chose, but also, when
she chose, she could say things that were perfect of their kind.
When one considers the difficulty of bidding a pleasant goodbye to a prisoner, the unsuitability of all the phrases used on
ordinary occasions, one realizes how admirable her sense of fit-
ness could be.

In 1906 the Sunday evening debates at Well Hall were given
up in favour of amusements not requiring so many burdensome
preparations. Amongst the speakers at various meetings had
been Cecil and G. K. Chesterton, H. G. Wells, Bernard Shaw,
Clifford Sharp, Hilaire Belloc, and several of the others whose
names have been mentioned from time to time; as well, of
course, as Hubert Bland himself, a debater of the first order.
Edith had sometimes taken part in these verbal duels. She has
been described as a good speaker, but somewhat cutting and
sarcastic in manner.

For herself she preferred private conversation to forensic eloquence, though nothing gave her greater pleasure than to see

her husband taking up his stand against a worthy opponent. When the debate was over the pick of the company would often remain and argue less formally into the small hours. This was something that she and everybody else at Well Hall dearly loved. At a very intimate gathering, she enjoyed drowsing in her chair while the others went on talking around her, rousing herself to join in when some subject of special interest was broached.

Discussing her idea of a perfect setting for conversation she pictured a room with a sort of continuous divan all round the walls. Here her friends should lie all night, those who wished to sleep sleeping, and those who wished to talk talking without hindrance; the others waking up to take part in the discussion when they pleased.

Hubert Bland was now at the height of his own career, and his personality was in its fullest vigour. He was well known as an author, a journalist, a propagandist, and a helpful friend to all promising and ambitious young men. "He, who was interested in almost everything," wrote Cecil Chesterton after his death, "was especially interested in youth. . . . I have known him argue with mere children, and pay them not only the compliment of listening carefully to everything they were trying to say, but the much higher compliment of consciously arming himself to maintain his ground against them as against equals. . . . Hubert Bland was a very big man. That was the first impression that anyone who met him received."

A man of fine presence and acknowledged intellectual capacity who readily engages in serious discussions with others half his age, and that without the least air of patronage or of merely wanting an audience, will naturally excite an esteem amounting to hero-worship in those whom he has favoured. Hubert Bland had an immense influence on the work and outlook of numbers of young men who afterwards achieved eminence. His train of satellites was longer than his wife's, and it is generally admitted that he eclipsed her as a personality just as, considered in perspective of time, she eclipsed him as an artist.

For all the wide range of subjects on which they shared the

same beliefs and tastes (hers being largely founded upon his), it did not by any means follow that the admirers of Hubert Bland were also admirers of Edith, or vice versa. It was very seldom, during these later years, that they had, in the full sense of the term, friends in common.

Among the few who felt equally attached to both were Gerald Gould and Clifford Sharp, two of the young men whose capabilities Hubert Bland had recognized while they were yet in the earliest stages of development.[9] He had approached Clifford Sharp as the result of an eloquent speech at one of the Fabian meetings, and had brought him to Well Hall, where he soon became an intimate of the family, and eventually, by marriage, a member of it. After his first few visits, he introduced Gerald Gould who, at the age of twenty-one, had just published a book of poems, and was distinguishing himself in scholarship.

Gould was already a lover of E. Nesbit's tales for children. He had begun reading them during an illness at the age of seventeen—an unlikely age, in most cases, for the enjoyment of juvenile books—and had been quite enchanted with them. He was eager, therefore, to know the writer, and was attracted to her as to Hubert Bland from the moment of meeting. She in her turn was charmed with a young man who was equally ready to make impromptu ballads or to join impromptu boating expeditions. Her friendship with him was typical of the sort of friendship that, in these middle years, she most enjoyed. She had very few companions of her own generation, for she loved play as much as she loved talk.

She was nearly fifty years old, but she might have been fifteen for all the change that advancing years had wrought in her habits and her attitude to life. She had all the caprices, the little petulances, the sulks, the jealousies, the intolerances, the selfishnesses of a child; and with them went a child's freshness of

[9] Gerald Gould (1885–1936) was one of the best known writers of reviews and essays of the 1920's and 1930's. He had held various academic positions, and had been assistant editor of the *Daily Herald*. Clifford Sharp (1883–1935) was the Editor of the *New Statesman* from its foundation in 1913 to 1931.

vision, hunger for adventure, remorse for unkindness, quick sensibility, and reckless generosity. When she was in an ill humour, she upset the whole household as inconsiderately as she had upset the Ursuline Convent nearly forty years before; her tempers were known as "blights" because of their devastating effect upon everyone who happened to come within the range of them. But her good humours were not less infectious. Nothing could shake them; her high spirits made light of every disaster.

In physical aspect a stout, aging woman who suffered from asthma and bronchitis and walked about in trailing gowns with a tin of tobacco and cigarette papers under her arm, in heart a combination of the whole Bastable family put together, in capabilities a great artist one day and no sort of artist at all the next, it is not astonishing that she inspired in many of her friends a devoted love which was never quite disentangled from awe and bewilderment.

15 The "Neolithic" Period

During her long holiday in France, E. Nesbit had begun another novel, *The Incomplete Amorist;* it was finished on her return to England and published in 1906. Its scenes were laid chiefly in such circles as she had caught a glimpse of through her daughter's being an art student in Paris, and Grez was also introduced. Although her people were seldom recognizably portraits from life, she was exceedingly literal in her descriptions of places. The book was dedicated to Justus Miles Forman, with whom she had been in the habit of talking "shop" incessantly, both in France and at Well Hall, and to Richard Reynolds, who subsequently became her nephew by marriage. Beyond the mere competence of the writing, there is nothing in this work to suggest that the author was a woman of brilliant capacities. The action is singularly uninteresting, and the characters behave according to the popular novelistic convention of the day, from the moment when the sweet and innocent young heroine falls in love with a gay adventurer who is only mildly flirting with her to the moment when (he being now as much hers as she could wish) she leaves him without a word because her rival very unconvincingly explains that she ought to.

So slight and trivial is the whole tale that one might believe she had written it with her tongue in her cheek in a contemptuous effort to give the public what it is supposed to want. But since she sent copies to critics and admirers, including Andrew Lang, the assumption would not be justifiable. Mr. Lang wrote: "I shall read the story but I very seldom receive novels for review, and have only offchances of saying a good word for what I like"—which seems to imply that she had expected him to form a favourable opinion of it, even though he had frankly disliked her *Red House*.[1]

In a pecuniary sense, the novel must have been well worth her while, for although its success in England was small, it was published serially in America in the *Saturday Evening Post,* a journal which paid exceptionally high fees. Mr. Forman wrote affectionately to congratulate her on this profitable arrangement, pointing out what excellent advertisement she would receive through a paper of such an enormous circulation.

Another volume for adults came out at about the same time. This was *Man and Maid,* a further series of short stories, dedicated to Ada Breakell, the friend who had known her since her eighteenth year, and was still in close touch with her. *The Story of the Amulet* now appeared in book form in the usual course, and besides this there was another new tale in her happiest vein, *The Railway Children,*[2] illustrated by C. E. Brock, who had provided drawings for a number of the Bastable stories. The family depicted here is not, perhaps, as skilfully and beautifully drawn as the Bastable family; its adventures are less credible. Nevertheless, it is a most engaging book. To an adult the author may have seemed unduly generous in providing her child characters with opportunities of saving lives and averting disasters of every description, but the readers for whom the tale was intended are not likely to complain about it on that score. The chapter in which the youthful hero and heroines save a train from wreck by waving flags made of red flannel petticoats is

[1] In the same letter Mr. Lang offers her the gift of one of his own tales for children, and adds that "it is . . . like everything of mine, utterly unpopular"—a rather curious assertion.

[2] First produced serially in the *London Magazine,* 1904.

quite superbly written and a masterpiece of its kind. The book has proved highly successful as a television serial.

The same year saw the beginning of another children's serial in the *Strand—The Enchanted Castle*. Good as it is compared with ordinary juvenile fiction, it is not quite in the same rank with the works that preceded it. The writing shows signs of haste, and the magic entanglements are not unravelled with that deftness she had led her admirers to expect. A certain slight falling off may be looked for almost as a matter of course, where an author produces so much and directs his energy towards so many different ends; but what comes as a surprise to the reader who has followed her career through all its phases is the absence of that sensitive touch which, in the earlier stories, constantly suggests the lovableness of the writer. In one of the principal boy characters, Jimmy, the Bastable frankness has degenerated into mere pertness. And there is a servant girl in the story whom the children treat with an unkindness which Oswald Bastable would have been quick to reprove. There is no reason why an author's heroes and heroines should be the mouthpieces of his own sentiments, but as E. Nesbit's obviously were so, or had been until now, the suspicion of hardness one gets here is a matter of some interest.

Another notable feature of the book is that it breaks a rule which she had hitherto always observed in this sort of writing —namely that she should exclude from her pages everything likely to awaken fear. The episode of the Ugly-Wuglies' coming to life, though it is from the adult's point of view one of her most original and amusing conceptions, is rather frightening to children. There is a sort of refinement of horror in the fact that these repellent creatures, whose faces are paper, whose arms and legs are covered hockey-sticks and umbrellas, and whose hands are stuffed gloves, have no roofs to their mouths and are thus only half-articulate.

The Ugly-Wuglies were invented for a game of charades at Dymchurch. One of the scenes to be acted required a larger number of players than were present, and Edith conceived the idea of hastily painting a number of grotesque faces on paper and mounting them upon coat-hangers, on which she hung clothes, and which were disposed about the room in the manner described in the story. It afterwards occurred to her that she might represent them as coming to life in the serial she was working on, and she did so with a realism almost too convincing. H. R. Millar, though he had not seen the original Ugly-Wuglies, portrayed them with remarkable felicity, notwithstanding the great difficulty he found in giving the look of life to creatures who were intended at the same time to look unlifelike. She thought his work for this book the best that he had done.

This was the first and last time E. Nesbit ever sounded any note of horror—and perhaps the word is too strong—in writing for a juvenile audience. For adults, however, she often contrived effects that were, or were intended to be, hair-raising. She had something of a child's morbidity in searching into subjects which she herself found terrifying. Like a little girl fascinated with ghost stories whose aftereffects she well knows to be disastrous, she would sit up at night writing tales of violence and death until she was afraid to go to bed. And she would read books and see sights which, as she was fully aware beforehand, were certain to upset her nerves. When in Paris in 1905, she had gone to the macabre waxwork show known as the Musée Grévin, and had afterwards prolonged the nervous repulsion it inspired by writing a short story about a man who had spent a whole night there.

She was always careful, however, as she had promised in her 1897 articles, to protect her children from the alarms she had herself experienced, sometimes using very peculiar means of doing so. Conspicuous in her house, for instance, she had kept for many years a human skull and a little collection of bones. Her reason for tolerating these disagreeable ornaments was that she herself, in childhood, had been liable to fits of terror at the sight of a skeleton, and she had no doubt that, if she familiarized her children with such objects from earliest years, this would be at least one childish fear averted. Her belief proved to be perfectly sound; but perhaps the medicine was rather worse than the disease, since it was forced upon friends whose distaste for these relics was beyond cure.

Her horror stories were probably more disturbing to her than to her readers. They fail to capture the emotions that she is so palpably bent upon arousing, for the same reason that an actor will fail to capture the emotions of his audience when he is so much moved by his part that he loses control of it. The terrors she wrote of were all actively her own. A great many of the stories, for example, concern cataleptic trances and premature burial [3]—a subject which it always distressed her to contemplate: yet she never succeeded in conveying the fear which she is known to have felt herself.

Apart from *The Enchanted Castle,* some magazine stories, and some contributions to Raphael Tuck's books, E. Nesbit published no creative work in 1907; but in January of that year she had a one-act play produced at Maskelyne and Devant's Theatre. It was called *The Magician's Heart,* and was devised to give the celebrated conjurers scope for the performance of "magic." As one who had long been an enthusiastic patron of "London's Home of Magic and Mystery," she must have been delighted with her opportunity of learning something of what went on behind the scenes there.

In the following month her daughter, Iris, was married to John Austen Philips—not auspiciously, as it turned out.

Shortly after the wedding, Edith took another holiday in Paris, and astonished the custodians of the Versailles gardens by paddling in one of the fountains! F. Ambrose Flower, known always to her as Florizel, Prince of Bohemia, was the only one of her four companions who was brave enough to enjoy this adventure with her. Their pleasures were terminated by the gendarmerie after five minutes. On another occasion she caused a disturbance at the Théâtre Comédie Française by going from corridor to corridor, accompanied by the same

---

[3] It is recorded that she had strong reason for a dread of premature burial which amounted at times to an obsession; a relation of hers, possibly one of her grandfathers, had been actually placed in his coffin when it was discovered that he was still breathing.

friend, opening windows because she found the atmosphere stuffy. In every corridor she was told by the military officials that the opening of windows was strictly forbidden, and with each frustration she held on to the curtains with a swaying motion and an alarming expression of being about to faint, while Mr. Flower assured the gendarmes that she was very ill, and must have air. It is not every woman of forty-eight who has the moral courage to gratify such whims as these, but she had not even begun to outgrow the high spirits of childhood, as two or three other anecdotes of this period will reveal.

At Dymchurch Arthur Watts and Gerald Spencer Pryse, another of the young artists to whom she was much attached,[4] had built a raft with pieces of old fencing which they set together and tarred. When it was finished they placed a wicker chair on it and invited E. Nesbit to go for a voyage with them. She readily consented, and when the raft capsized and completely ruined her beautiful and brand-new Liberty dress, quenched all embarrassment with her irresistible laughter.

A little later, when she and the same two friends were about to leave Dymchurch for London, she decided that it would be a splendid adventure—motoring being then in its infancy—to hire a car for the journey. Her companions pointed out that besides themselves and the driver, there were five dogs to be accommodated—two dachshunds which she took everywhere, two greyhounds belonging to Spencer Pryse, and Mr. Watts's bull-terrier. Nothing daunted, she persisted in arranging the trip by motor. It took twelve hours, for the engine failed repeatedly, the tyres were punctured one after another, and the dogs engaged in disturbing fights almost the whole way. The nerves of the others were distinctly rattled, but Edith remained in high good humour from first to last, and protested that she had enjoyed every moment of the day.

On another occasion, when the Dymchurch party included

[4] Commander Watts informed me that he and Spencer Pryse thought nothing of leaving London in the evening and cycling to Dymchurch, taking the whole night for the journey, and arriving early in the morning at E. Nesbit's house, where she would be delighted with them for throwing themselves upon her hospitality.

Gerald Gould, Cecil Chesterton, Clifford Sharp, her son Paul, and several girls, she suggested that they should all go out for a water-picnic. "I can see her now," wrote my informant,[5] "as she sat at breakfast that morning hung with beads and jingling silver bangles, and glowing in a flowery crimson dress like a poppy; and those young men about her all talking and arguing. We had our picnic at Hythe Canal and returned home in the evening—only to learn that there was no dinner! Our hostess had forgotten to order it. Quite unperturbed even by the appearance of several extra visitors, she disappeared while we went to dress, and when we came down, there was a perfect meal ready—an omelette about a yard long and some delicious strange drink with excellent coffee to follow. At about 10 o'clock we all bathed by moonlight."

Dymchurch, as might have been expected, was sometimes shocked by these goings on. E. Nesbit had been known in earlier years to cycle down the sea front in a billowing garment bearing some resemblance to a tea-gown, and even now she could be seen holding conversation with the Vicar from a seat on her rain barrel, her long quill cigarette holder between her lips, or walking about arm-in-arm with the humble woman who did her housework. But by degrees she prevailed over her antagonists, for she proved a useful inhabitant, and, busy as she was, helped to organize amateur theatricals for local causes, and even by strenuous efforts prevailed upon the authorities to give the little town its first dust-cart—the rubbish before her day having been dumped into the sea.

For all the time that she gave to such occupations as I have described—not to speak of the serious business of earning her living—she yet continued to be an omnivorous reader, and beside her bed a curious little assortment of books was always to be found. Nor had she abandoned her habit of writing to the authors whose work had given her most pleasure. Amongst these was William de Morgan whose recently published *Joseph Vance* had excited her highest admiration. He replied to her letter with the note that follows, addressed to "E. Nesbit, Esq."

[5] Mrs. P. T. Heady.

Florence.
7th May, 1907.

My dear Sir,

How can it be anything but a great pleasure to an author to receive a letter like yours to hand, re "Joseph Vance"?

The book has been, in one sense certainly, a great success; I mean that (judging from my correspondence) it has found so many readers who have read it more than once. One such reader is worth a thousand who never open a book twice.

Very likely my not knowing your work is only part of a huge and disgraceful ignorance of what is going on in letters. My excuse is that I have passed a life-time in other pastures.

Thanking you cordially, believe me, Dear Sir,

Yours very truly,
Wm. De Morgan.

Whether she ever met Mr. De Morgan I am unable to say, but she certainly sent him copies of some of her own works, and was appreciated in her turn, as may be seen from another letter of his already quoted.

She was soon to have an excellent opportunity of making approaches that needed no apology to the writers whose talent she found congenial: for towards the end of 1907 she became joint editor with three others of a periodical of short but by no means negligible career.

F. E. Jackson, who was master of the lithography classes at the Central School of Arts and Crafts, had for some time been turning over in his mind a scheme for the production of a college magazine that should be, both as to illustrations and text, a work of lithography. He discussed his idea with Graily Hewitt, the eminent calligrapher, who was one of his colleagues, and who undertook to write the script. The original plan was to make the whole work an affair of the school alone, but as it was discussed with one expert and another, it took on a wider scope. Spencer Pryse suggested a consultation with E. Nesbit, and in due course the prime movers met her at Well Hall, and a definite project was formulated. E. Nesbit was to find contributors and attend to the literary business, Jackson was to organize and to have control of the technical side of the production, Hewitt was to be the calligrapher, and Spencer Pryse the art editor: each of the four agreed to put up a capital of £10. The enterprise was to be in every sense co-operative, the contributors receiving instead of fees a share of such profits as might be earned.

Premises were taken in Royalty Chambers, Dean Street, adjoining the Royalty Theatre. They consisted of a flat which E. Nesbit used as her *pied-à-terre* in London, the rent of which was paid partly by her and partly from the funds of the new quarterly—now christened *The Neolith*. Here, installed in an office, the editorial staff proceeded to send out circulars to prospective subscribers. Several months were spent in preliminary work, and at last in November the first number was issued. It contained seven literary contributions, all printed in Graily Hewitt's beautiful script, and six pictures. The writers were G. K. Chesterton, Bernard Shaw, Selwyn Image, Gerald Gould, Graily Hewitt, E. Nesbit, and Alfred Bland: the artists, Edmund Sullivan, F. Ernest Jackson, A. S. Hartrick, Frank Brangwyn, Charles Sims, and C. Raven Hill.

Mr. Shaw had furnished a witty short story about the reception in heaven of a bishop and a drunken charwoman, and Selwyn Image a short essay on Thomas Bewick. E. Nesbit's own contribution was *The Criminal,* a reminiscence addressed to her dead son, some lines from which have been quoted in an earlier chapter. Mr. Chesterton, Mr. Hewitt, and Mr. Gould had provided her with poems. The magazine was handsomely, even splendidly, produced, and the subscription list, although not large, was adequate to assure the editors that no one, at the worst, would be out of pocket.

The barque had been launched successfully, but not in serenely fair weather. Its various captains had suffered from the effects of many delays and frustrations and there had been a good deal of internal dissension. Edith, who wept easily at all times, shed abundance of tears at editorial meetings. Mr. Hewitt, accustomed to work under what he described as "cut and dried conditions," was harassed by unpunctuality and technical difficulties. Material came in too late, temperamental artists failed to keep their promises, Edith took offence at well-meant criticisms from co-editors, and the atmosphere in the office was often one of storm and stress. But if she sometimes created obstacles, she was also skilful and energetic in surmounting them. Her resilience gave her power to throw off depression and disappointment with surprising ease, and she provided the motive force that made the others willing to continue. For all the discomfort that her fits of weeping caused, her partners were never on seriously bad terms with her: and by the time the first number had come from the press, everyone was ready to attend her party of celebration in good humour. It was a dinner at the Villa Villa Restaurant, followed by games and talk at the flat in Royalty Chambers. About twenty guests connected directly or indirectly with *The Neolith* were present, including most of the artists and writers who had contributed, and everything went off delightfully. But the preparation of the second number involved no less worry and disagreement than the first, although when the magazine eventually reached its small public it showed no falling off in the standard that had been set. The literature was provided by Laurence Housman, Andrew Lang, Lord Dunsany, Wilfrid Wilson Gibson, Robert Hugh Benson, R. Ellis Roberts, and—mysterious as it may seem—Oswald Bastable[6]: the pictures, by George Clausen, Frank Brangwyn, Charles Shannon, Arthur Watts, Spencer Pryse, Oliver Hall, and J. Kerr Lawson. As before, all the writers had been gathered in by E. Nesbit, most of them being friends of hers.

Lord Dunsany alone, I think, had been quite unknown to her until this time. She had approached him as the result of reading his first work, *The Gods of Pegana*. She was, in his own words, "probably his second reader, Spencer Pryse being the first." As his public—again in his own words—"consisted of something

[6] Oswald Bastable was the pseudonym chosen to conceal the identity of Oswald Barron who had been in the habit of comparing notes with E. Nesbit on their respective childhoods, and had thus been indirectly connected with the creation of the Bastable family.

like four people," he was pleased and astonished to receive this encouraging letter from her:

Royalty Chambers,
Dean Street,
Soho.
9th October, 1907.

My dear Sir,

I have just read with deep interest and delight your wonderful "Gods of Pegana" and I venture to ask whether you would consent to contribute to the Neolith. . . .

I enclose our preliminary prospectus. May I add your name —and can you let me have a short story or article (between 800 and 1,000 words) before Christmas? (Or even shorter if you would wish it so.)

So far I have, with one or two exceptions, only asked for contributions from personal friends—but I love your book so much that I cannot bear to let go any chance, however slight, of receiving a contribution from you. If you will give me one I shall be for ever your grateful debtor.

E. Nesbit Bland.

After a little further correspondence [7] Lord Dunsany furnished the desired contribution and received an invitation to lunch at Royalty Chambers. A rather curious circumstance distinguished their first meeting. Lord Dunsany was obsessed just then with the idea of Chronos, whom he had introduced into a good deal of his work as the most important of the gods. While they were sitting at luncheon discussing this favourite subject, the clock on the wall suddenly behaved in the most insane and unaccountable manner. Its hands rushed wildly round and round while a furious whirring noise was heard from within it. Lord Dunsany felt that this desire on the part of Chronos to make himself evident on such an occasion was not without significance. A little while after the luncheon he and Lady Dunsany together paid the first of several visits to Well Hall.

[7] In one of her letters she inquires with typical candour: "Do I address you correctly on this envelope? I am inexperienced in correspondence with Lords."

Another promising young writer to whom E. Nesbit made overtures on behalf of *The Neolith* was Richard Middleton, the poet and essayist whose tragic self-inflicted death in 1911 at the age of twenty-eight was the result of his futile struggle to gain even a bare livelihood from writing. As very few of Middleton's letters have been published, it will perhaps be of interest to his admirers to see one here:

> 45, Lambton Road,
> Raynes Park,
> Wimbledon, S.W.
> 1908.

Dear Mrs. Bland,

Thank you very much for your note; the Neolith passed it on the way, and I feel that I must thank you for having permitted me to enter its sedate pages. (For sedate please read select, my pen wanders.) When I shall have returned to town from these pastoral places, I shall certainly call at Royalty Chambers in the hope of seeing you. I hope the Neolith will continue. It would be a pity if it were to join the dodo and the great auk after a brief but glorious career. It might pay to advertise it in the Studio and the New Age and some of the other papers. A good many people who might have subscribed have never heard of it. But doubtless these things have occurred to you! Meanwhile I hope the rashes grow green in the neighbourhood of Dymchurch.

> Yours sincerely,
> Richard Middleton.[8]

The Neolith's contributors were nearly all to be seen both at Eltham and at Dymchurch from time to time. Henry Savage, Richard Middleton's biographer, recollected going to Dymchurch with him and finding that Joseph Conrad and Percival Gibbon were of the company. E. Nesbit had met Conrad some years before at H. G. Wells's Sandgate house and he had visited her several times, but he was not one of the familiar figures in her circle.

Besides parties at Well Hall and the seaside house, there was now a good deal of entertaining at Royalty Chambers. The

[8] This letter is printed by courtesy of Mr. T. A. Middleton.

company would dine out in Soho and would afterwards adjourn to the flat for charades and music, Edith playing sea-shanties and folk-songs on an old and not very helpful piano. One evening she borrowed a guitar from the foreign proprietor of a restaurant near by, who agreed to lend it on condition that he was invited to the party. I do not imagine that the consent was withheld. Sometimes there were luncheons, the meal being sent up from the nearest restaurant. On one of these occasions a guest of some importance was so late in coming that she decided to begin the meal without him. The principal course was contained in a huge casserole, and this had just been emptied to provide second helpings when the dilatory guest suddenly arrived. No sooner was he heard approaching than the hostess seized all the replenished plates, one after another, and plunged their contents back into the casserole, so that she would not have to confess that there was nothing left to eat.

Towards the middle of 1908 *The Neolith* appeared for the third time. The material was supplied, as to letters, by Richard Whiteing, Cecil Chesterton, Edgar Jepson, V. Mortimer, Denby Hughes, and Oliver Basingstoke, as well as E. Nesbit herself and Gerald Gould, a former contributor: and, as to art, by Walter Sickert, Otto Greiner, Joseph Pennell, "Belleroche," and others who have already been named.

Although their unique venture had met with a very favourable reception, the editors were finding that it involved them in more trouble than its little triumphs repaid, and it was becoming clear that they could not continue it much longer. There was no prospect of monetary gain from a magazine brought out in a manner so costly, and printed by a process both slow and delicate; each issue had been preceded by disagreements and by tearful outbursts on the part of E. Nesbit; Mr. Hewitt was dissatisfied with the technical results obtained from writing by hand on transfer paper; and Mr. Jackson was working on portraits which occupied the greater part of his time. They resigned themselves to bringing out a final issue, thus rounding off a year of interesting but disturbing experiment. The fourth and last number contained literary contributions from Richard

Middleton, Arthur Machen, and John Nicolas, and pictures by Francis Dodd and William Shackleton, besides work of both kinds by some of those who had provided material for earlier issues.

The partnership came to an amicable end. Despite her all too obvious defects as a business woman, E. Nesbit left a strong feeling of regard in the minds of her associates, and their friendship continued until, in the ordinary course, it subsided into passive cordiality.

The time devoted to *The Neolith* had been stolen from more remunerative pursuits, so that E. Nesbit was less productive than usual during the year that the magazine had engaged her; but the theft was very much to her advantage as an artist. *The House of Arden,* a *Strand* serial published in book form at the end of 1908, was little if anything inferior to the best work of four or five years before; the Mouldiwarp was worthy to take his place beside the Phoenix and the Psammead, and the charm of manner which pervaded the earlier books, but which had noticeably declined in certain parts of *The Enchanted Castle,* was once more gratefully in evidence. The second Arden book, *Harding's Luck,* begun a month or two after the first was finished, was as good or, as she herself and many others thought, better than the first. Those faint indeterminate traces which will give away, despite all the author's endeavours, the fact that his story has been written hastily and against the grain, were entirely absent and the tales were dovetailed together more precisely than those of the earlier sequences. Certain features of *The House of Arden* indicate plainly that she had deliberated the plot of *Harding's Luck* many months before she came to write it—an unfamiliar course for her.

The only works published in 1908 besides *The House of Arden* were *Ballads and Lyrics of Socialism,* a selection of her propagandist verses brought out under the auspices of the Fabian Society, and the first volume of a series known as the Children's Bookcase, which she edited for the Oxford Press. Her own contribution was *The Old Nursery Tales*—a skilfully revised version of the fairy stories handed down by tradition, with the gruesome parts omitted, and the cruelties and injustices likely to have a bad effect on a child's mind dexterously altered. There was also *Jesus in London,* a single poem printed in pamphlet form with illustrations by Spencer Pryse.[9]

She was preparing other material for the press, however, though not with the same speed and intensity as in former years. There was a novel under construction, and she was at work upon a play, *Absalom,* a verse-drama which she hoped to see on the stage. In November she wrote to Bernard Shaw—with whom, though she had seen little of him since his marriage in 1898, she had never completely lost touch—and asked for advice on the manner of obtaining licence and copyright for it. He replied giving her instructions of a Machiavellian nature, but it does not appear that they were ever carried into effect, and the play was banned by the censor on account of its Biblical characters.

There was possibly another reason besides E. Nesbit's connection with *The Neolith* to account for her comparatively small output during 1907 and 1908. It was at about this period that she inherited from an uncle by marriage the sum of £500—the first money she had possessed since Darcy Reeve's gift of 1892 that had not been earned by her own labour. As she and her husband always lived up to their means, and as the greater part of her writing was admittedly done to fulfil domestic needs, it is not unlikely that the legacy was mainly used as the purchase price of well-earned leisure.

I have had frequent occasion to mention E. Nesbit's habit of making friendly approaches to writers whose talents she considered distinguished. Her judgment seems sometimes to have erred on the side of enthusiasm, but on the whole she was remarkably sensitive in appraising new and curious qualities in

[9] At some later date, she apparently sent a copy of this to Maurice Hewlett, who wrote to say: "Your poem is a fine one—simple, sincere, and perfectly true. And I admire the Steinlenish illustrations." Hewlett (1861–1923) was then very famous as a novelist and essayist. He was an infrequent but appreciative guest at Well Hall.

work that had not yet won general recognition. None of the authors to whom she thus paid tribute failed to achieve the eminence she prophesied, although most of them were then known only to a very small public. The faculty of *self*-criticism was obviously wanting in her; but it says a great deal for her critical faculty in general that when E. M. Forster was still at the beginning of his career, and before he had met with any such almost reverential admiration as he attained later, she wrote to tell him how highly she thought of his ability.

Mr. Forster had written three novels, and it was the newest of them, *A Room with a View,* which inspired the letter she addressed to him. It needed no little discernment at the time for a much older author, bred in an entirely different tradition, to appreciate the fine shades of subtlety, the delicate poise, of work which his own generation took so long to applaud. E. Nesbit was among the very few who perceived immediately that this young author was writing with luminous originality, and her praises, coming at a time when praise was still new to him, were encouraging.

The correspondence she had opened resulted in an invitation to luncheon at the Dean Street flat. Mr. Forster arrived, shy and embarrassed as most people are when called upon to encounter a professed admirer; and the first few minutes were even worse than he had anticipated. In closing a window at her request he overturned with his foot a pile of plates lying on the floor near by. A number of them were broken, and his horror and confusion were beyond words. In despair of putting things right after so bad a beginning, he was picking up the fragments and reiterating his apologies when she surprised him by saying: "Now sit down, and let me tell you what those plates cost!" And then, to his relief, she explained that they were not part of some precious dinner service, but had been bought at the Caledonian Market and could be replaced without the least difficulty.

After this they met or wrote to each other from time to time, and although they never became intimate, they were always on terms of cordiality. It was not until 1911, however, that Mr. Forster visited Well Hall.

In 1908 E. Nesbit made another friend, and one destined to remain so through many vicissitudes. This was Mr. E. N. da C. Andrade,[10] the brilliant young scientist—from whom she attempted, not very successfully, to learn some of the principles of elementary mathematics. Her reason for trying to master a branch of learning so alien to her mental powers was a very extraordinary one. She had become engrossed with the Bacon-Shakespeare theory, had taken the Baconian side, and was endeavouring to prove by numerous ciphers and by the Napierian system of logarithms that Bacon wrote the works of Shakespeare.

When I say that she was endeavouring to prove this, I do not use the phrase with any merely casual significance. She never did anything half-heartedly, and if there was one subject in the world to which she applied herself with her whole heart it was this thankless attempt to set up Bacon in Shakespeare's stead. For a good ten years of her life she devoted time, money, and energy to the working out of theories in the realms of fantasy, and amassing a collection of books on ciphers and secret codes in general. During the First World War she wrote of her study as "a mental narcotic—such as some people find in playing patience"; this was the only benefit she ever derived from an occupation that her friends almost unanimously thought injurious to her work and unworthy of powers essentially creative.

Her first interest in this investigation was said to have been inspired by a propagandist to whom she was attracted—an acquaintance made through her connection with *The Neolith*. Apart from her tendency to make her opinions coincide with her feelings, she was naturally responsive, for all that was childlike in her character inclined eagerly to an hypothesis involving cryptograms, secret societies, and mysteries beyond number.

[10] Professor Andrade, D.Sc., Ph.D., Quain Professor of Physics in the University of London, 1928–50; Emeritus Professor, 1950; Director Royal Institution and Davy Faraday, 1950–52; Royal Society Hughes Medal, 1958.

Very soon she was surrounded by a little regiment of Baconians, certain of whom turned her credulity to their own advantage in diverse ways. One of them, who was supposed to be a great expert on the Baconian title pages and the Droeshout portrait of Shakespeare, was maintained in her flat, and traded upon her good nature for months on end.

As time went on she began to waste whole days on cipher research, deferring the work which she was under obligation to produce until it became necessary to rush it through with even greater haste than was customary; and the indifference or antipathy her friends displayed towards the new hobby horse seriously hurt her feelings. Meanwhile, the theory grew and grew until not only Shakespeare's and Bacon's works but Spenser's *Faerie Queene,* Burton's *Anatomie of Melancholy,* the Authorized Version of the Bible, and much other Elizabethan and early Jacobean literature was drawn in and had to be searched for hidden clues.

Bacon was also supposed to have concerned himself with the invention of Napier's logarithms, and these played a considerable part in her attempts to elucidate the problem. Professor Andrade, himself a student of poetry and a firm Shakespearean, was called upon to help her in the application of mathematics to the solving of imagined ciphers, and no amount of gently expressed doubt, even from this accomplished mathematician, could prevail over her faith. She would demand that a series of numbers should be unquestioningly subjected to certain processes, explaining that *she* would deal with the result. By bringing logarithms (which she could never understand) to bear upon sequences of letters in Sonnet CV, for example—which contains the passage beginning " 'Fair, kind and true,' is all my argument"—it was possible to make out various fragmentary statements, such as "I am F. B." or "I am Fras B." or "I am hog" or "F. Ba is W. Sha"; or, from other verses, she might deduce the number 1623 (the date of the first folio) or 1616 (the date of Shakespeare's death). But the results were far from conclusive, since the system often gave alternatives of eight different letters for one in the original.[11] Quite undaunted, she continued to choose whatever letter fitted in with the result she was aiming at.

Letters, again, could always be replaced by numbers and numbers by letters. B could, if necessary, count as 13, because 13 looks like B, and so forth. Yet the reward of all this ingenuity after several days of concentrated work, would be nothing better than some such unconvincing phrase as I have quoted. The books she felt obliged to buy were no light tax upon her purse. She was not content to work from a later reprint of Napier's *Mirifici Logarithmorum Canonis Descriptio,* but insisted upon possessing a copy of the 1614 edition, an extremely scarce and costly book; and many others not less rare were sought for and purchased. She studied Latin, too, in order to read familiarly the works supposed to be significant.

J. C. Squire,[12] another staunch anti-Baconian, often argued with her into the small hours, trying to convince her on literary grounds of the futility of her quest. On one occasion when he was staying at Well Hall he sat with her till two in the morning while she worked out a Bacon "proof" which rested on the assumption that four thirteens made forty-two. On his pointing out that her calculation was fallacious, she was surprised but not in the least shaken.

Yet another observer, John Bland's young tutor, George Scaver, a warm admirer, was embarrassed when she tried to enlist him as her amanuensis in her incessant work on illusory

[11] "She was by nature quite incapable of mastering the meaning of mathematical symbols and arguments," Professor Andrade explains, "and for a long time based theories on the supposition that the incommensurable number e was 2.7182, whereas these are but the first five figures of a number that can be worked out to as many as thirty decimal figures, and actually 2.7183 is a closer approximation than 2.7182. When she was told that the base of Napier's own system of logarithms was not e (strictly speaking his logarithms do not admit of a base), the reciprocal of this number was, by a misunderstanding, exalted into the position of the key number. As the figures were frequently copied down wrongly, this did not make as much difference as might be supposed."

[12] Subsequently Sir John Squire, poet and editor of *The London Mercury.*

ciphers, and amazed that so much knowledge of Shakespeare's plays could go with such "naive ingenuity in fitting facts to theories."

Many years after this sort of research had become an obsession, she applied to Bernard Shaw for the use of his facsimiles of the Shakespeare folios. He then had an opportunity of seeing what effect this long and arduous pursuit had had upon her, and came independently to the conclusion that it was responsible for many of the financial difficulties that embarrassed her last days.

16   *Last Edwardian and First Georgian Impressions*

In 1909 normal literary activity was for a time resumed. The novel begun in the preceding year was finished and went to press, the publisher being George Allen and Unwin; a small collection of stories about children, written at various earlier times, was brought out by the same firm under the title of *These Little Ones;* another book for adults—a thriller called *Salome and the Head*—was written for Alston Rivers; and *Harding's Luck* was running in the *Strand Magazine.* Neither of the novels was in any sense worthy of her genius. There was far less attempt to achieve credibility in them than in her books for children, where everything was at least consistent within its own world; the love scenes were conventional and forced in tone; and the action mechanical to a quite amazing degree. In the first of these two books, *Daphne in Fitzroy Street,* there is a child character whose every word and act belong to the sphere of palpable fiction. Even her natural aptitude for portraying children seems to have deserted her when she had an adult audience in view.

Salome and the Head, reprinted five years later by George Newnes as *The House with No Address,* was written, so she told her brother, "for £200 down (on account of royalty) and finished and typed in exactly 30 days!" It is easy to believe on reading it that she was speaking no more than the plain truth. She added that she thought it had "a few nice things in it." It also contained some things that were not at all nice. The inspiration for the plot was evidently drawn from the sensation caused by Maud Allan's first season at the Palace Theatre, when she performed a dance in the role of Herod's daughter, carrying a head upon a platter. E. Nesbit's heroine was likewise a fashionable young dancer, and the performance attributed to her was clearly based upon Maud Allan's. But the dancer in the book, by a series of unconvincing machinations, is tricked one night into dancing with the real head of a murdered man and is afterwards isolated with it in a remote and fearful house. The author's determination to make the reader's flesh creep is too obvious to result in success. The story is unusually "horrible" for its period, and yet it fails to achieve the desired effect.

It is pleasant to turn from this rather unattractive aspect of her employments to another much more likely to fulfil the expectations of her admirers—her affection and kindness towards children. I have said that she made a point of replying to all who wrote to tell her how much they loved her books.[1] Sometimes she sought them out and made friends with them. And by good fortune—for nothing can be more interesting than her relations with the readers who won from her the best she had to give—I am able to trace the whole course of such a friendship (one, too, which ended only with E. Nesbit's life) and even to quote a vivid impression of her recorded in a child's diary.

In 1909 she received an admiring letter from three children named Mavis, Kathleen, and Cecily; the reply she sent was apparently lost in the post, and they wrote to her again. Her answer was in a style much livelier than that rather terse and detached tone she usually reserved for correspondence.

---

[1] She kept a great many of their letters, most of which are amusing and some very touching. One was addressed to Oswald Bastable, Esq., 150 Lewisham Road, S.E.! The writer was a little girl who imagined that she was addressing the authentic Oswald. Some kindly grown-up had placed the letter in a second envelope before sending it.

My Dears,

I *did* write to you, in answer to your other letters. I wonder what became of *my* letter? Perhaps it perished in one of those conflagrations caused by bad boys who drop lighted fuses into pillar boxes. Or perhaps it was delivered at your house and was put in a drawer and then slipped over the back edge into the house the drawer lives in, and when the housemaid found it at spring cleaning time she thought it was an old letter and put it in the dustpan. But I suppose we shall never know. Its fate will remain forever a mystery like that interesting affair of the Man with the Iron Mask, or that never-really solved question "What became of the little Dauphin?"

I am very pleased to have your letters, and to know that you like my books. You are quite right to like Kingsley and Dickens and George Macdonald better than you like me, my dear Cecily. There is one other person whose books you ought to like better than mine—and that is Mrs. Ewing. Oh—and Hans Andersen is another. If I had a magic carpet I would lend it to Kathleen for a month. Then you could all come and see me on it, and that would be jolly for all of us. I wish Mavis could have magic adventures like my children: the best I can do for her is to call the next child I write about Mavis.[2] . . .

Your loving friend,
E. Nesbit.

The children, who were cousins, continued to write during their Christmas vacation. Then school-life was resumed, and the rest of the story—or as much of it as can be included in this chapter—appears in the little journal to which I have made reference. It was kept by Mavis,[3] who was at a boarding school in Folkestone. The extracts are from the entries for February and early March, 1910.

On Saturday 19th I was very happy and before tea was sent up to draw or read or talk to my friend Eileen in the Arts and Crafts Room, then presently we were told to go and get ready for tea, I

---

[2] She did not forget the promise. The heroines of *Wet Magic,* the last of her long tales for children, were called Mavis and Kathleen.
[3] Miss Mavis Carter.

went to the door and Miss Ethel . . . said to me in a very matter of fact voice "Mavis you are to go and get tidy to see your Mother." "My mother"?!—!? I said and flew downstairs to be made tidy. . . . I really was never so surprised in my life. I thought Mother was at Home and she is staying at Folkestone, and I shall see her every Sat or Sunday—and its perfectly delightful ——— and when I went, Father was staying there, he may be there still for all I know and there was love and chocolate cake and next Sat I shall see them again an' everything's jolly and rose-coloured. . . .

This diary is only about true events but I'm going to write something which happened to me on the 12th [of March] that at the time seemed so like a dream I could hardly believe it.

Well it was dear Mother's last Sat. here and at lunch Miss Ethel gave me a rowing about going and seeing Mother last Sat in a dirty blouse and told me I was to wear a silk one when I went out at 12 with Mother.

I felt cross but when Mother came to fetch me I cheered up. Mother looked awfully excited. Mavis! she said we are going to see E. Nesbit and have lunch with her now! We got into a carriage and had a ten mile drive to Dymchurch and on the way I besieged Mother with questions and she told me how it had happened. She had sent my photo to E. Nesbit and told her how happy it made me to be at school in the Nesbit county and the answer was a wire reply paid Can you come to lunch with me tomorrow 1.30.

So when we got there oh! well. She *was* a dear—rather stout, jolly brown eyes and brown hair and a funny old fashioned house. Of course I felt rather shy at first, but one doesn't feel like that long with Her.

We had dinner with a dear Puppy scrambling all over the place and then we went a walk [.] Mother and E. N.'s secretary went on the sands. E. N. and I talked she was glorious she gave me one of her books and wrote in it and sent Kay [Kathleen] a photo. At last we had to go and we drove away blowing kisses and I was the happiest girl in the world.

Things E. N. said to me

"There are two kinds of naughtiness one is being mean, and the other is carelessness."

"I like 'the Amulet' very much. I was reading it the other day and found it quite amusing." [4]

"If it hadn't been for Cromwell England certainly wouldn't be the country it is now." ["This," Miss Carter explains, "was because I, a Roundhead in those days, ardently defended my hero of the moment to her. I often wonder if she was being mildly sarcastic at my expense, and meant it ironically."]

Miss Carter's comments on this memorable occasion, examined later in perspective, are illuminating. Her picture tallies well with that of many adult observers:

I see her now as she stood in the doorway of that house at Dymchurch . . . her untidy brown hair pinned up in curls that were always coming down—the eternal cigarette—the trailing Liberty frock of some lovely faded colour, and her brown eyes looking at you over the spectacles—looking at you through and through; the meal to charm a child's heart, the country chicken "with its boots on," lots of bread sauce, and chocolate mould; a puppy . . . to set one's shyness at ease—the immediate feeling that here was a grown-up child to play with, and yet a very awe-inspiring person too.

There was another lovely time when she came to Edgbaston in 1911 or 1912 (I think) and stayed with her niece Dorothea Deakin, whose husband took us out in his car. . . . It was blazing summer, and there was much discussion as to appropriate garb for the occasion. We three children eventually went in bright coloured linen frocks and sun-bonnets to match—which delighted E. N., who deplored for the rest of the drive the fact that, while *we* were all in sun-bonnets *she* was in a little motor bonnet bought for the great event, and which she didn't like at all. We went to Leicester's Hospital and Warwick Castle and Guy's Cliff and Stratford, where she thought it very wrong that one had to pay sixpence to see Shakespeare's church. And we all had a picnic tea. Certainly the day remains one of the happiest I have ever known.

---

[4] The little girl was very much astonished at the idea of an author's reading one of her own books, just as if it had been written by some other hand, and finding it "amusing."

Early in 1910 E. Nesbit undertook to provide a weekly article for children in the *Daily Chronicle* describing the games and adventures of her own childhood. In a letter to Mavis Carter she says:

> What sort of stuff do you think children would like? And will you tell me whether you ever skip any parts of my books? And if so, what parts do you skip? Write me a letter full of information, won't you? And *soon*.

It will be seen from this passage that she was, as I have already indicated, far readier to accept criticism of the work she did well than the work in which she must, however she disguised it from herself or others, have felt to some degree uncertain of her ability. Her own family was at all times permitted to express opinions of her children's stories quite freely. Sometimes their judgment was harsh but she never resented it. On the other hand, adverse comments on her poetry or novels were not taken in such good part.

The terms on which she stood with her children and adopted children as she and they grew older are rather difficult to define. There was a good deal of inconsistency in her behaviour here as in other matters. Passionately affectionate, she yet had certain formal and forbidding qualities which kept her family aloof from her. She loved to be embraced, but she did not care to be ruffled. Even her caresses had an element of aloofness. Again, broad-minded as she was in theory, and usually in practice, she was capable of sudden fits of prudery. Encouraged at one moment to be independent in thought and action, at another the children would find themselves in her bad graces for some such mild offence against the conventions as she herself, in her youth, had committed time without number. There is one instance of this disparity between principle and practice which, though it belongs to a period much earlier than that I am writing of, is sufficiently typical of her conduct in general to be worth quoting.

Her daughter Iris, when fourteen or fifteen years old, had been invited by a very harmless youth to go to a performance at the Queen's Hall. Edith suddenly took it into her head that it would be improper for the young pair to attend the concert, and to Iris's enormous disappointment, forbade her to go. Meeting with a strenuous opposition to such an unjust decree, she eventually permitted the engagement to be kept on the understanding that the boy's sister should accompany him—a condition which involved a good deal of embarrassing inconvenience. The incident is trivial, but not irrelevant.

Left to herself, she might have been not less genuinely unconventional as a mother than she was as a friend, but Hubert Bland held nearly all the orthodox views on the upbringing of growing daughters—at least, his own—as may be seen from his many essays on the subject of feminine propriety; and his wife almost invariably paid deference to his judgments. He was on the side of "good appearances." And so she whose book heroines were always throwing off chaperonage and insisting on the right to "live their own lives," by no means approved these sentiments in her daughters.

Both the girls were now married, however, and only one child was left at Well Hall. In the autumn of 1909 Rosamund had become the wife of Clifford Sharp, a family friend of three years' standing. At the time of the wedding E. Nesbit had written Lord Dunsany to say that life seemed all packing and unpacking and that waves of straw and tissue paper surged around her. But wedding preparations did not loom so large in her affairs as if she had been an ordinarily feminine matchmaking woman. Formal as she could become where one might have expected informality, she was a little unworldly and bewildered when called upon to play the conventional role of a bride's mother. As for match-making, no occupation could have been less congenial to her. There was no marriage in her family which she had raised a finger to bring about; indeed, her activities generally tended in the direction of frustrating matrimonial designs whenever she suspected them—and not always, it is thought, to the advantage of the persons concerned.

Concerning love affairs, mothers, it may be supposed, seldom receive the confidences of their daughters, and E. Nesbit, for all her vivacity and the general youthfulness of her outlook, was no exception to this rule. Becoming suddenly aware perhaps that she might enter into the spirit of Rosamund's courtship a little more fully than she had so far tried to do, she once asked her with a mixture of shyness and motherly interest whether her young lover had kissed her. On being told that he had, she paused a moment and then enquired solicitously "And was it *satisfactory?*"

She was more at ease with her children when they were still small and dependent, but even here she could not always be said to resemble the serenely kind and competent young matron who appears as mother, aunt, or temporary guardian in so many of her works. If that delightful woman was a projection of herself, as many readers have thought, it was an idealized projection. She had all the charm of the mother of the Railway Children or the Bastables' Mrs. Leslie, but she had not the patience to be uniformly tactful with a family whom she saw every day.

She did not respect her children's right to privacy, and at times her apparently wanton curiosity alienated confidence. Yet she ardently desired confidence and was wounded if it was withheld. As a companion she was all that youth or childhood could desire; as a parent she constantly defeated her own generous ends. She loved giving presents and delightful surprises, but sometimes spoiled the savour of the gift by a too obvious demand for gratitude: she threw open her house to her children's friends as to her own friends, and yet she was capable of distressing them and their guests by those sudden displays of illtemper which young minds cannot readily understand and pardon. Wonderful as her memory was for the emotions of childhood, there was one thing which she seldom seemed to remember—a child's self-consciousness.

Often this forgetfulness went hand in hand with the kindliest intentions. When, for example, Well Hall garden yielded more flowers than could possibly be used in the house, or when there had been a dinner party with lavish floral decorations which were no longer needed, John Bland and any friends who hap-

pened to be with him, would be sent down to the gate with bas-
kets of roses, which they were instructed to give to passers-by.
It would be hard to think of any pleasanter idea than this, but in
making the children her emissaries she overlooked the fact that
they felt "silly" in approaching strangers with unlooked-for
offerings. Her family were often asked to do things that made
them feel "silly," and though doubtless the effect in the long
run was to give them a moral courage, a mental independence,
well worth the price they paid, there were occasions when her
demands seemed unmaternally selfish.

Two or three further anecdotes touching her conscious kindness and unconscious or half-conscious cruelty may be told appropriately here, though in the sequence of time, their place is
slightly later.

John Bland had been out on some excursion with a friend,
and had arrived home rather late for the evening meal—than
which few transgressions could be more serious. She was cold
and brusque not only to John but to his companion, casting
over both boys one of those "blights" that only adults—brave
adults, too—could afford to smile at. Later in the evening, while
still under pain of her displeasure, John had the misfortune to
upset a vase of flowers. Thinking his friend, Stephen, responsible for this accident, in itself very trifling, she turned upon him
sharply and upbraided him in terms that drew a natural remonstrance from John. Much offended she retired majestically to
her study, leaving two wrathful boys behind her. Suddenly
Stephen had a happy inspiration. He went after her and reminded her with all the eloquence in his power that she was
being *inhospitable:* she was treating him discourteously, and he
was her guest. There was no better way in the world of appealing to her finest qualities. Hospitality was sacred; Admetus
himself could scarcely have placed a higher value on the claims
of a guest. She burst into tears of real penitence, and the rest of
the evening was spent in making handsome amends.

The boy who had the courage to face her with a just reproach
could not fail to command her affection. Stephen Chant as he
grew up was numbered among her friends. While he was still
at school she once sent him an invitation to Dymchurch which he

was obliged to refuse on account of being short of the pocket-money to cover the expense of the journey. He did not confess this as his reason, but she quickly divined it, and wrote again to insist that he must be her guest from Victoria Station, adding, as a salve to youthful pride, that when she was old and in the workhouse he should bring her "little quids of tobacco."

But acts of the most exemplary graciousness were often succeeded by others ruthlessly inconsiderate. There was a holiday that John and his friend had been much looking forward to, and which was rendered even more inviting by fine weather. E. Nesbit chose this day of all days to set them to the unwelcome task of repairing two tumble-down pigsties that she had made some years before with her own hands—to her lasting satisfaction, though they never served the purpose for which they were intended. Protest was useless; she had impulsively renewed her determination to keep pigs: and the two boys were obliged to spend the precious hours in labour they knew was destined to be wasted. The pigsties, as they foresaw, continued empty.

For all these perplexing whims, she was devotedly loved by many children. It is easy to forgive an unkind caprice when the offender is willing to admit the wrong and, moreover, to be openly repentant. E. Nesbit never pretended to be sacrosanct even outside the circle of those daily associates who would have seen through the pretence. A letter of what was—for her—very unusual length, addressed to Mavis Carter, shows that she was not unconscious of her besetting faults, and that if she allowed them to prevail it was rather because they were stronger than herself than for want of taking thought. I am glad to quote it, for it is the only one I have seen, belonging to adult years, that touches even distantly upon religion—a matter on which she was always exceedingly private. The sentiments are couched in language fitted to the comprehension of a child who had confided in her, but there is no reason to assume that they were other than sincere:

My dear [she writes], I know what it is to have a temper: I've had a long and hard fight with my own. One thing I think one can do is always to say one's sorry directly one *is* sorry. Because sometimes, right in the middle of a quarrel one feels "How silly!" or "What a beast I'm being" and yet one goes on quarrelling because one doesn't know how to stop. Stop at once: say "I'm sorry." If the other quarrelling person hasn't reached the being-sorry stage it will perhaps say "Oh yes—it's all very well—you always *are* sorry when it's too late" or something like that, which makes one long to say every disagreeable thing one ever thought of in one's life. But its better not to say them. Its better to say nothing. And take what the other person may say, in *its* temper, as a little penance for losing your own.

Losing one's temper is a sort of madness, and the moment you are sane again *stop the row,* no matter how nasty the other person may be about it. I know all this is easy to say, and jolly hard to do. But you have to try, and to try every day. I find it helps if you just say in the morning "Dear God I don't want to lose my temper today, and you're going to help me, and I'm not going to lose it—am I?" And at night—if you haven't succeeded as you meant to succeed own that you've failed—and tell yourself that tomorrow you aren't going to fail.

About your Mother and doing things for her—I can only say that since my Mother died things come back to me from years ago—little things that I might have done for her and did not do. And I would give the world if I had done those little things. On the other hand Mothers understand a great deal, and make enormous allowances.

Sometimes, I know, one tries to be extra nice, and then everything goes wrong, and the people one is trying to be nice to misunderstand and don't appreciate. But God understands and He is pleased.

You know when people are very clever and very athletic everyone admires their feats. And people don't mind saying "I took a first class at Oxford" or "I won the two mile handicap"—but no one thinks of saying "I have been good" or "I am good"—the only person you can say that to is God.—It's a great mistake to think that one ought only to talk to God about one's sins, or when one wants something. He is our Father, and He is pleased and proud of us when we come to him and say "Dear Father, I have tried to be good today, and you have helped me, and I think I have been good. Thank you dear Father"—

You *did* ask me, didn't you? If you hadn't, of course I wouldn't have written what looks very like a "preachy" letter.

The little sermon was clearly the result of self-examination. She was not the sort of adult who would preach to a child of virtues that she did not think it worth while to aspire to herself. Her practice often fell far beneath her aspirations, but her failures were at least as grievous to her as to those who felt the sting of her sharp tongue and the injustice of decisions made when she was out of temper. If she exacted much she gave back more. Ill humours came and went, but the sparkling stream of gaiety, ingenuity, generosity was never quenched for long. Her quick anger soon melted into repentance. Her capacity for enjoyment was measureless; and when she set aside her work to play with a child, she played not as an adult pleasantly condescending, but as another child released from bondage.

"I remember," Margaret Bondfield wrote to me, "calling at the Moat House one day when she was playing with some children. They were building a wonderful house with such immense attention to detail—no scamp work allowed—and she identified herself so completely with the feeling that to build that house securely on the best possible plan was a matter of supreme importance. . . . Her marvellous understanding of the young child mind is the most vivid impression she left on me."

This childlike aspect of her character—for she understood children with a fellow feeling rather than with the detachment of a psychologist—made her the most charming of guests to people of a congenial turn of mind. Most of her friends naturally were thus congenial, and none more so than Lord and Lady Dunsany, who welcomed her and John at Dunsany Castle at the beginning of 1910. They were not less eager to play than she was, nor did it distress them to have their drawing-room turned upside down so that she might make what she called "a magic city" there.

This was the month in which her serial, *The Magic City,* was begun in the *Strand;* and to build little towns out of all sorts of objects, useful and ornamental, like the boy hero of the book,

was now a favourite occupation. Lord Dunsany also had a flair
for this sort of building, and they were able to compare notes on
the respective merits of clay bricks in the garden or wooden
blocks indoors. But these were merely the basis; decorative
effects were obtained with dominoes and chessmen, boxes,
books, silver candlesticks, little ivory figures, and brass bowls
and ash-trays. "A room," as Lord Dunsany explained to me, "is
full of miniature domes and cupolas if you turn things the
wrong way up." The material for the new story took shape,
very literally, at the Irish castle. The evenings were spent in
charades, and such games as hide-and-seek and writing contests,
and altogether the holiday was one after Edith's own heart, as
her letter written the day after her return to England will show:

My dear Lady Dunsany,
    The sea was very rough, and the wind was very cold, and it
rained a little, and hailed a little, and everything was detestable;
and we were sorry because we were coming away from you, so
the whole thing was in keeping. We spent the night at Holyhead,
in perhaps the worst hotel in Europe, and thought of you and
talked of you, and wished that we were again where we had so
happily been. We reached home in time for dinner last night, and
John is already arranging to have the picture of your joyous
Castle framed for his room.
    Gracious and dear Lady, it is not possible to thank you ade-
quately for all the kindness with which you wrapped us round
while we were in your house. But we shall never forget it.
    Please bring us to the kind remembrance of Lord Dunsany.
John sends you his love. And I, if I may, send you mine.
Yours,
E. Nesbit Bland.

Magic cities continued to be built even after the book about
them was finished, and she became so adept in constructing
them that one of them was exhibited very successfully to the
public at Olympia. The source of the book's inspiration was, I
conjecture, Dr. Hoffmann's story about a boy called Reinhold
who built a little town of toys which grew larger and larger

until it reached full size and the inhabitants were as big as himself. She had used the bare outline of it a dozen years before in a short story called *The Town in the Library in the Town in the Library,* with Rosamund and Fabian, under their own names, as the two adventurers; and now it was dexterously elaborated.

It cannot be said that *The Magic City,* notwithstanding the competence of its style and the novelty of its matter, stands on the same high level of excellence as her eight or nine best books. The construction is somewhat loose and rambling, and there are passages which seem to indicate that the author was taking the easy rather than the interesting course. For the first time too—unless I am guilty of some oversight—she begins to obtrude personal reminiscences to the detriment of her artistry, and this was a habit which persisted and increased in nearly all her subsequent work. The Bastable books had consisted very largely of personal reminiscences, but they were so transmuted in the recounting that they appear as fiction convincingly written. Now, however, that she was actually writing fiction, she would interrupt her narrative to bring in recollections extraneous to the theme. *The Magic City* was only slightly marred by this new fault; later it became disconcertingly noticeable.

She had always been inclined to introduce into her stories references to matters which engrossed her—Socialism in particular—but she had done so with an adroitness which disarmed criticism. By degrees the habit grew upon her until any perceptive reader might easily have formed a pretty clear idea of numerous likes and dislikes of hers in no way relevant to her subject matter. One would need to be fairly obtuse not to gather, from the study of two or three of her later books together, that she was a Socialist, a Baconian, and a resister of the Women's Suffrage movement. *The Magic City* itself, though intended for children, contains a cut at the women who were then fighting so vigorously for equal franchise. The "Pretenderette" is an obvious caricature of a militant suffragette. The behaviour of certain feminine agitators was exciting derision at that time all over the country, and E. Nesbit showed no greater sympathy towards them than was felt by women whose political views were less advanced than hers. Nevertheless, two or three of her friends were of opinion that she was by no means opposed to the breaking down of sex barriers on principle, and might have taken part in the movement herself had it not been for Hubert Bland's influence.[5] A letter of hers seems to confirm this view. Miss Evelyn Sharp [6] had written to her to suggest that she should sign an authors' memorial to the Prime Minister, asking him to allow facilities for the passage into law of the Conciliation Bill for Women's Suffrage—a measure which, if it had succeeded, would have given the vote to about a million women. E. Nesbit sent the following reply:

13th June, 1910.

Dear Miss Sharp,

   I am sorry I cannot sign the enclosed Memorial as it does not embody my views. I am for adult Suffrage, but primarily my political interest is all for Socialism, and I do not wish Socialism to be endangered by an extension of the franchise to a class of women mainly Conservative.

Yours sincerely,
E. Nesbit Bland.

This very concise explanation savours more of Hubert Bland's manner than his wife's. His politics were coolly reasoned, hers emotional. Although it is probable that she would have taken an ardent interest in social reform whatever sphere of life she had lived in, it does not seem as if, without Hubert Bland's guidance, she would have been likely to attach herself unequivocally to a political party and call her social creed by a definite name. But whether it came naturally to her to be concerned with politics or not, once having made her profession, she was consistent in it. At Lord Dunsany's house in London,

[5] See note concerning Mr. Laurence Housman and the Women's Suffrage movement on p. 116.
[6] Evelyn Sharp (1869–1955), journalist and author of a large number of novels and books for children; prominent in the Women's Suffrage and other political movements and twice imprisoned. She married Henry W. Nevinson, the war correspondent.

many years after she had ceased to take an active part in the enterprises of the Fabian Society, she met the poet, W. B. Yeats, who had known her in the early Fabian days. He asked her if she had entirely dropped out of the Society, and she protested almost vehemently that, on the contrary, she still took a zealous interest in it.

Capricious as she was in practice, and quickly as one enthusiasm was supplanted by another and then revived again, I have not yet come upon any instance of her wavering in a single one of her more serious beliefs.

17 The Decline of Prosperity—
Hubert Bland's Death

Hubert Bland had long been suffering from a diseased heart, and at the end of 1910 his health broke down so completely as to leave little prospect of its ever being fully restored. In the New Year he went with his wife to Looe in Cornwall to get the benefit of the mild air there, and she wrote to several friends expressing her fervent gratitude for his improved condition; but soon after his return to London he began to have serious trouble with his eyesight, and between this and the low state of his health in general, he was obliged to give up some of his work, and to resign the office he had held in the Fabian Society for twenty-seven years.

In the spring, E. Nesbit, desiring a change from Dymchurch, took as her seaside retreat Crowlink Farm House, at East Dene, between Eastbourne and Seaford, a very pretty and ancient place lying on the downs, yet only half a mile from the shore. It was of substantial size, providing bedroom accommodation for twelve and various amenities she had not been able to boast at Dymchurch. "Part of the house is Tudor and part earlier," she wrote to her brother, perhaps not quite accurately, and added proudly, "it used to be a smugglers' retreat." She was delighted with her find, and having nailed charms over all the doors to keep away evil spirits (for she was superstitious to an extreme degree), she settled down to intermittent residence for five or six years, sometimes letting the house during holiday seasons when she could not leave London herself. Maurice Hewlett was one of her tenants.

Meanwhile, she was working, not with the same intensity as formerly, but harder and better than she had worked for some little time past. In the previous year her only publication, apart from *The Magic City* and her weekly contribution to the *Chronicle,* had been a dozen or so of horror stories, some of them first printed a good while before, gathered together under the title *Fear.* Now with revived energy she set about a novel, a new serial for children, a volume of poems, and the usual amount of miscellaneous work.

The novel, *Dormant,* was perhaps the most efficiently written of all her books for adults, not excluding the much more popular *Red House.* It was a sort of combined romance and thriller with a plot so frankly fantastic that one does not feel as strongly inclined to grumble at its improbabilities as in reading the stories she based upon conventional themes. The interest was far better sustained than in any other novel of hers, past or to come, the central characters were more like real men and women; and the love scenes less often cheapened by that "bantering playfulness" which, though occasionally admired, was oftener deplored.

Magic and near-magic play a large part in the story, and she was so much more at ease in handling these fanciful materials than in drawing from the common stock of not very ambitious novelists, that one wonders why she spent so much time in trying—as she had tried when a child—"to write like everybody else."

On receiving the proofs of the new book she wrote to Lady Dunsany:

My dear Lady Dunsany,
    Here is the proof of Dormant. Will it be too much trouble for you to look through it and to let me know if you see any reason why I should not have the pleasure of dedicating it to you? Also if

I've made footmen or butlers do anything foreign to their beautiful natures will you please tell me?

We have been making a chart of the moat, with soundings, and
buoys and creeks and shoals and things named after the people
we like who have been on the moat. We have the Lady Beatrice's
Haven. I hope you don't mind. We couldn't put Lady Dunsany's
Haven very well, because we have a great tract of country in quite
another part called Dunsania, and far inland on that happy shore
are all the beautiful cities of which Lord Dunsany is the architect.
Jimmy [1] has made the chart; it is a thing of beauty—and I wish
you could see it. John and I send our love.

> Yours,
> E. Nesbit Bland.

The passage about the Well Hall moat calls for a double
comment. It was to her the foremost of all the delights that the
house afforded—not merely as an interesting relic of bygone
times, but as a sort of glorified toy. She would sail miniature
yachts on it, or float round it in a punt for hours at a time, her
pad of writing paper on her knee, her attention divided between
her task and the sheer enjoyment of her favourite element. Her
friends, too, were encouraged to consider the moat as a retreat
for work or pleasure. J. C. Squire, to name but one, was accustomed to make for this cool, dark stream, with its overhanging
boughs, trailing grasses, and straggling barbed stems of black-
berry, on every possible occasion. That the moat should be
charted and its features named after honoured friends was a
typical Nesbit fancy. Nicknames were very much to her mind.
She was fond of re-christening places, things, and people, and
the names she gave them had a way of becoming fixed.

She herself was almost invariably called by one of two titles—
"Madame" and "Duchess." Why the first was given I have not
learned; as the mode of address used for royal ladies, it had no
doubt the significance of homage. The second was originated
during the Paris holiday of 1905. E. Nesbit was in the habit of
sending little notes by hand to her friends asking them to come
round to her flat for coffee, and Berta Ruck, quoting—or, if she

[1] Horace Horsnell.

will forgive my pedantry, misquoting—from *Alice in Wonderland,* would exclaim: "Ah, an invitation from the Duchess!" The pet-name derived from this allusion remained in use for many years.

In 1911 Mr. E. M. Forster paid his first, and, I think, his only visit to Well Hall. He had recently brought out *The Celestial Omnibus*—the first volume of his short stories—to which he makes oblique reference in a letter [2] concerned with E. Nesbit's work:

Weybridge.
22, 5, 11.

Dear Mrs. Bland,

How very kind of you to send me the Other Omnibus. I enjoyed it so much, and of the other stories was particularly delighted with The Town in the Library, in —. I tried in yet another to trace resemblance between Denis and Daisy who were of royal birth and Denis and Daisy who came with an Aunt that memorable day, but concluded that I did not see any.[3] Thank you so much; we have enjoyed the book greatly.

I should very much like to come to Well Hall, but fear it cannot be for the Wed. night, as you so kindly suggest, since my class ends late in the evening. Perhaps I might come down some Wed. afternoon, rather later on in the year. Considering the only social action I have yet performed in your presence was to smash a pile of plates, I take it very kind of you to imagine me in the midst of butlers and valets. Perhaps, though, they have rendered me unaccustomed to handle plates. I will leave it there.

Again thanking you—and I am so glad that you liked my short stories—

I remain,
Yours sincerely,
E. M. Forster.

[2] Printed by kind permission of the writer.
[3] The "Other Omnibus" was *Nine Unlikely Tales,* E. Nesbit's book of short stories first printed ten years before; "The Town in the Library in the Town in the Library" was the tale which was later elaborated into *The Magic City;* the two pairs of children named Daisy and Denis were the prince and princess in "Fortunatus Rex & Co.," and the cousins who made their inauspicious appearance in the first chapter of *The Wouldbegoods.*

At the period of Mr. Forster's visit, the making of "magic cities" had given place for a time to another and still more curious pastime. E. Nesbit had always felt a passionate detestation of modern industrial and speculative building—so much so, indeed, that there is scarcely a single prose work of hers, either for adults or for children, that does not contain some indignant comment on it: and as she passed her zenith and became less careful of her artistry, these comments grew to be indictments, often tediously inappropriate to their context. The abhorrence was such that, not content with the mere statement of it, she thought out a way of expressing it tangibly. She could not go about setting fire to factories and rows of villas, but she could burn them in effigy, so she amused herself and her friends by making hideous little edifices of cardboard and brown paper and setting them up in the garden, where, at sundown, they would be fired. Mr. Forster assisted at one of the burnings.

Her taste for the dramatic in private life rather surprised him; it seemed hardly to accord with her unaffected charm and kindliness. Taking him round the garden that day she paused at some place which she said was the scene of an incident in one of her books, and suddenly speaking in her theatrical voice, embarrassed him faintly by a kind of acting which he did not know whether he was to take seriously or to smile at. Afterwards, playing him Beethoven's Seventh Symphony on the pianola or discussing her work and his, she resumed the direct and natural manner which sat so much more happily on her.

The hatred of industrialism which found vent in the burning of miniature factories was extended to almost all the products of modern civilization. Again and again in her writings her reverence for the past and her condemnation of the age she lived in, are thrust upon the notice of the reader. But her belief in the superiority of our ancestors was rather romantic than reasoned. She thought that the first years of the twentieth century were full of such squalor and misery as had never had their like in the world before—from which it would appear that her studies of living conditions in past eras had been largely confined to their pleasanter and more glamorous aspects.

She was seldom either precise or logical in her mode of thinking, but she was at least consistent, even when—to write what may seem paradoxical—she could not remain so without self-contradiction. In this respect she sometimes proved more reasonable than her husband, though his intellectual powers excelled hers. Hubert Bland, to give one instance, bitterly resented the rows of workmen's cottages which were springing up all over Eltham and destroying the cherished dignity of his own house. She shared his resentment, until one night H. R. Millar laughingly pointed out to them both that they were only getting what they had asked for, since as Socialists they had long been demanding some such attempt to solve the housing problem. Hubert Bland was anything but pleased to be thus reminded of his inconsistency, but Edith acknowledged at once that Mr. Millar was in the right.

The Well Hall district was certainly going down, and the Blands' home itself was no longer kept up so lavishly as in the first days of their success. They had spent their money freely, had been generous beyond their means, and now their earnings were much reduced. *Dormant* went into two editions, but its royalties could not have increased the year's income substantially; *Ballads and Verses of the Spiritual Life* was not more profitable than most volumes of poetry; a few little tales written for one of her early publishers were likely to have brought in only a very inconsiderable sum. And when *The Wonderful Garden* reached its last instalment at the end of 1911 it was not immediately followed by another serial according to the long-accustomed procedure.

"It was a great blow to me," she wrote to her brother in Australia, "when, owing to the muddle-headedness of an agent, the *Strand* did without me last year. It made me very hard up, and added considerably to the worry of life."

Whether it was because she seriously needed to turn to account every source of income, however trivial, or whether simply from a love of having as many irons as possible in the fire, she now decided to sell day by day the garden products of Well Hall. The chief attraction of the plan was certainly that she would be able to supply fruit and flowers to the poor of the district without the intervention of the profit-grasping middleman.

She therefore opened her own little market-gardening stall at the main gate of the house and sold—or very often gave—her garden stuff to humble customers. It could hardly have been a lucrative employment, for during the War, when her gardening activities were at their height and prices greatly inflated, she told her brother that her stall was making twenty-five shillings a week, and in these pre-War days the proceeds must have been very much less. Profit, however, was not her first consideration, as might be shown by many stories of her charity. A single one will suffice.

One day an old, poorly dressed woman came to the gate to ask for funeral flowers—the best that could be obtained for the pathetically small sum which was all she could spare to grace her daughter's funeral. Edith promised to do her best, and by the next day she had made with her own hands an exquisite wreath of narcissi and white lilac and pinned to it some verses specially written for the mother's consolation: nor would she consent to take the proffered payment.

In 1912, when she herself was in low water financially, her brother evidently wrote to her to suggest that she should buy some shares in a newspaper or magazine which he was founding in Brisbane. She replied:

Dearest Harry, . . .

We are awfully hard up at present, so I can't take any shares in your paper, but I send you a poem which you can use if you like. It has not been published. If you don't care for it send it back please. I wish your paper every success. And I will send you something else for it, if you like, later on.

I wonder whether you would care for me to send you Baconiana—are you a Baconian or a Shakespearean? I have been investigating the question of ciphers in the works of Shakespeare —and have found several—but I don't know enough about figures to get very far. I wish you were here to help me! . . .

I have had a one-act play accepted by a London manager, but it won't be performed till the autumn. Best love to you and yours.

Your loving sister

Daisy.

Although she had not seen her brother for over twenty-five years she still kept up an intimate correspondence with him, and took a great interest in the Australian branch of her family, which now contained many members whom she had never seen. Her next letter gives a fairly comprehensive résumé of all the matters which occupied her at the time. Nothing is missing but a reference to her current literary work, of which there was less in hand than at almost any time since the beginning of her career. Her only publication was *The Magic World,* which consisted of twelve stories for children reprinted from magazines. It is generally thought that the chief reason for her comparative sterility, as well as for the impoverishment that was the natural consequence of it, was her intense pre-occupation with the Bacon-Shakespeare question, which, as may be seen, finds its place in both the letters quoted: and certainly her fellow Baconians sponged on her ruthlessly. At the same time, it cannot be overlooked that her usual *Strand* serial had remained unwritten through no wish of her own, and that she was now fifty-four years old and had been toiling incessantly for thirty years. Her hand would probably have begun to slacken even if she had not become engrossed in a costly and unproductive hobby.

My dearest Harry,

Thank you for your nice long letter. Do just what you like with the poem—and if you get any money for it give the same to Collis as a little present from his Aunt. I think the *idea* of the last verse is all right, but I agree with you that it might have been more poetically expressed. On the other hand I felt it needful to *condense* at that point. . . .

We live very quietly now that the girls are married, and Hubert's eyes are so bad.

I am frightfully busy. Rehearsals of my play every day. It will be performed next Tuesday.[4] In addition to this (bother this pen!) I have undertaken to build a "Magic City" of bricks and dominoes and odds and ends, at Olympia for the Children's Welfare Exhibition. And in order that it may be advertised beforehand I

---

[4] The play was *Unexceptionable References,* licensed to Vedrenne and Eadie of the Royalty Theatre.

have had to build a part of it—about 10 ft. x 6, in the flat which I share with Iris (she does dressmaking; and has a work room and reception room at Rathbone Place, close to Winsor and Newtons, and I have the other rooms). The bit of the city which I have built looks jolly nice, but it is a most awful fag to do. I will try to send photographs of it when they come out. I am to have a "stand" 32 ft. x 20 which will be like a room, open on one side, and lined with blue (to shew like sky). Millar's Illustrations are also to be shown. The tables on which the city will be built will be about 18 ft. x 8 so you see its no light job, to cover all that space with towers and bridges and palaces and gardens, all made of common objects of the home, such as biscuit tins and bowls and chessmen and draughts and tea-kettle lids . . .

I had no idea when I undertook this Magic City building what a bother it would be, or I should never have undertaken it—but they say it will be a very good advertisement. I am also to read fairy tales aloud at Olympia.

I will send you the House of Arden. I'm glad you like Harding's Luck. I am extremely fond of it myself. I am sending you the Incomplete Amorist and Daphne. If there are any others you want let me know.

Its a good thing for you that the thick of the world's between us, or I should certainly insist on your teaching me how to deal with logarithms, because the Shakespeare Cipher I am after involves the use of Logs not Briggs but Napiers—I can get no book dealing with Napier's Logs to the base E. i.e. $\dfrac{1}{2.2121396}$—and so on. And I am quite incapable of learning such things from books even if there were one, which I don't believe there is. Best love dear, to you and yours,

Your loving sister,
Daisy.

Although she found the building of a "magic city" on a large scale a more arduous labour than she had expected, there were few of her enterprises which left a more lasting sense of triumph in her. A dozen years later she still remembered it with pure enjoyment. Thousands of visitors to Olympia, including Queen Alexandra and other royal personages, admired the beautiful little town with its glittering palaces and marvellously intricate temples. She was in charge of the stand herself, and sold copies of her book, *The Magic City,* and came face to face with many faithful readers whose existence she had hitherto only been able to surmise from impersonal royalty statements. The unconcealed pride and excitement of the children whose purchases she autographed must have been extremely pleasant to her.

When the exhibition was over she wrote *Wings and the Child,* a book on the building of magic cities and on children's amusements in general. It was an extraordinarily sane and sensible piece of work expressing the most advanced views then current. If she was not an irreproachable mother, her failings were rather temperamental than intellectual, for she had a most delicate comprehension of the difficulties. And there was one of them she thought it impossible to surmount, though—as writer at least—she had come nearer to surmounting it herself than any other woman of her time.

> There is [she says] a freemasonry between children, a confidence and give-and-take which is and must be for ever impossible between children and grown-ups, no matter how sympathetic the grown-up and how confiding the child. Between the child and the grown-up there is a great gulf fixed—and this gulf, the gulf between one generation and another, can never really be bridged.

The book contains a good deal of enlightenment about her tastes, and many reminiscences of her childhood. Her professed aim is to tell: "Something of what I know about children—know by the grace of memory and by the dreams of childhood, to me, thank God, persistent and imperishable."

Her two last full-length tales for children [5]—*The Wonderful Garden,* published in 1911, and *Wet Magic,* which first appeared serially in the *Strand* in 1913—show that the grace of memory was in her as fresh and pervasive as it had always been. There are passages of description in both books that give an al-

---

[5] *Five of Us and Madeline,* published the year after E. Nesbit's death, is not a full-length book, but a number of short stories dovetailed together by Mrs. Clifford Sharp.

most physical sensation of contact with the realities of child-hood. There are phrases that shine like lamps upon forgotten treasures, and shine, too, without any hint of vanity. Not a word suggests the conscious cleverness of an author bent on showing how much he remembers and how skilfully he can set it down. Yet this is not, on the whole, as good as her best work: it is only better of its kind than almost any hand except her own could have written.

And of its kind it was the last she ever wrote. She was weary, miserable, out of health, beset with difficulties. Hubert Bland, suffering from a disease of the retina of both eyes, was going blind, and in the face of this disaster even such high spirits as hers could not survive. He was only fifty-seven years old, and the unimpaired vigour of his mind made his physical affliction seem doubly tragic. He bore it bravely, but his wife, the loyal, admiring companion of thirty-three years, felt a weight upon her heart that utterly suppressed her accustomed zest and geniality.

Two pathetic letters show the state of her feelings at the time, and explain why she was never again to write with sheer, spontaneous gaiety. One is to her brother in Brisbane, the other, which is uncommonly revealing, is to Lady Dunsany, who had asked her advice on the bringing up of an only child. They were both written towards the end of 1913:

My dearest Harry,
    I am very glad that things are looking brighter for you, and that your health is better. Things are pretty black for us—Hubert has practically lost his sight—he is undergoing a very expensive treatment which *may* do some good, but so far has done very little, if any. I am getting very tired of work, and the expenses of life don't seem to get less. I wish everyone had a small pension at 50—enough to live on. I have had a novel in hand for some time, but I have been too worried to get on with it.
    I am now going into the country for a few weeks, in the hope of getting some work done.
    Love and best wishes to you and yours—
                                        Your loving sister
                                                    D.

My dear Lady Dunsany, . . .

Thank you for your letter. The problem of the lonely child is a difficult one. If I had an only child to bring up I think I should get another little boy to educate with him, and let them grow and live together. It would be very jolly for the other little boy, too. Failing that I should get him a tutor, not too old or too young to be able to play as well as teach. For the two little boys I would have that tutor, too—and I would never never never send the boy to a public school.

If I am ever able to accept your kind invitation and to come and see you again, as I hope to do, I will try to write an article about the lonely child and you shall tell me what to say—if you will.

I am very glad you like "Wings and the Child". I enjoyed writing it. Indeed I am getting very tired of writing stories and wish I need only write verse, and set down the things I think. Any success my stories have had is due I think to a sort of light-hearted outlook on life—and now that Hubert's eyes have failed him a steam-roller seems to have gone over all one's hopes and ambitions, and it is difficult to remember how it felt to be light-hearted.

I am down at Crowlink trying to get well and to do a little work. It is a lonely little house on the downs, not a sound all day but the wind and the sea, and on sunny days, the skylarks. The quiet is like a cool kind hand on one's forehead. There are no flowers now, except the furze which as you know only goes out of flower when kisses go out of season—so I have cut two standard furze trees and put them in pots. They look exactly like Japanese Dwarf pine-trees—only they are covered with the sweet-scented yellow furze-flowers. They are a great solace. I am alone here except for the dogs, and my new secretary, a quiet youth who types what I write and in the evenings plays chess with me. Neither of us are chess-players, so it is quite a pleasant amusement—and not the weighty business that your real chess-player makes of the game.

Yours with love,
E. B.

It is gratifying to be able to quote one further letter—sent within a few weeks of the other two—by which it may be seen that if E. Nesbit's high spirits had at last succumbed to fatigue and worry, her desire to perform unlooked-for acts of kindness was still unquenched. *The Clarion* had organized a children's book-reviewing competition, in which the second prize was won by a little girl [6] who had chosen to review *Five Children and It*. Realizing with what great pleasure this admirer would receive a completely unexpected letter from her favourite author, E. Nesbit addressed her as follows:

Dec. 10 1913.

My dear Reviewer,

I have just read your article on "Five Children and It" in the Clarion. Thank you! It is the best review I have ever had. It gives an idea of the events of the story, and expresses charmingly your opinion of it.

I am glad you like the children—I am rather fond of them myself. They are second cousins once removed of the Bastables whom you may have met.

Have you read the other two books of the adventures of Anthea, Robert and the rest?

The reason why those children are like real children is that I was a child once myself, and by some fortunate magic I remember exactly how I used to feel and think about things.

I am sorry this letter is so badly written, but my fountain pen is not very well today. It is suffering from cramp in the iridium, a very painful disorder, but not, fortunately, dangerous.

If you go on as you have begun you ought to be a successful author. You have a grasp of essentials. Do you ever write poetry? It is the best possible training for writing prose. It teaches you the value of words and cadences.

I send you my love—
Your friend,
E. Nesbit.

Early in 1914 Hubert Bland lost the last remnant of his sight, and with his blindness the melancholy that had lately overhung Well Hall sank deep. The parties, which for some time had been growing rarer, were now entirely given up. Only intimates visited the house, no longer kept up in the lavish style of bygone

[6] Miss Joan Palmer, afterwards Mrs. Thomas Platt.

days: illness and weariness had seriously reduced the income of its tenants. In spring, Edith went to Crowlink with John Bland, Stephen Chant, and Cecil Gould.[7] Hubert Bland's heart was always a source of anxiety to his family, but there seemed no immediate danger, and he was being left in the hands of two devoted friends, Miss Breakell, who had for some time been living at Well Hall, and Miss Hoatson.

He died on an April evening scarcely a moment after he had finished dictating to Miss Hoatson his usual article for the *Sunday Chronicle*. There had been nothing about his condition that day to suggest that he was in worse health than at any time in the past year, and he had composed his essay without, apparently, the least premonition that it would be his last. But as he rose from his chair, having completed the final sentence, he declared that he felt giddy. Miss Hoatson, alarmed by his voice, ran to his support, calling to Miss Breakell to get the doctor. His weight was too much for her and he sank to the floor, gently rejecting her aid. The last words he uttered were, "I am not hurt." He died instantly afterwards.

A telegram was dispatched to Edith at Crowlink calling for her to return as Hubert was "very ill." She understood the import of the words at once, but for the sake of those who were with her, she concealed her knowledge. She hired a car, and the party set off in silence, nor did she make any remark during the whole journey.

If it were possible to measure grief, one might say that never —not even, perhaps, at the time of Fabian's death—had she known an hour so desolate as this. Her married life had never been serenely happy, but she had not loved her husband the less because he had called for sacrifices and taken the full measure of her generosity. She had wanted him to lean upon her, and she in her turn had leaned heavily upon him. In all distresses and perplexities, even those which the average wife or husband would have been concerned to hide from each other rather than to reveal, he had turned to her and she to him in truth and

[7] Gerald Gould's brother—killed in action in 1916.

comradeship. They had given each other a motive power, and with his death something ardent and vital in her seemed to perish. It was a long time before she gave any sign that the spark still burned, and might flame up again.

No original work was done by her this year, but by May she was busy with the task of selecting and editing a number of Hubert Bland's essays for publication. Cecil Chesterton [8] wrote the introduction to the book and paid homage to the ability and the personal charm of its author. Of Hubert Bland's work he speaks thus:

> He was a great journalist and those articles, some of which are reproduced in this volume, represent, I think, almost the high-water mark of English journalism. The triumph of his genius was this, that he could interest a huge popular audience in things in which all the self-satisfied prigs and all the routine professionals would have combined to tell him that ordinary men could not be interested. . . . Yet so powerful was his gift of lucid exposition, so happy and vigorous was his method of illustration, that it was incontestable that his most purely philosophical articles were immensely popular with the working men of the industrial North, from whom he was continually receiving letters asking for further elucidation of the ideas of Hegel or Nietzsche or Bergson.
>
> He possessed [the writer adds] a sense of human equality and brotherhood rare in literary men, and still rarer in those who profess what are vaguely called advanced views.

Gerald Gould, who became a celebrated critic, said: "He had considerable private standing among men of letters, but he never put the best that was in him into writing. Yet his essays had power enough to make the artisans of the North country interested in sheer hard thinking, and he never shrank from tackling any subject."

E. Nesbit herself spoke of him thus in an epilogue to the essays:

> Hubert wrote as he spoke and he spoke as he thought. He never did for money or for fame sell himself. He had, in the

[8] Brother of G. K. Chesterton.

highest degree, the quality of intellectual honesty. He would not deceive himself, nor would he suffer others to be deceived. . . . He hated the Pharisees, the Prigs, and the Puritans. All men else he loved.

As a journalist he had a strong influence on the tastes and views of thousands of eager readers both in London and the provinces; as a lecturer, debater, and pamphleteer he was directly instrumental in shaping the destinies of many distinguished politicians and economists of a later day; while in his private life he unweariedly sought out and fostered the talents of younger men whose promise, in many cases, he was the first to recognize; and by the encouragement and the material help he gave, he did great service to art and letters.

Whatever may have been his frailties, his character was loved and respected by a wide circle of friends drawn from all ranks of life, and most of all by the wife who had had thirty-four years in which to see the best and worst of him.

18   *The First World War*

Shortly after her husband's death, E. Nesbit went to stay near her friends, the Courlanders, in Paris, and, though the general tenor of her thoughts was clearly unhappy, there were moments there when she seemed to have recovered something of her youthful capacity for enjoyment. One afternoon in a little cinema where a ludicrously bad picture was being shown, she laughed so heartily that an usher came up, and, tapping her on the shoulder, exclaimed: "You mustn't laugh like that here!" With this he took a seat near where she sat with her companion, and began to watch them as if waiting for some further outburst of mirth. For a few minutes she was nonplussed, but soon she beckoned politely to the usher, and as he approached, addressed him in her excellent French: "Monsieur, if we are not to laugh at the picture, may we please be permitted to cry?" And with that she burst loudly into mock tears.

She had always loved France and the French profoundly, but on this visit, her last, she thought she detected signs of a disagreeable change in the national character, and this she attributed to the decline of religious authority. She was conscious, too, of a sinister and oppressive atmosphere pervading the whole capital, but of the imminence of war she had no suspicion.

Her journey back to England was an urgent and unpleasant one. After a few weeks in Paris she became seriously ill and was obliged to write to Miss Hoatson at Well Hall begging to be fetched back, for she felt herself—and not wrongly—to be in danger. On arriving in England in a state that gave cause for anxiety, she was found to be suffering from a duodenal ulcer. Within a day or two she was taken to Guy's Hospital for an operation, and came through it so badly that she was all but given up for lost. Her daughter Iris, visiting her on the following day, found her at death's door. Her temperature was alarmingly sub-normal, and she was so weak that the surgeon had little hope of her recovery.

Her one desire was for food, which had been rigidly denied her. The refusal struck her as absurd, for she thought that, if her death were inevitable, she might as well have what she wanted in her last hours. Mrs. Philips agreed, and going out returned with a tin of beef essence, which she administered by the half-teaspoonful every hour during the day. The patient's temperature slowly rose, and to the great surprise of those in charge of the case, by nightfall there was a very evident improvement. On leaving the hospital she seemed for a time to make good progress, but after a few weeks she had a grave relapse, and it was only by virtue of a strong constitution and careful nursing that she was restored to something approaching normal health.

If any human being was ever born whose life seemed carefully planned to prove the old adage that misfortunes do not come singly, E. Nesbit must have been that person. Every major calamity she had to face was followed by a series of lesser or greater calamities, and no year ever brought so many misfortunes in its train as 1914. Even the gloom of Fabian's death had been a little lightened by the enormous success of her literary work at that period. But now she knew that success on a large scale could never be hers again. The war had begun and had turned everything most hideously upside down. There was no chance left of regaining her lost prosperity, and one by one her friends and the members of her family went to fight, to make munitions, to work in hospitals or government offices, until she could see nothing before her but loneliness and a struggle to keep house and home together on ever-diminishing means.

The war itself she detested but saw no help for. She would have preferred some less cruel and wasteful method of settling the quarrels between nations, but once England was involved she was carried away, unresisting, on the tide of patriotic fervour, and took her part as eagerly as almost everybody else. During the Boer War, when a little glamour still clung to the idea of fighting, her attitude had been that of a schoolboy. There is a passage in the *Wouldbegoods*—one, indeed, of many—which shows with clarity what view she then held. A kindly officer has been allowing the children to examine some guns, and when they have eagerly admired these and the soldiers and himself, he tells them that his company has been ordered to the front and will sail in a few days. "We were very sorry they were going," the illuminating comment runs, "but Oswald, as well as the others, looked with envy on those who would soon be allowed—being grown-ups and no nonsense about your education—to go and fight for their Queen and country."

As E. Nesbit grew older and saw something of warfare at closer range, the glories doubtless seemed to her rather poorly balanced against the horror, but she was never a pacifist. Her judgments were personal, and it happened that she had disliked the Germans heartily from her childhood. Soon after England's declaration of war she sent E. M. Forster a letter of such violently orthodox patriotism that he felt both surprised and disappointed. Her first "war work" was an attempt to fire popular sentiment by means of an anthology of *Battle Songs* published in 1914. Two years later her attitude was still that of any other public-spirited British matron. "If I can," she wrote to her brother, "I will send you an article I felt it my duty to write about the Germans. It was a horrible thing to have to do, but I did it."

Her natural anti-German bias, however, did not lead to such an infatuated bigotry as some of her compatriots gloried in. She was most active in her attempts to save an elderly German friend of hers from being interned, and sheltered him at

Well Hall regardless of all that prudence might have urged. Again, when a Zeppelin was brought down in flames within sight of her house, she was shocked by the behaviour of Miss Hoatson who applauded the spectacle as if it had been an entertainment. "Do you realize," she inquired in her most imperious voice, "that there are people being *burned alive* over there?"

As the long months of struggle and misery dragged on, E. Nesbit touched the very nadir of her fortunes. Her earnings were almost negligible, her health was poor, and she was separated from her children and most of her friends. Her son Paul was in the army; her daughters had occupations away from home—Iris being in charge of munition workers at Woolwich Arsenal, and Rosamund abroad with her husband, Clifford Sharp, who had been entrusted with a Government mission to the Baltic Provinces.

John Bland was still at school, and in those days there were few grants or scholarships to enable a boy so situated to continue his education, so that, talented as he was, provision for his future might have been an additional difficulty. Here, very luckily, an early friendship was to come to the rescue. When Hubert Bland was dying, he had been greatly troubled about John's prospects, and had implored Bernard Shaw to do something for him. Shaw, with characteristic generosity, arranged to pay for the training at Cambridge which enabled John to take a medical degree, and subsequently distinguish himself as a research worker.[1] Though at the time he believed himself to be E. Nesbit's child, John, of course, was actually the son of Miss Hoatson. E. Nesbit would undoubtedly have furthered his career by her own efforts had she been called upon to do so, but fortunately this was not required of her. When I mentioned to Mr. Shaw that I believed John himself was quite unaware to whom he was indebted, he said, "Then don't tell him!" John's expenses at Cambridge, he remarked, had been "extraordinarily small" compared with those of the sons of his friends.

In 1915 E. Nesbit was awarded a Civil pension of £60 a year in recognition of her services to literature. The tribute was a wel-

[1] He became Senior Demonstrator of Bacteriology at Bart's Hospital.

come one from every point of view, though she was a little disillusioned when the payment arrived with a deduction of several pounds for income tax. The Royal Literary Fund also, in close secrecy, came to her aid, but the sums granted were still insufficient to place her beyond need, and she found it necessary to take paying guests at Well Hall.

At the same time the market gardening activities were extended, her fruit and flowers being sold at a reasonable price to munition workers and to the Government for the provisioning of military hospitals. She also ran a poultry farm for the same purpose. The house at Crowlink was a luxury no longer to be indulged in, and she was obliged to sacrifice the seaside holidays which had enabled her to bear with so little effect the strain of her crowded life.

Her letters for this period make melancholy reading. I give extracts here from two of them, one to Miss Carter and one to Henry Nesbit:

8.6.15.

Dearest Mavis,

I must finish my novel, before I go anywhere or do anything and I *can't* finish it. Now that my husband is gone, the close and constant companion and friend of thirty-seven years,[2] my life seems broken off short. And this horrible war adds to the desolation and the feeling that nothing is worth while.

I am so sorry, my dear, that the war has come home to you so terribly, in the loss of your cousin and friend. It is a nightmare of horror, the whole thing. Yes—it's good for *them* to be out of all the horror, and happy and at peace—but for us who are left . . .

Goodbye, my dear. God bless you.

Your loving

E. Nesbit.

To her brother several months afterwards she wrote:

I am much better in health—but I do not find I can take much interest in life. Without Hubert everything is so unmeaning. I

[2] She had first met Hubert Bland in 1877.

don't do much writing, though I am always hoping I shall be able
to again. I have taken in paying guests since last October—If I
could get a few more I should get on all right. Also I sell flowers
out of the garden, and apples and vegetables. In the last eight
weeks I have made by that alone 25/- a week. Then there is the
pension. If I could live without writing I should like never to
write another line. The War makes everything more miserable. It
seems too horrible to be true. . . .

My love to your wife [she ends]. I *should* like to see her, and
you and the boy—but I suppose I never shall now!

For all her depression and her difficulties, she was still ready
to give help and counsel to fellow-authors, though the society of
literary people no longer in itself attracted her. Opportunities
were fewer than they had been, but when they came she never
failed to welcome them. In the early days of the war G. K.
Chesterton wrote to her saying that his friend, R. Brimley Johnson, wanted to talk over a scheme for the production of a children's newspaper on entirely original lines. "I thought of you,"
he said, "not only as the ablest child's novelist I know, but also
more generally as one who understands the heroic simplicity of
all revolutions of the right sort." She was delighted to see Mr.
Johnson, and keenly interested in the novel idea of a newspaper
wholly for children, and intended to contain social and political
news of all kinds as well as the usual juvenile features. She
promised her support, and he left her, as he has written, with a
greater feeling of confidence and security than he had received
elsewhere, and an unforgettable impression of "her gracious,
generous, and vivid personality." Unfortunately, though many
celebrated names, including her own, appeared on the prospectus issued soon afterwards, the scheme fell through owing to
the difficulty of obtaining financial support for it at such a
time.

The novel mentioned in the recently quoted letter to Mavis
Carter was *The Incredible Honeymoon,* published in America in
1916, but in England not till 1921. Wartime shortages affecting
book production may have been responsible for this long delay,
but it is probable that the work failed to appeal to London pub-

lishers, being almost the least attractive she ever wrote. The theme is little better than puerile and the tendency to air theories which have no connection with the story is worryingly manifest. There are pages of Bacon-Shakespeare propaganda almost lacerating to the reader's feeling for artistic unity.

She had nobody now to offer criticism even if she had been disposed to ask it. The old groups had broken up and she saw little of her former intimates. The house, too, was a changed place. Its tried and trusted servants, now employed in filling shells at Woolwich Arsenal, had been replaced by a staff that was untrained and far from adequate in size. The economies were stringent. Leg of mutton and suet pudding appeared on the table instead of beautifully served French food, and water instead of wine. "But she looked," in the words of Mrs. Courlander, "as much a châtelaine as ever, and there was still a baronial air hanging over the frugal feasts." She did not allow her own low spirits to depress her guests. Those of them who were new acquaintances had no suspicion that she was concealing weariness and a deep-rooted grief. She still had children about her—first of whom was her little granddaughter Pandora, Iris's child—and still invented games for them, prepared birthday surprises, and delighted in contriving small but interesting gifts.

Among the newer visitors was a very young author later to become eminent as novelist and playwright, then a wartime volunteer nurse. Enid Bagnold had lived on Shooter's Hill in the Well Hall neighbourhood when in her teens she first longed to write and to know writers. "On every walk I took," she told me too late for the text of my first edition, "I hoped to meet Hubert Bland. It was a romance. I had never seen him, but I knew he wore a black, very wide eyeglass ribbon. I could recognize him by that. Often I rehearsed what I should say if I came across him in my walks. . . . How by my fiery tone he would recognize my talent, by my opening words he would know, etc., etc. I never met him, but I saw his funeral. Later I was introduced to Well Hall and went to tea several times with Mrs. Bland. I was then a V.A.D. at the Royal Herbert Hospital, and got certain times off, when, in white apron and dress I used to ride sideways on a Douglas motor-cycle—sideways for fear of crushing my apron. The house was romantic, the garden lovely, and Mrs. Bland so kind. But the experience of the great military hospital which I had just left and would re-enter again after tea over-shadowed all other impressions. Not a word—nothing—remains, but a table spread in a comfortable nurseryish way for tea, people talking warmly to each other, and my wrist turning constantly up towards me that my watch might tell me when I was at my last margin of time."

Two of E. Nesbit's paying guests made contributions to this book. One of these was Peter Blundell, a well-known humorous novelist of the day, who was there with his wife. Mr. Blundell, who had been trained as an engineer, and was in charge of one of the departments of Woolwich Arsenal, where Mrs. Philips was also employed, met E. Nesbit first through Munitions Welfare Work. His recollections of the days he spent in her house will serve to counter-balance the rather gloomy records of the last two chapters:

We were a large party [he wrote], and E. Nesbit was never tired of doing her utmost to entertain us and keep us all happy. We used to dance in the drawing-room, and she could dance well, although easily fatigued. We used also to act charades planned and stage-managed by her, and she would make the costumes during the daytime, when most of us were away at our work. Often we had exhibition dancing in which her daughter, Mrs. Clifford Sharp, took a share as well as her granddaughter Pandora.[3] All sorts of people used to come to these entertainments . . . most of them intelligent and interesting. Amongst those I remember best were E. Nesbit's son-in-law, Clifford Sharp, J. C. Squire, just beginning to be well known, Professor Andrade, on leave from the front, and Enid Bagnold, now Lady (Roderick) Jones, who had just won fame with her book, *A Diary Without Dates.*

I can see E. Nesbit now with her ample figure rather untidily

[3] Later a member of Pavlova's company. This only granddaughter was killed in a motor accident in the 1950's. She left two children.

dressed in black, her dark masses of hair done sketchily, a ciga-
rette-holder stuck in the corner of her wide, generous mouth, and
her round, ruddy low-browed face and the grey-blue eyes behind
the big spectacles, eyes that shone with a wish to make everybody
happy (except Mr. Lloyd George). "The handsomest woman
when she was young that I ever met," John Lane, the publisher,
once said she was. And although she was well on in years then,
the vivid beauty he remembered was there still.

It was hard to believe, seeing her presiding over the evening's
amusement, that she had been busy since early morning, writing
newspaper articles, looking after her big household, working at
the Bacon-Shakespeare ciphers, selling vegetables at her munition-
workers' stall, and helping with the poultry farm! I knew that
after everyone else was in bed she would still be working with the
greatest absorption in her bedroom at the top of the house; and
that if one of the frequent air raids occurred, she would be the
first to come down to the stone-floored dining-room where we all
used to assemble. The trams when a raid was on stopped outside
the house, and she was in the habit of taking coffee out to the
drivers. With her, standing on the top of a tram, we saw the first
Zeppelin brought down. . . .

She cared nothing about money. What she did care for was that
all about her should have, as far as she could afford it, the best of
everything. But with the best of intentions—her mind being busy
with other things than food—we sometimes came off rather
badly.

I remember one day at lunch, she said to us: "Mr. G. S. Street [4]
is coming to dinner tomorrow night, and I've ordered a turkey,
for I know he's fond of turkeys." When I returned home that
evening I found her in the hall looking pale and distracted. "A
terrible thing has happened," she said. "I've just looked at the letter again, and Mr. Street is coming to dinner tonight, not tomorrow night. And all we have is curry!" The knowledge that Mr.
Street should have been eating turkey instead of our very British
curry spoiled that dinner for me, as I am sure it did for E. Nesbit.
But if his feelings bore any resemblance to ours, he hid the fact
well.

[4] G. S. Street, the essayist; for many years Censor of plays.

It is not easy to realize that the woman whose prevailing characteristic was infectious good humour, and who, as Mr. Blundell has said, "seemed to have a genius for getting the best out of life," was at that very time feeling that she was "shivering in a sort of Arctic night," with nothing before her but misery, but that this was the truth may be judged not only from her contemporary letters but from those in which she surveyed the whole transition period in retrospect. For it was indeed a transition period, and one from which she was soon to emerge triumphantly. Life still had as great a gift to offer her as any it had ever given. She was on the verge of a happiness equal to the best that she had tasted at the height of her success and power, and of a peace exceeding any that she had known.

19   *Second Marriage*

E. Nesbit had never lacked for friends, but when the war scattered the circle on which she had so long relied for sympathy and fellowship, she was often miserably lonely. She was still in touch with a great many well-wishers; but by contrast with her former way of life—the baronial hospitality, the innumerable fêtes and holidays—her present lot seemed unendurably hard. It was not only that she missed her old companions, but she missed the little services that other hands had always done for her and that she was now obliged to do for herself. She was far from being a helpless woman, but during twenty or thirty years of writing for a living she had been obliged to leave the more tedious duties involved in running a large house to well-rewarded deputies; and now she had got out of the way of bearing such responsibilities herself, and so found them doubly worrying.

She had one friend, however, on whom she could rely at all times for useful counsel and practical assistance—a man of what would then be called humble origin but a disposition after her own heart and very closely akin to her in several important characteristics. Thomas Terry Tucker, invariably known to friends and acquaintances alike as "Skipper," was a marine engineer by profession, and by habit an alert observer of life, a courageous adventurer, a cheerful philosopher, and incidentally a most ingenious expert in describing every conceivable species of action and object in nautical language. Of Edith's own generation, he was yet, like her, tenaciously young in spirit, but, unlike her, notably level-headed in the small concerns of everyday life. He shared her enthusiasm for experiments, for doing and making things, for discussion, reading, the society of youth—everything, in fact, that she enjoyed, and he was sensitive to all her moods without being so much affected by them that his optimism gave way before her fits of despondency.

He had been on friendly terms with her for some years, and had known her by sight and reputation from the days of her early youth, when he had attended Fabian lectures or organized Sunday meetings at the Poplar Town Hall, where Mr. Shaw and other friends of the Blands frequently came to speak. At a much later period he had visited Well Hall from time to time to discuss politics with Hubert Bland. He had liked Bland and Edith had liked his (Mr. Tucker's) wife,[1] so that when both were widowed within two years of each other, they had a special link of sympathy and understanding.

Mr. Tucker's life had contained both hardship and happiness in full measure. He had begun his career before he was in his teens as rivet boy to Sir Alfred Yarrow, the famous builder of torpedo boats, and after many years of travel and adventure he had given up seafaring for good, and was running the Woolwich Ferry for the County Council. It was his pride that, as a general "handy man," friends, employers, and strangers alike would find him ready to be of service; and it seemed to him that if anyone had ever needed a handy man it was the bewildered and over-driven mistress of Well Hall. Whenever he had leisure, therefore, he went, in his own words, "to see if he could make himself useful," and his chivalry so won her confidence that he soon knew more about the state of mind her outward

---

[1] Mr. Tucker's first wife, Sophia Tucker, was a worker for progressive causes, and a woman whose exceptional qualities were widely honoured among the poor of South London, to whose welfare she devoted many years of her life.

gaiety concealed than even the kindest of those who surrounded her. He saw her growing wearier and wearier, he saw her weeping over affairs that became more and more chaotic, and, feeling as he did the strongest affection for her, he decided that such conditions could not be allowed to prevail.

One day he made his proposal, thus: "It looks to me as if you need a tug round here!"

"I wish I had one," she replied, and so it came about that, after she had talked the matter over with her children and one or two of her oldest friends, the wedding was arranged. She wrote at once to Bernard Shaw and several others with whom she had never completely lost touch saying that she was about to begin a new life; and all of them who had known anything of her three years' ordeal were heartily glad to learn that another prospect was opening up before her. Among the letters she preserved was this from Maurice Hewlett:

> Elm Tree Farm,
> West Wittering,
> Chichester.
> 10th Feb.

My dear Mrs. Bland,

You give me good news of yourself indeed. Nothing could be better, for I know only too well that we weren't intended to live alone. Don't let us suppose we are not to meet again. It's true that I don't live in London any more—but when our nightmare is over, and we begin to live again I shall expect you to come and stay a day or two with me here. This is a place after your own heart—just now under the grip of ice—but you must know it in the Spring, when it is as hot as Provence.

God bless you upon your new life—and thank you for telling me about it. I always knew we were intended to be friends—and am glad that you have treated me like one.

> Yours always,
> M. Hewlett.[2]

Another friend to whom she wrote delightedly of her altered circumstances was Professor Andrade, then on active service.

[2] This letter is printed here by kind permission of Mrs. Welby Everard.

"Everyone is very much surprised," she said, "at my marrying Mr. Tucker—but no one is more surprised than I am. . . . It is extraordinarily rum that I should have found someone who suits me like this. It is like a consolation prize for all sorts of failures. And the knowledge that I have a friend and comrade to sit on the other side of the hearth where life's dying embers fade, is incredibly comforting." How different was this letter from those addressed to the same correspondent a few months before, in one of which she had said: "Nothing seems worth while, somehow. It is like doing work on the seashore when you know the tide is soon coming that will wash away you and your work together."

She was married at St. Peter's Catholic Church in Woolwich on the 20th of February, 1917, and the "new life" that she had counted upon was at once auspiciously begun. Within a week or two she announced the news to her brother, telling him that she was very, very happy, and that her husband was the best man she had ever known.

He is the soul of goodness and kindness [she said], and he never blunders in matters of sentiment or emotion. He doesn't blunder in anything, for the matter of that, but you know in those matters how fatally easy it is to go wrong. After the cold misery of the last three years I feel as though someone had come and put a fur cloak round me. Or like one shipwrecked on a lonely island, and I have found another shipwrecked mariner to help me to build a hut and make a fire. He is a widower and I knew his wife and he knew Hubert, so we can talk about *them*. . . . His whole life seems to have been spent in doing good. Also he is fond of laughter, and likes the same kind of jokes that please me. . . . I feel as though I had opened another volume of the book of life (the last volume) and it is full of beautiful stories and poetry.

Her favourable hopes were more than realized, and to the very end of her life she still described the last volume as the best. She spoke of Mr. Tucker always as of a knight errant who had come to her rescue, and she congratulated herself for having known, if only for a few years of her existence, what it was to have won a love that was incapable of vacillation. When she had been married some little time she wrote to Henry Nesbit again giving him a further account of her husband's qualities, which she admired the more as she had better opportunities of proving them.

> I feel peaceful and contented in my new life with him. . . . He has a philosophy of life which makes all things easy to him. He never worries and he never lets me worry. So, though we are pinched for money, and hard put to it to keep going I am quite at ease. He cares absolutely nothing for material things and *possessions,* though he enjoys life and is very merry and jolly. He has been all over the world as ship's engineer, and is a born *observer.* Also he has words to clothe his thoughts and observations. If we had time I am sure we could do some good writing work together. I send you a paper with a sketch in it I wrote with Mr. Tucker's help, and an article about a *ship!*

Mr. Tucker did, as she foresaw, become her collaborator, and after a long barren period she began to produce stories and sketches inspired by his reminiscences. The excellent tale called "Tammy Lee's Jack," which appears in *Five of Us and Madeline,* was a true one recounted to her by him. The manner of telling it is very like his own crisp narrative style, which she evidently followed closely. Occasionally they wrote sketches of nautical life together, and these were published in the *Westminster Gazette* and other papers. She had always felt a strong attraction towards the sea and everything belonging to it, and his sailorly way of living and talking was not the least of his attractions for her. Sometimes when his work at the ferry kept him out till the small hours of the morning, she would go with him to the boat, and grill a beefsteak and make coffee in the cabin with the same delight in the novelty of her surroundings as she might have taken in her childhood. She would address him then as "Skipper" and he would call her "Cook," and none of the child characters she created could have kept up the game of being a real member of a real ship's crew better than she. At other times, she would wait up at home to give him a hot supper, and as they ate they would begin to exchange the little records of the day and eventually become so engrossed in conversation that the morning had dawned before they went to bed. Gradually her speech took on something of the seafaring idiom she loved, and she was proud to be known to the Skipper as his "Mate."

Besides giving her the impetus towards creative work which she had needed, Mr. Tucker set about reorganizing the management of Well Hall, and he found that many retrenchments might be made which she had scarcely contemplated. The first step was to ensure that hospitality was kept within reasonable limits; that is to say, that she should only entertain guests whom she liked and really wanted to see. Her various employments during the War had brought her into contact with a number of people who were not of her world, and in whose company she could take no pleasure. Yet they were fascinated by her and, mistaking her general charm of address for signs of preference, they paid her frequent visits and made demands of all kinds on her good nature. It was by no means uncommon for her to be expected to receive, not only these well-meaning but tedious acquaintances themselves, but also their friends and relations. Mr. Tucker saw that their presence was a strain on her nerves as well as on her purse, and since she would never have had the heart to deny herself to them, took the law into his own hands, and politely but firmly kept the unwanted satellites at a distance.

In the meantime, paying guests continued to occupy two or three of the Well Hall bedrooms, and there was a great deal of tiring work to be done. But she had recovered much of her natural energy and resilience, and no longer shed secret tears over her difficulties. Although many of her old childlike qualities had vanished, the share of youthful vivacity that still remained to her was immeasurably beyond what might have been expected in a woman of her years and her experience of life: and in exchange for just so much lightness of heart as she had lost during the days of war and widowhood, she had attained a serenity perfectly new in her. It was as if her spirit had grown up.

I am indebted to Mr. Russell Green, who spent three months at Well Hall during the autumn of 1920, for a vivid picture of E. Nesbit as she then appeared—in her last days as "châtelaine" of a house whose hospitality had been celebrated for twenty years. Mr. Green had advertised in *The New Statesman* for a home away from the noise and grime of London, and E. Nesbit replied to his advertisement, and accommodated him in a room that overlooked—as she told him with pride—the site of the house to which Margaret Roper had brought her father's severed head.

As a writer of the youngest generation,[3] against whose methods she had firmly and unquestioningly set her face (one of the few prejudices in which she showed herself "elderly"), Mr. Green often gave her material for the sort of whimsical banter she enjoyed. Pretending to regard him as a sinister advocate of all the revolutionary theories she so much disapproved, she would ask his opinion on a piece of *vers libre* which she said had taken her five minutes to write, or challenge him to defend on aesthetic principles some little water-colour sketch which she had done "in the cubistic style." She could not see how work which might be thrown off so easily could possibly have any merit, whatever pen or brush produced it. Mr. Green refrained from raising the point again when she boasted that she had once done three thousand words of a story while waiting for a concert to begin!

"Her manner," he wrote, "was sprightly and sharp. Her apt retorts and humorous asides would be made with a kind of sparrow-like uplift of the head that gave her a look of almost impudent pertness. Yet, with her grey hair and gold-rimmed spectacles, she looked her full age for all her liveliness of expres-

---

[3] He had recently come down from Oxford where he had won the double distinction of being Newdigate Prizeman and Chancellor's English Essayist, and had moved in the advanced set which contained Aldous Huxley, Thomas Earp, Wilfred Childe, etc. He was then editing an esoteric quarterly called *Coterie*.

sion. She fulfilled admirably, in fact, the role suggested by her books for children; she might have sat for the model of a fairy-godmother. This was always the first thought that came to mind when one saw her, as one often did, in the midst of a group of children. I seem to remember no assembly round the long oval dining-table without several little girls, of ages between six and ten, on whose long plaits fluttered extravagant butterflies of gay ribbon. Our hostess herself, rather tall and stately, would sit gravely engrossed in their conversation—sometimes delighting them with a lively fancy, but more often absorbed in listening to their chatter as if this were all she really lived for.

"So much did she seem to be their fairy-godmother, that one would scarcely have been surprised if she had suddenly produced a wand with a sparkling star, and if the old house, standing gaunt and weathered in the midst of masses of foliage, had at her own behest vanished into some fairy realm. The atmosphere of the tales by which she is best known seemed to have become her natural element, so that in her contact with the modern world—and even with her own children—she was strangely aloof. And although she was charming and wonderfully sympathetic, there was, in the pressure of her lips, a hint of sternness and of a strong and irresistible will.

"I sometimes thought that her remoteness might be due to her preoccupation with religion. She was frequently visited by an exceedingly amiable priest, and I gathered that she was often privately immersed in spiritual considerations, though she never at any time discussed them. One sensed beneath her gaiety that she was devout and, in a religious sense, unworldly. Yet in the long drawing-room, with its Oriental carpets, its long windows, and its human skull grinning on the top of the piano, she threw off that distant air, and became a woman essentially sociable. Here, on Sunday evenings, she would play cards, or accompany her husband while he sang nautical songs, the guests joining in at appropriate passages.

"She still entertained very freely, notwithstanding the straitened means which were implied rather than stated in her man-

ner of living. That she concealed her want of money was not
due to any snobbery in her, but rather, I should imagine, to
avoid depression. The concealment had grown to be such a
habit that it might have been mistaken for a kind of happy
thrift. With the accumulated possessions of a lifetime gathered
about her, it was not difficult for her to hide the economic
pinch: but certainly there were subterranean dilapidations
which became noticeable little by little. Yet even towards these
she bore herself with an air that suggested a sort of reverence for
them as relics of the past.

"Her sympathy for the distresses of other people was inex-
haustible. She gave to a tale of hardship or betrayal no mere
perfunctory hearing; she bent her whole mind and knowledge
of human nature to it, striving to convey from her store of wisdom some possible escape, remedy, compromise. One still seems
to hear her clear voice suggesting, advising—about the griefs of
others, never about her own."

E. Nesbit had become softer and kinder with age; she had
lost many of her old intolerances. Her attitude towards the
world in general may have been sterner, yet with the people
about her she was more yielding, less fretful, than she had ever
been before. If the childish capacity for fun was no longer as
great as it had been, the childish petulance and thoughtlessness
had diminished too. And she was still interested in everything
under the sun, and still a fanciful humorist even among the
commonplaces of domestic life. Not many women of sixty-two,
for example, would have taken the trouble to caution the inhabitants of her house against misuse of the bathroom in such
terms as appear in this notice:

THE ORDER OF THE BATH

We know Hygeia's votary refrains
From throwing bits of matches down the drains,
Yet some there be who must be better taught,
Don't use Hygeia's temple as they ought.
They leave the fountains dripping, bang the door,
And pour libations on the temple floor,

Not in the vessel which her Grace provides
For votaries to scour their foul outsides.
Who, in the madness of life's low pursuits,
Invades the temple in his muddy boots?
And, with impiety the gods abhor,
Rubs off the mud upon the temple floor,
(And even on the temple's mat once whiter
Than snow—the impious, sacrilegious blighter!)
Who shuts the windows up, that steam may fall
In tears and slowly sap the temple wall?
Who strews old shoes about the bather's path?
Who leaves the soapy water in the bath?
Miscreants, repent! And sin this year no more!
With reverent heart approach the bathroom door;
Thus shall Hygeia's blessing still attend
Upon you till one-nine-two-one shall end.

And the little doggerels she wrote in her letters are not the
sort of fun one might reasonably expect from an elderly and
stately lady. She recorded at this time some of the curious verses
which came into her mind during sleep, bringing her, as she explained,[4] a firm though fleeting conviction that they were mas-
terpieces. Here are two of them:

Bachelor bears compare combine
  To cheat me out of my mortal span
They've had their dinner, and I want mine—
  That is the difference, said Timothy Bann.

Of this dream-poem she wrote that she awoke with a strong
impression "that Timothy Bann was an important unconventional person—a kind of Mark Rutherford or Theophrastus
Such." Of the next, she had the idea that it would be "very
beautiful set to music"—though the air of *Coming through the
Rye* did not occur to her in the dream.

Mr. Oddy
Met a body
Hanging from a tree;

[4] In the *Westminster Gazette,* 25th June, 1921.

> And what was worse
> He met a hearse
> As black as black could be.
> Mr. Oddy
> Said, "By God, he
> Ought to have a ride!"
> Said the driver
> "I'd oblige yer,
> But we're full inside."

She would have been willing now to write children's fiction again, and from the few short stories that she did produce during this period there is little reason to believe that she had lost her cunning; but no publisher encouraged her to raise the Phoenix from its ashes or to add a new member to the Mouldiwarp family.

In 1921 Miss Clemence Dane, who was known to E. Nesbit only by repute, sent her an appreciative letter, telling her how long she had read and loved her books for children, and enquiring when she would gratify her admirers with another. "No one alive to-day can write children's fairy tales as you do," she said truly, but E. Nesbit was obliged to reply: "Publishers tell me that children don't want my sort of books any more."

Towards the end of 1921 it became apparent to Mr. Tucker that, with all the economies he could devise and with all the help his wife received from him and from her useful and devoted companion, Miss Olive Hill,[5] the expense and effort of keeping up so large a house as Well Hall were an insupportable drain upon her resources. It was imperative, in his opinion, that they should find a smaller home, and one which could be run without such great exertion. It might not have been easy to induce her to leave the house she had loved for twenty-two years, but by a stroke of rare good fortune they were given the opportunity of buying a sort of double bungalow at Jesson St. Mary's,

[5] Miss Olive Hill, herself a writer for children, was one of those who had approached E. Nesbit for literary advice. As the result of their mutual liking and interest, she came to live at Well Hall, and remained constantly with E. Nesbit till the last day of her life.

a mile or so from Dymchurch—the very district where she had
spent some of the happiest days of her life; and it was clear
that, with certain alterations and additions, they might make
the place as comfortable in all essentials as the somewhat dilapidated mansion at Eltham. The purchase was arranged, and by
the spring of 1922 Well Hall, within whose walls there had
been so much brilliant talk, so much laughter, so much cheerful
activity, passed into the hands of others.

No one was destined to live there long after the liveliest, the
most audacious, the most hospitable of all its many inhabitants
had departed, for, like a champagne-glass broken after the royal
toast is drunk, the house was razed to the ground within a few
years of her death.

"When you were at Well Hall," she wrote to Berta Ruck a
few months before her death, "I used often on summer evenings to slip away from the table and go and look through the
window at the rest of you finishing your desserts and your flir-
tations and your arguments amongst the flowers and fruits and
bright glasses, and think 'This is how I shall see it all some day
when I am not alive any more.' Well, it won't be Well Hall I
shall go back to now when the time comes, for it died before I
did, and it is quite dead."

At the time when I visited Eltham to gather material for this
book in 1931, Well Hall was indeed like the realm of a banished
enchantress. Tangled foliage overhung the moat, and in its
stagnant waters lay the remnants of the little boat in which E.
Nesbit had browsed and worked through the summer afternoons. The orchards where she had wandered in the long evenings, planning the tales that opened a kingdom of magic to
thousands of children then unborn, were rank with weeds, and
the crumbling red brick walls of the garden were propped to
keep them standing.

But since then there has been a most complete transformation. The grounds have been cleared and turned into a public
garden known as Well Hall Pleasaunce. The old red wall with
the moat and the old moat bridge have been preserved, and the
upper floor of the Tudor barn, restored, was a temporary Art

Gallery for the Borough of Woolwich. For some years the public was promised a children's library which was to be dedicated to the memory of E. Nesbit, but it has never materialized and the lower floor of the last remnant of her home is now a restaurant. At the time of going to press I cannot learn that the authorities have any intention of conferring official recognition on the most endearing resident in Eltham's long history.

20   *Jesson St. Mary's*

The bungalow at Jesson consisted of two buildings which had been used for military purposes during the War—one of them as a photographic laboratory for the Air Force Staff and the other a storehouse for medical materials. They required a great many internal alterations to make them habitable, and E. Nesbit devised all these herself. Never was an architect happier, though the means at her command were so limited that professional workmen had to be dispensed with wherever she and Mr. Tucker, both expert at odd jobs, could take their place.

In order that the Skipper and his Mate might feel appropriately housed, everything was arranged in the most nautical manner possible. The trim little bedrooms were "cabins," the kitchen was "the galley," the big drawing-room was "the saloon"; the two houses themselves were named the Longboat and the Jollyboat in allusion to their shape (the Jollyboat being "short and fat"), and the passage which joined them was known as the Suez Canal. As soon as her curious new home was—in a double sense—shipshape, E. Nesbit began to receive a succession of visitors. Week-end after week-end new friends and old were gathered about her, and the parties, though much smaller than those at Well Hall, were not less amusing. A number of the people who came to them had belonged to the old Dymchurch group in the days when her star was at its most brilliant. Amongst these were Mrs. Thorndike and her son and daughter, Sybil and Russell, both of whom had now become famous.

One day Mr. Russell Thorndike who, like the rest of his family, was an enthusiastic admirer of E. Nesbit's work, astonished her by saying that he had always thought the sandpit described in *Five Children and It* must have been the one at St. Margaret's, Rochester, where he and his sisters had played in their childhood. "Why," she replied, "so it was! That was the very sandpit I had in mind!" The coincidence struck them both as extraordinary, for she had not met Mrs. Thorndike's children when the book was written.

E. Nesbit had known many dramatists and dramatic critics, and had been on terms of pleasant acquaintanceship with not a few of the renowned actors and actresses of her day (one of them was Ellen Terry, to whom she bore, in these later years of her life, a striking physical resemblance), but she had seldom if ever been intimate with anyone belonging wholly to the theatrical world. Yet now that she had come to live in a remote bungalow on Romney Marsh, she suddenly found herself in close contact with several players celebrated or destined for celebrity. Among them none was more attached to her than Athene Seyler, who had been brought to see her by her old friends, the Griffiths.

By the time that Miss Seyler came to know her it was not easy to guess that her irrepressible high spirits had once been a byword. She had recognized the slow approaches of the bronchial illness that was to be her last, and, without a trace of sanctimoniousness, she was anxious to be at peace with God and with the whole world. Religion was the subject which most deeply interested her, and she was no longer reticent about it, but talked often of the future life. She had ceased to be more inclined to one church than another, holding now that all Christian creeds were worthy of respect, and the best of all a simple faith in the teaching of Christ as it might be learned in the Gospels, unencumbered by the interpretations and arguments of man.

There were moments when something of the old ardent gaiety would flicker up within her, and she never lost her whimsical turn of speech and expression; there were moments, too, when the autocratic manner which had always kept a certain discreet distance between her and her associates was very much in evidence. She could still be a martinet when the humour took her. One evening there was a party to which a group of friends illustriously connected with the theatre had been invited. They arrived rather late, and Edith—clearly a little out of temper at their tardiness—greeted them on the doorstep with the uncompromising command: "You are to act charades. All the guests are waiting for you. You had better go to the dining-room and think out something." Not one of the astonished latecomers could find courage to protest against so stern a pronouncement, but their reluctance to play an impromptu scene to an audience of strangers was by no means lessened when they caught a glimpse of the crowd in the drawing room, arranged expectantly in several rows. Edith, perceiving their intention to rebel, ushered them firmly to the dining-room and locked them in.

Professional actors are perhaps more nervous even than laymen when called upon to perform under unfavourable conditions, and the members of the little group which had been told to think out a charade behind locked doors felt anything but easy in mind when they considered that the anticipations of the waiting company were probably worked up to the highest pitch. They stared at each other with blank faces, nothing further from their thoughts than a subject offering possibilities either for wit or drama. From time to time their hostess rapped on the door demanding in an increasingly peremptory tone whether they were ready.

They had just begun discussing a project for taking flight by the window when she flung the door open, and assured them that she could brook no further delay. The only charade they could work out on such terms was "Silly Billy," a fortunate choice, for they played it with so much awkwardness that the audience had every reason to think their acting superb.

E. Nesbit felt a very strong regard for Mr. Noel Coward, the last of all that long line of promising young men whose companionship had been a source of undisguised enjoyment to her. Mr. Coward had the double merit of being both interesting in himself and an almost lifelong admirer of her work. As a child he had saved up year after year to buy her books. He had not been able to afford the bound copies, but there was a second-hand bookshop on the way to his school where he could get back numbers of the *Strand Magazine* for a penny each, and he had systematically saved a shilling at a time so as to get twelve numbers together. As he grew older his enthusiasm did not wane, and when, in 1922, he went to St. Mary's in the Marsh to work and learned that the author was living near by, he decided to call upon her.

Even if his personality had been lacking in the qualities she approved, which it was not, E. Nesbit would not have felt disposed to give a cool reception to a young man who held that she was "the only children's writer of recent times who was first-rate." As it was, she made friends with him at once, and as long as he lived in the district they continued to see a good deal of each other. She read his early plays and liked them: when she found anything in them that displeased her she expressed her opinion pungently and without equivocation, but she had no doubt as to his future. He found that her technical knowledge of the theatre was slight, but an excellent sense of character made her criticisms worth hearing.

The themes he treated, though wholly different from those that had been favoured in her theatre-going days, and different, too, from any she had ever been disposed to treat herself, did not shock her. "Her moral attitude," he told me, "was quite genuine—that is, not belonging to any fashion or period. It was clear that she would have held just the same views in the most rigid Victorian epoch as in the most dashing years of the twentieth century. She was a strange case of being a *real* Bohemian."

Preoccupied as she was with religion at this time, she never—to his delight—adopted the manners of "a sweet old lady." He, at any rate, found that her tongue could be as caustic as it was witty and amusing, and that her temper was not of the most even. But if she became quite frankly angry because a guest was late for tea, her bearing in the face of serious affliction was so splendid that one could well support the little remnants of her old asperity.

A few months after E. Nesbit's first meeting with Noel Coward, his friend, Miss G. B. Stern, came to the Dymchurch district with her husband, Geoffrey Holdsworth, and they, too, decided to pay her an informal visit. Each of them had encountered her on one earlier occasion. Mr. Holdsworth had read *Dormant* while at the front, and had written to the author to tell her that he had enjoyed the story but had been disappointed with her manner of disposing of the characters at the end: she had replied by saying that she would have arranged it differently if she had not grown too tired of the book to finish it as she had wished, and by inviting him to come and see her when on leave—an invitation that had been accepted. Miss Stern, not then married to Mr. Holdsworth, had been taken to Well Hall by Mrs. Courlander, and had found E. Nesbit making innumerable cakes and pies, and so concentrated upon the task as to be somewhat negligent of her guests; the first impression had thus not been favourable.

Now, however, they were welcomed with a hospitality so far beyond anything that might ordinarily be expected, that they desired nothing better than to spend their whole time with her, and discovered each day some fresh aspect of her "almost divine kindness and understanding." Both of them were in need of complete relaxation after illness and worry, and E. Nesbit, instinctively casting down that little barrier of formality that had always encompassed her, true Bohemian though she was, let them come and go as they pleased, and behaved towards them with unofficious motherliness. On leaving Jesson Miss Stern was able to write in all sincerity: "You are quite the nicest and most comforting person I have ever met."

Although for some years past the woman of letters in E. Nesbit had been subjugated to the woman of domestic interests, many writers of the younger generation visited the Longboat, and she realized with pleasure what numbers of those whose careers were only just beginning owed their first joy in literature, their first conscious flights of fancy, to her. Whatever publishers might urge as to the changing tastes of children, she saw that the children for whom she had written were still faithful to her. Her correspondence with admirers who knew her only by her work was hardly less extensive than it had been fifteen or twenty years before. Amongst those whose praises heartened her in the last year of her life was Mrs. Naomi Mitchison, who thought that she had exercised an untold influence for good over countless children—an opinion not likely to be disputed by those who remember to what heights of chivalry, of noble candour, of almost reckless generosity one could rise, fired by the example of the Bastables, the three C's, or the four friends of the Psammead.

No other such gallant bands as these were to be created, but E. Nesbit's writing life was not yet ended. In 1922 she published *The Lark,* her last novel, and *Many Voices,* her last book of poems; in 1923 the last series of short stories followed. The poems were largely reprinted from earlier volumes, or from newspapers to which she had contributed during the War. Those that were new showed plainly how her mind had matured during the years of misfortune. The reluctance to expose her deeper feelings that had filled so many of her verses with insincerities seemed to have been almost overcome (though, strangely enough, only a few weeks before her death she warned a young poetical aspirant against self-revelation); and had her new courage been coupled with her old fertility of ideas, she might have written better poetry now than ever before: but she was apparently constrained for lack of fresh inspiration to use themes which had served her often and sometimes even to repeat phrases and similes from other poems. The same tendency, careless or deliberate, may be seen in her later prose work.

The novel brought out at about the same time as *Many Voices* is, I should imagine, the only thing she ever did or wrote in the guise of that typical "sweet old lady" whom she so little resembled. It has all the air of having been produced by a dear, gentle, very elderly woman of rather sprightly humour, whose notions of girlish behaviour were based on impressions three or four decades old, but who was anxiously determined to be tolerant and "move with the times." No one who knew anything whatever about E. Nesbit's life and views could have guessed that it was the work of her hand if her name had not appeared on the title page, and yet she did not write it with her tongue in her cheek, but took it seriously as the very thing it was not—"a girl's story." So she referred to it with emphatic self-commendation in a letter to a friend. Compared with the average novel of the post-war years it is absolutely naive, and yet it is meant to be dashing. That the writer could have been exchanging astringent and sagacious comments on the state of modern morals with Mr. Noel Coward and others just after this novel was finished is a very astonishing thing indeed.

Ladylike innocence of the manners of independent youth at the beginning of the twenties sets the prevailing tone in every chapter. The two heroines, earning their own living and described as "perfectly fearless, perfectly unconventional," are not prepared to visit a theatre together without a chaperon unless the performance be a matinee; they have qualms about the respectability of going on the river with two young men; after seeing these two young men nearly every day for weeks in circumstances of great intimacy, they invariably address and refer to them, even when talking to each other alone as "Mr. Rochester" and "Mr. Dix." When Mr. Rochester himself—and his old-world courtesy is if anything even greater than the girls' modesty—uses the Christian name of one of them, she instantly rebukes him, although by this time they both love each other. When he, with marked propriety, embraces her and utters an endearment she breaks away, exclaiming: "I want you to understand that I'm not at *all* that sort of girl." If the author had not been concerned to show how modern and adventurous the girls were, this sort of conduct would seem less incredible, but as that was her object, it is very incredible indeed—more especially since she herself in her girlhood had never had the least hesitation in doing anything she pleased.

The only conclusion to be reached is that E. Nesbit had never been intended by a providence that had lavished so many gifts upon her to be a novelist, and that in order to write a novel at all it was necessary for her to assume a false attitude which, as she worked, she had to try and believe a true one, because she **could** do nothing without faith in its goodness. She held, as one of her last letters explicitly states, that to write anything that was less than one's best was "the sin against the Holy Ghost," and as she would not consciously commit this sin, she was compelled to resort to self-deception. In *The Red House* and *Dormant* she had found subjects which she might treat with less disguise of her real taste and feeling than was generally called for; the one book dealt with childlike people, the other with magic. But, on the whole, the more profoundly one admires her genius as a writer for children, the more regretfully must one contemplate her desire to be a novelist.

Her handling of short stories was altogether more competent, for these did not so often require the assumed attitude, and when they did, it could, of course, be kept up more convincingly for a day or two than for the time it takes to write seventy or eighty thousand words. Many of her stories are uncommonly good and nearly all of them are entertaining. *To the Adventurous,* the last of all her books, contains at least half a dozen tales really excellent of their kind.

Taking all the enormous body of her work together, there is undoubtedly a great deal that has not, and never can have, any value except to the student of her development as an artist. We who belong to a generation not far from her own in time may deplore the fact of her ever having written so much that was unworthy of her, but the generations of the distant future will have no such grievance, since only her best is likely to survive. And if that best is, indeed, handed down from parent to child for many and many a year to come—as who can doubt it will be?—at least a dozen volumes bearing the cherished name "E. Nesbit" will be read and treasured by our descendants. No other English writer for children has produced an equal quantity of wholly admirable work.

21 The End

Until she grew too ill to see anyone but her doctor and the members of her family, E. Nesbit continued to be surrounded by devoted friends, and when it was no longer possible for her to receive them under her roof she knew what place she would always hold in their thoughts. Physically she was in agony throughout all the last months of her life, and could not but long for release; yet spiritually she had seldom been more tranquil. Her husband and Olive Hill tended her with unwearying affection. Her children constantly came down from London to spend the week-ends with her, and their number was now augmented by a daughter-in-law [1] who loved her not less than if she had been a daughter. In her granddaughter Pandora she saw with pleasure almost a replica of herself in her girlhood. "My own ghost," she called her.

Towards the end Miss Berta Ruck, who had lost touch with her fifteen years before, wrote her a letter which showed that she had treasured the memory of the friendship that outwardly had been allowed to lapse. E. Nesbit replied in terms of warm regard, and her letters to Miss Ruck were the last she ever wrote with her own hand. This correspondence presents an extraordinary testimony of her courage, her kindliness, and her inexhaus-

[1] Paul Bland had married Miss Gertrude Nebel in April, 1917.

tible interest in life. Even in speaking of the illness that was tor-
turing her she could still reveal her dauntless humour.

"I suppose I shall not get well again," she wrote in June, 1923,
"but, like Charles II, I take an unconscionable time over the
business. You would not know me—I am so thin. Once a
Rubens Venus in figure but now more like a pre-Raphaelite
Saint Simeon. I suppose you have thousands of stately motor-
cars," she added, in oblique reference to her friend's success as a
novelist. "Why don't you get into one of them and come and
see us?"

Miss Ruck did go to see her and was distressed to find her
lying on a couch, instead of moving about the room while she
talked according to her old restless habit. The small active
hands that had always been so brown from rowing, swimming,
and gardening, were now strangely white, but their gestures
were still quick and expressive. She was thin and wasted, as she
had said; yet her eyes were as bright and her smile as eager as
when her vitality had seemed unquenchable. Through some
unforeseen delay in the journey, Miss Ruck had failed to arrive
at the hour stipulated, and it was not without a qualm that she
heard E. Nesbit greet her—her rich voice as imperious as ever
—with the words: "You're late, girl!" She looked at the
changed figure before her, hardly able to repress her tears, and
replied gently: "Yes, fifteen years." Then, as the moment hung
delicately suspended, she added, glancing towards the prepared
tea-table, "And I see you've still got something for me." This
was all the reconciliation needed to enable them to take up their
friendship where they had left it.

E. Nesbit had followed with interest the career which she
herself had helped to launch, and was grateful for the dedication of *The Clouded Pearl,* a novel offered as "a tribute to her
fadeless power." Even when it had become an intense effort to
write letters, she dealt with Miss Ruck's work in detail, praising
and candidly advising. From the same friend she received a
constant and most welcome supply of fiction by other authors
and of magazines. She read and commented upon them all; but
when a periodical which specialized in gossip and photographs

of fashionable society was included in the customary parcel she asked that it might not be sent to her again. "It presents an aspect of life which disgusts me," she said. "Its general tone quite horrifies me." She could still be moved to resentment at the sight of a paper devoted almost solely to chronicling the amusements of people whom she thought useless and idle.

As the months went by she grew more and more helpless, and was obliged to dictate her correspondence to her husband or Miss Hill. She was as resigned to death as anyone can be who has enjoyed life enormously and whose mental vigour is still unimpaired. She grieved only because the end was delayed so long and because her illness was an affliction to her household. When Mr. Tucker tried to cheer her up with hopes of her recovery, she would reply with a smile and a shake of the head, "No, no, Mate, you're too sanguine." That she was quietly and firmly convinced of the imminence of her death may be judged from her reply to an admiring reader who, not knowing that she was ill, had asked her if he might look forward to any continuation of the Bastable series. The enquirer was Mr. Angus MacPhail, later celebrated as a scenario writer; and this is the answer she wrote him:

18 Nov. 1923.

Alas, my dear Angus, your poor E. Nesbit lies dying and it is a long business and very tiresome. I fear the last of the Oswald Saga has been sung.

I fear I shall never write anything again though I feel now as though I had never written anything comparable in importance and interest to what I could write now if I could hold a pen.

It is very pleasant to hear that you are teaching your friends to like E. Nesbit books. Morden House [2] was nowhere in particular, just any old red brick house on that side of the Heath. I suppose you've read Oswald Bastable and Others (Gardner Darton and Co.).

We are in a government hut in the middle of Romney Marsh,

[2] Morden House, Blackheath, with the address of the Bastables when they lived with their "Indian uncle."

if ever you should pass this way you can come and see me—if I am still here.

> Yours, pleased that you like her,
> E. Nesbit Bland-Tucker.

In December, 1923, it seemed as if she could stand the strain of suffering no longer, but she rallied and lived bravely through four more lingering months of it. "I did nearly die last week," she told Berta Ruck in a letter, "and I assure you that the hitch in the arrangements was no fault of mine. I'm sorry to be such a copy-cat of poor Charles II, but better luck next time."

To Mavis Carter in the same month she wrote: "I have everything to make me happy except health, kindest and most loving nursing and care . . . a four-post bed like a golden shrine and a view of about eight miles of marsh bounded by the little lovely hills of Kent."

At about that time Miss Carter, who had guarded as a treasure all E. Nesbit's letters and the diary in which she had so joyfully recorded her first schoolgirl impressions of her, came to pay her last visit. They talked with pretended gaiety about the days of their first meeting and the motor excursion to Warwick when Edith had envied the children their sun-bonnets. Suddenly the sentimental reminiscences were interrupted by a flaring up of the old petulance: Mavis was sitting with a curved back and crossed ankles, and her hostess would not proceed with the conversation until she had adopted a more elegant posture. But, repenting of her brusque rebuke a moment afterwards, she cried: "Forgive me, dear! You must allow me a sick woman's privilege to be disagreeable—and I am very ill." Leaning heavily upon her husband's arm, she saw her visitor to the garden gate, and having kissed her, stood there waving till she was out of sight. The girl who knew that she would never see her again, and who had loved her and looked up to her from childhood, could only go towards the Dymchurch sands and lie there weeping.

Miss Carter was able to gratify a long-standing wish by doing her a service that she greatly valued. This was the preparation of a scrap-book containing a number of her hitherto uncollected stories, articles, and poems, and intended as a birthday present for Mr. Tucker. E. Nesbit herself supervised the work from the distance with minute care, and sent several letters describing the size, shape, and style of volume she desired. For the most part they were businesslike communications devoted entirely to one subject, but sometimes a little individual touch appeared in them:

"I strongly disapprove of your marmalade recipe," she wrote immediately after a comment on the precarious state of her health. "Far better cut up each orange in eight—don't squeeze —and soak before cutting up. But, dear me, marmalade is far behind me."

When the work was finished, very shortly before her death, she dictated the following letter, one of the last she ever sent:

April 19th, 1924.

Kind Mavis,

I have been hoping against hope to be able to write to you myself about the scrap-book which you have so beautifully done for me. I never expected when I asked you to do it that you would produce such a delightful result from these old things. Everything is perfect, lettering, paging, and all, in fact the lettering is most beautiful. . . . Mr. Tucker for whose birthday-present the book was designed is delighted with it and will hardly let it out of his hands, declining firmly to lend it to anyone. You have often said, my dear, that you wished you could do something for me. Well! now you have done it, and no small thing either!

With sincere thanks and love
I am,
Yours always affectionately
E. Nesbit.

In the meantime, she continued to read the various books Miss Ruck sent her, and to find interest in them and, despite intense pain, in a hundred other matters. Nor had she lost her readiness to help aspiring talent. A young girl from New Romney had come to take down her letters and do small tasks about the house, and E. Nesbit soon discovered that she was writing poetry, and began to give her well-meant counsel. "I tried to let her know," she said, ". . . that if you write *only* about your heart's core you give yourself away to everyone who reads a verse of yours, whereas if you write about indifferent subjects as well, your jewel soon becomes concealed among the pebbles on the beach. This, I told her, is the use of the dramatic lyric."

Her last pronouncement on her own work [3] shows that she was still quite ignorant of the lasting worth of her contribution to prose literature: "Poetry . . . is really what I should naturally have done, that and *no* prose, if I had not had to write for a living." And she added in answer to a question: "Tell your boys that *all* the reviewers took me for a man, and I was Mr. Nesbit in the mouth of all men till I was fool enough to dedicate a book to my husband, and thus give away the secret."

"Talking of poetry," she said in the same letter, "I don't believe I have ever told you how very, very much I like Frances Cornford. I wish I could have written 'The Watch' instead of only endorsing it. Do you know her? If you do, do please tell her how passionately pleased I am with her work." At another time she wrote "I do like F. Cornford. She says

> I am so sick, so sick,
> O Death come quick, come quick, come quick!"

She read Dostoevsky's *Insulted and Injured,* which enthralled her and cost her a night's sleep; she read Clemence Dane's *Regiment of Women* and thought it a wonderful piece of work; side by side with these in her bookshelf would be a volume of poetry, a novel, perhaps, by Gene Stratton-Porter (who was, incidentally, one of her ardent admirers), a treatise on some recent scientific discovery, and a curious medley of other books, new and old, deep and shallow. And so between reading and pain and visits from the doctor and talks with her children, her last weeks slowly ebbed away. For all her eagerness to be set free she could not leave the world without a sigh. "The human

[3] In a letter to Berta Ruck.

span of life is far too short," she said. "What things there are still to see and to do, and to think and to be, and to grow into and grow out of!"

But she was convinced that she was not to be annihilated, and spoke sometimes of her hope that she might be allowed to help people still living when her body was dead. She was at peace with all her fellow-creatures; there was not one individual whom she had ever known against whom she would utter a word of bitterness. She had always been a generous and forgiving woman, incapable of spite, and now the last dim sparks even of justifiable resentment were finally extinguished. She would remember only kindnesses.

Her thoughts turned often to the days of her prime and oftener still to her childhood. She, who had set down with incomparable vividness a thousand little childish memories that have slipped beyond the reach of most adult minds, now recaptured impressions even older than those she had recorded —impressions of things that she had seen and marked in early infancy, the pattern of a flowered carpet, the shape and colour of a vase, the little soft kid shoes she had flung into the font at her christening.

One day her daughter Iris asked her whether she would live her life over again up to this time if every moment of it, happy or unhappy, had to be repeated. She answered that she only wished she could, for, good and bad alike, it had all been so unutterably interesting: there had scarcely been a moment of indifference. To the end this passionate interest remained, and with it a lively gratitude to those who had contributed to her last pleasures.

"Goodbye, my dear," she wrote to Berta Ruck. "Whenever you think of me do not forget to think how much happiness your loving kindness has given me, and how you have helped my last, long months. I really think the door will open soon now, and I may be able to scurry through at last. But I shall remember you wherever I wake."

One further letter followed this. Only a few lines of it were in

her own hand, but, notwithstanding the great effort they cost
her, the gentle humour, the strong courage, still inspired them:

> I *will* try to write to dear Berta myself. . . . Changed the Doc-
> tor, who now gives me morphia to take the edge off the pain, but
> I am still as sick as a dog (or cat. I think a cat is sicker don't
> you?) I have a poem coming with its form nebulous, but its con-
> tent all arranged and a few really good lines done—it is for you
> when I have (if ever I have) done it. (. . . The D. has come! I
> hope I can hold the pencil till the D. has gone. Still got him!)

But her husband had to relieve her of the pencil—and the
poem did not come. On 4th May, 1924, thirteen days after this
letter was written, the door outside which she had waited so
long and so valiantly opened at last.[4] The four days preceding
her death were terrible indeed for her and those who loved her.
She did not cross the threshold without an agonizing struggle.
But around her bed were gathered her son and daughter, her
husband and Miss Hill—those two whom, in one of her valedictory letters to her friends, she had called "my dear darlings."
And when the door closed upon all her suffering and all the
delights of the world that she had cherished, her daughter's
arms held her.

She was buried in the little churchyard of St. Mary's in the
Marsh, and by her own wish there is no stone upon her grave
—only two posts carved by her husband's hands, and between
them a wooden panel bearing the simplest of inscriptions. She
needed no more elaborate monument, for she had built one
stronger than stone and warmer. And the last of all the ornaments with which she decked it was a gracious one.

When she was dying she had longed to have a fair view of
the Kentish hills whose aspect had always rejoiced her. Hearing
this, her friend, Mrs. Thorndike, had sent her some contrivance
by which she could raise her four-post bed to a level with the
window. She replied with the poem that follows, the last she
ever completed, and one of the most charming:

[4] Her death certificate states that she died of bronchiestasis and cardiac
dilatation.

On bed of state long since a Queen
Would wake to morning's starry beams
Silvering the arras blue and green
That hung her walls with cloth-of-dreams;
And, where the fluted valance drooped
Above the curtains' broidered posies,
The pretty carven cupids trooped
Festooning all her bed with roses.

Mother of Stars! enthroned I lie
On the high bed your kindness sent,
And see between the marsh and sky
The little lovely hills of Kent;
And, 'mid the memories old and new
That bless me as the curtain closes,
Come troops of pretty thoughts of you . . .
And mine, too, is a bed of roses.

Thus she ended her career with such a gesture as one would expect of her—a graceful and a gallant gesture.

Bibliography of E. Nesbit's Works

N.B.—The dates given are those of English publication in book form. The list does not include the anthologies in which selections of E. Nesbit's verse appeared.

1885 *The Prophet's Mantle.* A Novel. (In collaboration with Hubert Bland under the pseudonym, Fabian Bland). Henry J. Drane. pp. vi, 322, 8°.

1886 Four booklets [1]—*Spring, Summer, Autumn,* and *Winter Songs and Sketches,* selected and arranged in collaboration with Robert Ellice Mack (and containing poems by E. Nesbit). Griffith, Farren & Co., London. 8°.

1886 *Lays and Legends.* Longmans, Green & Co. pp. viii, 197, 8°.

1887 Two booklets—*The Lily and the Cross.* Griffith, Farren and Co., 4°; *The Star of Bethlehem.* Ernest Nister. 16°.

1888 Five booklets—*The Better Part, Easter-Tide* (with Caris Brooke), *The Time of Roses* (with Caris Brooke and others), *By Land and Sea, Landscape and Song, The Message of the Dove.* Henry J. Drane.

1888 *Leaves of Life.* Longmans, Green & Co. pp. x, 185, 8°.

1889 *Evergreen* from the Poet's Corner, selected and arranged by Robert Ellice Mack. (Contains two original poems by E. Nesbit). Ernest Nister 16°.

1889 Two booklets—*The Lilies Round the Cross* (with Helen J. Wood); 4°; *Corals and Sea Songs.* Ernest Nister. 16°.

[1] The publications referred to as "booklets" invariably consist of illustrated verse.

1890 Two booklets—*Life's Sunny Side* (E. Nesbit and others). Ernest Nister; *Songs of Two Seasons.* Raphael Tuck and Son. 8°.

1891 *Twice Four* (short stories by E. Nesbit and others). Griffith, Farren & Co. pp. 50, 8°.

1892 *The Voyage of Columbus.* A narrative in verse. (Illustrated). Raphael Tuck & Son.

1892 A booklet—*Sweet Lavender.* Ernest Nister. 4°.

1892 *Lays and Legends,* Second Series. Longmans, Green & Co. pp. 160. 8°.

1893 A booklet—*Flowers I Bring and Songs I Sing* (written under the name of E. Bland).

1893 Contributions in verse and prose to illustrated books for children —*Our Friends and All About Them, Listen Long and Listen Well, Sunny Tales for Snowy Days, Told by the Sunbeams and Me.* Raphael Tuck & Son.

1893 *Grim Tales* ⎱ (short "horror" stories). A. D. Innes and
1893 *Something Wrong* ⎰ Co. 8°.

1894 Contributions in prose and verse to illustrated books for children —*Hours in Many Lands, Tales that are True for Brown Eyes and Blue, Tales for Delight from Morning till Night, Fur and Feathers, Tales for all Weathers, Lads and Lassies.* Raphael Tuck & Son.

1894 *The Girls' Own Birthday Book,* selected, written, and arranged by E. Nesbit. Henry J. Drane. pp. 252, 16°.

1894 *The Butler in Bohemia* (short stories) in collaboration with Oswald Barron. Henry J. Drane. pp. 142, 8°.

1895 A booklet—*Rose Leaves.* Ernest Nister. 4°.

1895 *Holly and Mistletoe,* a Booklet of Christmas Verse (with Norman Gale and Richard le Gallienne). Marcus Ward & Co.

1895 *A Pomander of Verse.* John Lane. pp. ix, 88, 8°.

1895 *Poets' Whispers,* a Birthday Book (quotations selected and arranged by E. Nesbit). Henry J. Drane. pp. 252, 16°.

1895 *Pussy Tales* ⎱Illustrated by Lucy Kemp-Welch. Marcus Ward
1895 *Doggy Tales* ⎰ & Co. 8°.

1895 Contributions in prose to illustrated books for children—*Dulcie's Lantern.* Griffith, Farren & Co.; *Treasures from Storyland.* Raphael Tuck & Son.

1896 *As Happy as a King* (a children's story in verse). Illustrated by S. R. Praeger. Marcus Ward & Co. Obl. 8°.

1896 *In Homespun* (short stories). John Lane. pp. vi, 189, 8°.

1897 A booklet—*Dinna Forget,* two poems by Clifton Bingham and E. Nesbit. Ernest Nister. 16°.

1897 Three illustrated children's books—*Tales Told in the Twilight,* pp. 120, 8°; *The Children's Shakespeare,* pp. 96, 4°; *Royal Children of English History,* pp. 94, 8°. Raphael Tuck & Son.

1898 *Songs of Love and Empire.* Constable & Co. pp. xii, 168, 8°.

1898 *A Book of Dogs.* Illustrated by Winifred Austin. J. M. Dent & Co. pp. 60, obl. 8°.

1899 *Pussy and Doggy Tales* (a combined edition of the two volumes issued in 1895, with new material). J. M. Dent & Co. pp. x, 132, 8°.

1899 *The Secret of Kyriels.* A Novel. Hurst & Blackett. pp. 391, 8°.

1899 *The Story of the Treasure Seekers.* Illustrated by Gordon Browne and Lewis Baumer. T. Fisher Unwin. pp. xii, 296, 8°.

1900 *The Book of Dragons.* Illustrated by H. R. Millar, with decorations by H. Granville Fell. Harper Bros. pp. x, 290, 8°.

1901 *Nine Unlikely Tales for Children.* Illustrated by H. R. Millar and others. T. Fisher Unwin. pp. xiii, 297, 8°.

1901 *Thirteen Ways Home* (short stories). Anthony Treherne & Co. pp. 306, 8°.

1901 *The Wouldbegoods.* Illustrated by Arthur H. Buckland and others. T. Fisher Unwin. pp. 331, 8°.

1901 A booklet—*To Wish You Every Joy.* Raphael Tuck & Son.

1902 *The Revolt of the Toys* or *What Comes of Quarrelling* (two stories). Illustrated by Ambrose Dudley. Ernest Nister. pp. 32.

1902 *Five Children and It.* Illustrated by H. R. Millar. T. Fisher Unwin. pp. xv, 301, 8°.

1903 *The Literary Sense* (short stories): Methuen & Co. pp. 299, 8°.

1903 *The Rainbow Queen and Other Stories.* Illustrated by E. and M. F. Taylor, M. Bowley, etc. Raphael Tuck & Son. pp. 64, 8°.

1903 *The Red House.* A Novel. Methuen & Co. pp. 274, 8°.

1904 *The Phœnix and the Carpet.* Illustrated by H. R. Millar. George Newnes. pp. xi, 236, 8°.

1904 *Cat Tales* (with Rosamund Bland). Illustrated by Isabel Watkin. Ernest Nister. pp. 64, 8°.

1904 *The New Treasure Seekers.* Illustrated by Gordon Browne and Lewis Baumer. T. Fisher Unwin. pp. 328, 8°.

1905 *The Rainbow and the Rose.* Poems. Longmans, Green & Co. pp. x, 143, 8°.

1905 *Oswald Bastable and Others* (short stories). Illustrated by C. E. Brock and H. R. Millar. Wells, Gardner, Darton & Co. pp. x, 369, 8°.

1905 *Pug Peter* (a dog story). Pictures by Harry Rountree, Vignettes by John Hassall. Alfred Cooke, Leeds and London. pp. 63, 8°.

1906 *Man and Maid* (short stories). T. Fisher Unwin. pp. 312, 8°.

1906 *The Story of the Amulet.* Illustrated by H. R. Millar. T. Fisher Unwin. pp. 374, 8°.

1906 *The Railway Children.* Illustrated by C. E. Brock. Wells, Gardner, Darton & Co. pp. viii, 309, 8°.

1906 *The Incomplete Amorist.* A Novel. Constable & Co. pp. viii, 311, 8°.

1907 *The Enchanted Castle.* Illustrated by H. R. Millar. T. Fisher Unwin. pp. 352, 8°.

1908 *Jesus in London.* A Poem, with seven pictures by Spencer Pryse. A. C. Fifield. pp. 14, fo.

1908 *Ballads and Lyrics of Socialism, 1883 to 1908,* published for the Fabian Society. A. C. Fifield. pp. 80, 8°.

1908 *The Old Nursery Stories* (No. 1 of the Children's Bookcase series). Illustrated by W. H. Margetson. Oxford Press. pp. 165, 8°.

1908 *The House of Arden.* Illustrated by H. R. Millar. T. Fisher Unwin. pp. 349, 8°.

1909 *These Little Ones* (short stories). Illustrated by Spencer Pryse. George Allen & Sons. pp. 210, 8°.

1909 *Harding's Luck.* Illustrated by H. R. Millar. Hodder & Stoughton. pp. xi, 281, 8°.

1909 *Daphne in Fitzroy Street.* A Novel. George Allen & Sons. pp. viii, 417, 8°.

1909 *Salome and the Head.* A Modern Melodrama (A Novel, reprinted by George Newnes in 1914 as *The House with No Address*). Illustrated by Spencer Pryse. Alston Rivers. pp. vii, 309, 8°.

1909 *Cinderella,* A Play with Twelve Songs to Popular Airs. Sidgwick & Jackson.

1910 *Fear* (short stories). Stanley Paul & Co. pp. 318, 8°.

1910 *The Magic City.* Illustrated by H. R. Millar. Macmillan & Co. pp. xiv, 333, 8°.

1911 *Ballads and Verses of the Spiritual Life.* Elkin Mathews. pp. 105, 8°.

1911 *My Sea-side Story Book* (with G. Manville Fenn). Illustrated by W. Rainey, A. Webb, and others. Ernest Nister. pp. 108, 4°.

1911 *The Wonderful Garden* or *The Three C's.* Illustrated by H. R. Millar. Macmillan & Co. pp. xiv, 402, 8°.

1911 *Dormant.* A Novel. Methuen & Co. pp. ii, 312, 8°.

1912 *The Magic World* (short stories). Illustrated by H. R. Millar and Spencer Pryse. Macmillan & Co. pp. x, 280, 8°.

1913 *Our New Story Book.* Illustrated by Elsie Wood, Louis Wain, etc. Ernest Nister, pp. 200, 4°.

1913 *Wet Magic.* Illustrated by H. R. Millar. T. Werner Laurie. pp. vii, 274, 8°.

1913 *Wings and the Child* or *The Building of Magic Cities.* Illustrated with photographs and diagrams by George Barrand. Hodder & Stoughton. pp. xiv, 197, 8°.

1914 *Battle Songs* (chosen by E. Nesbit). Max Goschen. pp. 96, 8°.

1914 *Children's Stories from English History,* by E. Nesbit and Doris

Ashley. Illustrated by John H. Bacon, A.R.A., Howard Davie, and others. Raphael Tuck & Son. pp. 140, 4°.

1914 *Essays* by Hubert Bland, edited by E. Nesbit-Bland. Max Goschen. pp. xv, 284, 8°.

1921 Second Book of *The New World Literary Series* (short stories for children), edited by Prof. Henry Cecil Wyld. Illustrated. Collins Clear Type Press. pp. 164, 8°.

1921 *The Incredible Honeymoon.* A Novel. Hutchinson & Co. pp. 286, 8°.

1922 *The Lark.* A Novel. Hutchinson & Co. pp. 288, 8°.

1922 *Many Voices.* Poems. Hutchinson & Co. pp. 94, 8°.

1923 *To the Adventurous* (short stories). Hutchinson & Co. pp. 286, 8°.

Date not traced—*Garden Poems.* Collins Clear Type Press. pp. 95, 16°.

POSTHUMOUS

1925 *Five of Us—and Madeline* (short stories linked together by Rosamund Sharp). Illustrated by Norah S. Unwin. T. Fisher Unwin. pp. 310, 8°.

Index

Doris Langley Moore

Doris Langley Moore was born in Liverpool, England, but spent much of her youth in South Africa, where her father was a distinguished journalist. His influence was felt not only by his daughter, but by many others who benefited from his advice and interest and later went on to writing careers of their own.

Her first published book was *Anacreon: Twenty-nine Odes,* a verse translation. Her second, though brought out anonymously, made an immediate impact. It was called *The Technique of the Love Affair,* and was a light-hearted but not in the least light-headed disquisition which was re-issued at intervals over many years.

In addition to *E. Nesbit: A Biography,* which was her first entry into the biographical field, Doris Langley Moore also wrote, during her early career, a number of novels. At the end of the Second World War, she wrote an inquiry into the tendencies of public opinion which she called *The Vulgar Heart* from Shakespeare's lines about "a habitation giddy and unsure." This was both a best seller and a work which won the admiration of critics. She followed it in 1953 with *Pleasure, A Discursive Guide Book.* That was the year in which American readers enjoyed her novel about fraudulence in the art world, *All Done By Kindness.*

Since then Mrs. Moore has been widely praised for her monumental book of posthumous Byron dramas, *The Late Lord Byron*. Another and very different variation on the same theme is her novel, *My Caravaggio Style,* which has gained devoted American fans.

Doris Langley Moore, in addition to being a biographer and novelist, is a famous authority on costume, has written two books on this subject, and founded a Museum of Costume at the Assembly Rooms, Bath, England. She has designed period clothes for many film stars, among whom are Katharine Hepburn (*The African Queen*), and Montgomery Clift (*Freud*), and she has also written the scenario of a ballet which had Ashton as choreographer, Fonteyn as ballerina, and William Walton as composer.